Innovation and Internationalization of Small and Medium Enterprises

A Crossroads Perspective

PETER LANG

Bruxelles · Bern · Berlin · New York · Oxford · Wein

Business & Innovation

Vol. 29

The creation of new activities, of news production and consumption modes, of new goods and services, of new markets and new jobs (etc.) depends as much on the heroic action of entrepreneurs as on the strategies of big corporations which develop their activities at a global scale. Innovation and business are interlinked. The main themes of the books published in this series are: Entrepreneurship, enterprise and innovation; Innovation strategies in a global context; Innovation policies and business climate; Innovation, business dynamics and socio-economic change. The synergies between innovative entrepreneurship, firms' strategies and innovation policies is of major importance in the explanation of technological paradigms change and of the transformations in economic and social structures of wealthy and less wealthy countries. In this series are published books in English or in French specialized in economics, management and sociology of innovation and also dealing with change and entrepreneurship in a local, national or international perspective.

This series is supported by the Research Network on Innovation.

Manon Enjolras, Mauricio Camargo
and Christophe Schmitt (Eds.)

Innovation and Internationalization of Small and Medium Enterprises

A Crossroads Perspective

Business and Innovation
Vol. 29

This work has been supported by the Innov4SME project from the Université de Lorraine (Research program "Lorraine Université d'Excellence" PIA2 ANR-15-IDEX-04-LUE.

Information bibliographique publiée par "Die Deutsche Bibliothek".
"Die Deutsche Bibliothek" répertorie cette publication dans la "Deutsche National-bibliografie"; les données bibliographiques détaillées sont disponibles sur le site <http://dnb.ddb.be>.

ISBN 978-2-8076-1820-6 • ISSN 2034-5402
E-ISBN 978-2-8076-1821-3(ePDF) • E-ISBN 978-2-8076-1822-0 (EPUB)
• DOI 10.3726/b19169
D/2021/5678/81

Éditions scientifiques internationales
Bruxelles, 2022
1 avenue Maurice, B-1050 Bruxelles, Belgique

Cette publication a fait l'objet d'une d'une évaluation par les pairs.

www.peterlang.com

Table of content

Innovation and internationalization of SMEs: A crossroads perspective

Introduction

Manon Enjolras, Mauricio Camargo, and Christophe Schmitt

Since 2020, with the Covid-19 crisis, the world has suffered a shock with impacts that nobody could predict. Moreover, everyone could agree that climate warming and its effects are not anymore a perspective on the scientific papers. These breaking-point situations have led to significant changes in our lives but also for all instances in our society.

Whatever the future will bring the current context poses a large number of challenges and uncertainties for companies. Indeed, globalization, acceleration of product life-cycle, changes in customer requirements and the technological environment, as well as the successive economic, political, environmental and health crises, have changed the rules of the game in terms of competitiveness and then the strategy. This is true for all companies, and more particularly for small organizations.

Small and medium-sized enterprises (SMEs) constitute the bigger contributor of employment and added value for the economies worldwide (OECD, 2018). Nonetheless, if one considers the main figures associated with small structures, it appears that they remain under-represented in world trade. Indeed, SMEs perhaps more than others, are forced to face the current upheavals of their ecosystem and anticipate them to secure their activities and guarantee their survival. However, while SMEs have well-known weaknesses, linked in particular to their limited resources, they also have many assets that enable them to constantly renew themselves. Flexibility, responsiveness, and resilience are therefore the watchwords that enable them to create new opportunities to grow, innovate, and position themselves on international markets.

Nowadays and for several years, the race to technological innovation has reached its limits. Innovation is now associated with major societal issues: sustainable development, digital economy, renewal of housing and urban planning, mobility, product "servitization" ...

Regarding companies' international activities, instead calls for protectionism and for reducing the international exchanges, some research works underline that a regulated commerce of a "moderated globalization" is still needed to take advantage of the local comparative advantages and competencies. For example, the Covid-19 crisis has greatly increased the internationalization potential of companies. By radically accelerating the digitalization of business development and trade, reducing delivery and supply chains, and promoting more local governance, it is now providing the opportunity for accelerated and reasoned internationalization strategies that are managed in a more agile and sustainable way. Indeed, paradoxically some international exchanges could be beneficial in terms of environmental impacts (Rajan, 2019).

Thus, reshaping innovation and internationalization in the current evolving environment appears as a joint challenge that SMEs must face. International activities represent a way to diversify sales and reduce risk when domestic sales are slowing down. In parallel, innovation helps firms to adapt their products, processes, and organization to embrace these new opportunities. However, these two activities are generally considered independently of each other both in terms of management within companies and in terms of the support offered by external bodies. A joint and cross vision of these activities nevertheless represents an interesting way of managing the complexity of SMEs under these new circumstances and takes all its importance in the changing context in which they evolve.

How does this new context call into question the dynamics, approaches, and strategies for evolving in the international market? What role does innovation play in pursuing these changes? What skills are now required? What new dynamics still need to be created?

To address these issues, a community of researchers and practitioners has been mobilized around the topic of SMEs' innovation and internationalization capabilities, thanks to the support of the Innov4SME project of the Université de Lorraine (Research program "Lorraine Université d'Excellence" PIA2 ANR-15-IDEX-04-LUE),

These shared reflections have then given rise to this collective and multidisciplinary book, through which we confront the point of view of management sciences, engineering, and the professional world, to provide a rich and complementary multifaceted insight into innovation and internationalization in SMEs. Based on the experiences of the authors, we thus have had the opportunity to cover different perspectives of the SMEs' international and innovative capabilities in various countries: Switzerland, France, Spain, Canada, Costa Rica and Chile.

First of all, this book aims to promote the paradigm according to which innovation and internationalization are intimately linked among SMEs, both for their growth perspectives and for their daily operations. Thus, this relationship is explored by the authors in several chapters:

Through Chapter 1, P. Wild and R. Baldegger investigate how international activities impact the innovation capacity of companies. They propose an interesting study on the influence of the Degree of internationalization (DoI), Entrepreneurial Orientation (EO), and Firm Size on the SME innovation performance. Their analysis is based on data from more than 1,500 internationalizing SMEs in Switzerland that were collected over a period of 10 years. Their empirical results demonstrate that SMEs Innovation Performance is significantly influenced by the Degree of Internationalization (DoI).

In the same vein, Chapter 2 is a contribution from the Think Tank "La Fabrique de l'Exportation" co-authored by J.P. David and J.C. Gessler. "La Fabrique de l'Exportation" is the main French think tank dedicated to the internationalization of companies. Its objective is to identify best practices and promote them to French companies and the exporting ecosystem. This chapter aims to explore how and why the international activities of a company induce an increase in its innovativeness. Relying on empirical cases and examples from Canadian firms, the authors illustrate this phenomenon from a practitioners' point of view and highlight the effects of market and entrepreneurial orientation as drivers of innovative development of companies via their internationalization.

In Chapter 3, D. Galvez, C. Muñoz, M. Enjolras et M. Camargo investigate the relevance of an integrative assessment model of innovation and export capabilities in order to establish common strategies and simultaneous improvement plans. Focusing on the specific context of SMEs, this joint innovation/export model relies on a synergistic vision enabling to address the main issue of small businesses: the lack of internal resources. By providing simultaneous improvements plans and joint strategies, the model proposes an optimization of the implemented actions, by minimizing the resources involved and maximizing the potential impacts. The authors also propose an application case within a Chilean wine SME, enabling to test the model in real conditions.

Considering this strong relationship between innovation and international activities, one of the ambitions of this book was also to look at the way in which it was concretely implemented within companies. Several authors have therefore sought to identify the characteristics of innovative and exporting SMEs in order to identify their specificities.

In Chapter 4, G. Benito, J. Pla-Barber and C. Villar, from the University of Valencia contribute to a better understanding of resilient companies through the business model framework. To achieve this objective, they propose a taxonomy of the business model of traditional manufacturing exporting SMEs in Spain, explaining how they have managed to compete, survive and succeed in international markets.

Chapter 5 exposes the case of SMEs' export performance in Costa Rica. S. Arce, M. Faith and J. Martinez share with us the results of a long-term qualitative and quantitative study over a population of firms regarding factors determining their export. Data obtained from SMEs' detailed exporting records are used to calculate the Export Performance Index (EPI), enabling the measurement of each company's export performance. The index considers an SME's exporting continuity, exporting dynamism, market diversification, and market access conditions.

Chapter 6, authored by M. Enjolras, M. Camargo and C. Schmitt, provides an explorative taxonomy of innovative and exporting companies' management practices. Considering that the behavior of a company depends both on its own characteristics, but also on the nature of its environment, this study aims to highlight the convergence and divergence of internal practices, exploring a sample of 25 firms and analyzing contextual and structural variables as differentiating factors. Mobilizing data analysis techniques, the authors highlight several companies' behaviors profiles in terms of innovation and export management, showing specific context- and structure-related orientations.

Finally, with the objective of fostering an efficient support to innovative and international SMEs, this book has attempted to provide some success factors that enable companies to create new dynamics and strategies for value creation. Thus, some authors have highlighted key drivers favoring the emergence of new opportunities both in the field of innovation and international development.

In this perspective, Chapter 7, proposed by J.C. Gessler, exposes how SMEs can benefit from shared innovation in order to reach international markets. From the academic literature and a survey of a sample of 117 French SMEs, he states that SMEs have an interest in engaging in collaborative approaches enabling the firm to acquire innovative capabilities to constitute an "innovation ecosystem" leading to an international expansion.

Additionally, in Chapter 8, our colleagues A. Hervé, C. Schmitt and R. Baldegger explore the potential of digital technologies to reduce barriers as regards reaching the global marketplace. Authors argued that the integration of digital technologies into internal and external dimensions of a firm is central to reinforcing the strategic posture of entrepreneurially internationalizing MSMEs (micro-, small- and medium-sized enterprises) and proposed that individuals are the central driver of this strategic approach. To reach this, firms should demonstrate a strong entrepreneurial orientation (EO). EO refers to strategic behaviors that are entrepreneurial in nature, in other words, it consists of decision-making practices that demonstrate innovativeness, proactiveness and risk-taking. Based on parallel mediation analysis, the model was empirically tested using 143 Swiss internationalizing MSMEs.

In conclusion, this collective work, mobilizing researchers and practitioners around the issue of innovation and internationalization of SMEs, aims to raise awareness of the many challenges currently faced by SMEs, as well as their crucial role in the development of innovation and international trade at the global level. In these challenging times, it seems essential to rethink the ways in which companies operate, and this requires a systemic and global approach to business management practices and the support provided to them. Therefore, this book is primarily intended for researchers in the field of innovation and international management. It is also intended for students in training programs related to engineering sciences, international business, and strategic management, at the bachelor and master/engineer levels. The book is also aimed at business practitioners and consultants seeking to gain expertise in the support offered to SMEs.

References

OECD. 2018. "Fostering Greater SME Participation in a Globally Integrated Economy." SME Ministerial Conference – Plenary Session 3. Mexico: Organisation for Economic Co-operation and Development.

Rajan, Raghuram. 2019. The third pillar: The revival of community in a polarised world. Harper Collins. ISBN: 978-0-00-827626-3.

Chapter 1

Analyzing SMEs innovation performance: Exploring the role of Degree of Internationalization (DOI), Entrepreneurial Orientation (EO), and firm size

Pascal Wild and Rico Baldegger

Introduction

In recent years, the patterns of SME innovation – especially in countries with a small domestic market – have increasingly become more focused on a dimension of economic policy and found its way into media coverage. In large parts of the world, SMEs make up more than 99 % of all economic entities and are a major source of job creation. This is true for North America as well as for the European Union. In the latter, approximately two-thirds of all employees work for an SME (Muller et al., 2018). It has been recognized that SME growth is essential for any national economy (Coviello and Munro, 1995), they have a strong influence and are considered the engine of economic growth in small and open economies, so-called SMOPEC (Gabriellson et al., 2008; Neubert, 2016), in developed markets as well as in many emerging markets (Bruque and Mayano, 2007).

Not only policy makers, but the SMEs themselves perceive growth as a necessity for various reasons and in consequence thereafter, decide to penetrate foreign markets. Hence, expansion abroad is increasingly seen by SMEs as a fundamental strategic option to gain competitive advantage. However, due to the heterogeneity of the SME landscape and its internationalization behavior, it is difficult to measure success or identify the success factors (Baldegger and Wild, 2019).

We analyzed the data of more than 1,500 innovating and internationalizing SME from Switzerland and tested our model in an explorative manner. Our aim is to shed light on the relationship between an SMEs strategic posture respectively its entrepreneurial orientation (EO) and thus "behavior" as well as its internationalization progress and innovation performance. Whereas the strategic posture is perceived to impact the progress of internationalization, both of these variables are hypothesized having an impact on the SME innovation performance. Our result support the proposed relationship between the variables even though their explanation power is not particularly high. Additionally, we discovered that firm size has an impact on all variables. Consequently, we tested the model separately for micro-sized and medium-sized SMEs and discovered that the innovation performance of the former is principally influenced by its strategic posture whereas the latter principally record an impact of internationalization on their innovation power.

Our chapter is structured as follows. First, we describe the literature in the field of SME innovation and SME internationalization. Then, by providing more theoretical insights, we establish a relationship among entrepreneurial orientation (EO), the degree of internationalization (DoI) and Innovation performance, followed by our hypotheses. We then describe our sample, the measures as well as the survey instrument and the analytical procedures executed in order to test our model. In the findings section we assess the model and describe our results. Finally, we discuss our results and describe its managerial implications, limitations as well as future research to be held on behalf of this topics.

1. Literature review and hypothesis development

1.1 Innovation in SME

Contemporary SME of various kind of industries are increasingly exposed to global competition. This development is not least due to declining trade barriers and improved logistical technologies and processes (McDougall et al., 1994). Consequently, many industries are recording rapid technological and structural change. This trend creates growing uncertainty among the industry actors and fosters the need for competitive advantages through knowledge creation and R&D. Innovation allows SMEs to stay competitive since it leads to product and service differentiation and cost reduction (Rosenbusch et al., 2011; Genc et al., 2019). Innovating SMEs are also a consequence to an increased technological sophistication in product markets and a rising demand for complex and individualized services. Companies of various sizes and age are constantly searching for new knowledge and capabilities. Multinational corporations (MNCs) from the most advanced economies of the northern hemisphere have accelerated their investments in R&D as a response to an increased sophistication in global markets (Penner-Hahn and Shaver, 2005; Hsu et al., 2015). Since they command fewer resources than their MNC counterparts, SMEs in general conduct less R&D (Genc et al., 2019). SMEs are also more prone to the risk of bankruptcy than multinationals. Nevertheless, their growth and economic well-being is increasingly important for the countries of the OECD (2013). Innovation capability has been found to be among the most effective (and thus important) factors for competition (Zahra and George, 2002). Geroski et al. (1993) found that most SMEs with greater innovation rates record a higher productivity and are more profitable. Despite the above mentioned disadvantages relative to MNCs, SMEs agility and nimbleness can allow them to react more flexible on latest innovation developments. They can quickly develop new products and services for sophisticated niche markets and also enter and/or create new niches (Rosenbusch et al., 2011). Compared to big multinationals that need to make their investments profitable through maximizing economies of scale, innovating SMEs are less prone to the risk of cannibalizing their own products and processes when creating new markets (Shane, 2009). However, not every SME, whether it is internationalizing or not, is innovating. An entrepreneurial posture can help the SME in overcoming the challenges of "smallness". The founder and managers entrepreneurial orientation (EO) triggers the creation of important networks (Frey et al., 2013) and allows them to act proactive on market changes (Covin and Slevin, 1989; Wales et al., 2013, 2019). EO itself can become an important driver of SME innovation (Chesbrough, 2003; Genc et al., 2019).

1.2 SME internationalization

Even though the phenomenon of firm internationalization already emerged in the early 1920s, when imperialism as the dominant organization principle gradually disappeared and cross-border interactions between market economies started to emerge, it massively accelerated after the post-second-world-war era (Ruzzier et al., 2006). In these early stages of this field of research, scholars mainly focused on multinational corporations (MNCs) international activities in general, and foreign investments in particular, and searched for theoretical reasons why their existence is economically explainable at all (Rialp and Rialp, 2001). The subject of internationalizing small and medium-sized enterprises (SMEs) has mainly been studied conceptually and empirically since the 1970s (Che Senik et al., 2011; Fujita, 1998; McDougall et al., 1994; Rialp and Rialp, 2001; Zahra and George, 2002; Zucchella et al., 2007). The Internationalization of SMEs refers to non-domestic activities, usually categorized as exports of goods or services, marketing and technology partnerships and Foreign Direct Investment (FDI) overseas (Régnier and Wild, 2018). Even though in its beginning many theories on SME internationalization have been derived from MNCs theories, such as transaction cost theories or the ownership location internationalization (OLI) paradigm, they cannot be fully applied to the context of SMEs (Paul et al., 2017; Ruzier et al., 2006). Differences in terms of resources, management and external outreach strategy between MNCs and SMEs make it difficult to compare these two fields of research. The process of SME internationalization and its impact on the firm has been famously conceptualized by the scholars of the Nordic school, describing that the SME increases its international commitment in a gradual process of market knowledge and commitment decisions (Johanson and Vahlne, 1977). New competences are acquired incrementally to enter ever more distant markets as the process involves not only rising geographic distances but also the overcoming of differences in language, education, and business practices, otherwise labelled "psychic distances" (Vahlne and Johanson, 1977, 1990; Ojala Tyrväinen, 2009), with foreign partners. In the 1990s, a new type of internationalizing SMEs identified as 'born global' or 'international new ventures' (McDougall et al., 1994; Bell et al., 2003) has been described. Such firms target global 'lead markets' (Bell et al., 2003) and have global activities since the very early phase of their creation (such as some starts-up in ICT branches). They have generally high and specific skills and/or proprietary technologies used as competitive advantage. These global start-ups internationalise rapidly and do easily cope with 'psychic' distance. Definition efforts have been proposed in recent years, and have contributed to the identification of a new research domain in international entrepreneurship, whose boundaries are still being discussed (McDougall-Covin et al., 2014). Bell et al. (2003) propose an integrative model of SME internationalisation, which explains the differences between traditional, born global and born-again global firms. It suggests a causal link between the SME internal knowledge and the chosen mode of internationalisation. Schwens et al. (2018) argue that SMEs opt for entry modes with a higher commitment in the new foreign market throughout their process of experiential learning. Finally, the authors of the most significant contribution (Rialp and Rialp, 2001; Ruzier et al., 2006) that initiated the Nordic school from the 1970s, revisited their original model in the light of the network approach (Johanson and Vahlne, 2009). They concluded that relationships inside foreign business networks and the SMEs commitment to learning and trust-building are essential factors in increasing the firms degree of internationalization (Johanson and Vahlne, 2009). However, not a single theory has been able to encapsulate the whole SME internationalization process (Bell et al., 2003; Coviello and Jones, 2004; Gankema et al., 2000; Kraus, 2011; Ruzzier et al., 2006; Schueffel and Baldegger, 2008; Zahra and George, 2002; Zahra et al., 2005; Zucchella and Scabini, 2007). Nevertheless, it can be stated that SMEs active internationally are seen as more performing than non-internationalising ones (Fujita, 1998; Bell et al., 2003; Ruzzier et al., 2006).

Following the explanations from the previous sections, analyzing the driving forces of SME innovation in combination with its process of internationalization is a task of growing importance for various scholars. In the following sections we hypothesize on the relationship between the SMEs entrepreneurial posture as measured by EO, its degree of internationalization (DoI) and innovation performance. We demonstrate EO and DoI as driving factors of SME innovation performance.

1.3 The impact of EO on SME innovation performance

Entrepreneurial Orientation (EO) is considered having a positive impact on the firm's capability to explore and exploit new market opportunities (Lee et al., 2001; Wiklund and Sheperd, 2003). Firms with a high EO level are consistently searching for product and process-improvements through the acquisition of new knowledge (Zahra and George, 2002). They are also quickly responding to changing conditions in their environment. Baker and Sinkula (2009) found that in small businesses EO, together with market orientation, is positively affecting innovation and consequently boosting small firm profitability. Genc et al. (2019) found, while analyzing internationalizing SMEs from the middle east, that EO is positively related to SME innovation performance and has mediating effects on the DoI – Innovation performance relationship.

Regarding the individual dimensions of EO, it can be argued that EO obviously needs to be associated to SME innovation performance through its innovation dimension. Wiklund and Sheperd (2003), however, have suggested that EO's positive influence on firm innovation can be considered as universal. Due to their smaller amount of resources available, in particular financial and human resources, SMEs have to overcome high barriers in order to innovate. EO helps firms being more proactive in establishing exogenous networks from which new knowledge can be generated (Chesbrough, 2003; Wiklund and Sheperd, 2003). In a similar vein, Salomon and Shaver (2005) describe that learning advantages through newly acquired knowledge, such as generated through expanding international business networks, makes SMEs also more prone to be proactive and risk-taking and thus impacts positively the remaining two dimensions of EO.

Thus:

Hypothesis 1: the entrepreneurial orientation of SME is positively related to SME innovation performance

1.4 The impact of EO on SME internationalization

EO is considered stimulating SMEs client acquisition and improving their export performance (Mostafa et al., 2006). New market entry of an SME is often associated with SME innovation (Wales et al., 2019). This goes in hand with the dimensions of EO. SMEs that are exploring global opportunities are unavoidably taking risks, considering their limited amount of resources available for this purpose, and act in a proactive manner. Wiklund and Shepherd (2011) highlight the idea that international expansion is rather a sign of exploring (international) opportunities instead of exploiting existing (home) markets. A strong entrepreneurial posture can be associated with being ahead of competition by pursuing international opportunities and being a first mover in new markets. Alternatively, there is also evidence that EO stimulates both, international opportunity exploration as well as exploitation (Thanos et al., 2017). In a study among 150 Indian SMEs, Javalgi and Todd (2011) discovered that the EO relates positively to the SMEs share of foreign sales. Jantunen et al. (2005) combined the share of foreign sales with the scope of countries into a Degree of Internationalization (DoI) variable and found a strong positive impact resulting from EO at the case of a quantitative sample of Finnish firms.

Thus:

Hypothesis 2: the entrepreneurial orientation of SME is positively related to the degree of internationalization

1.5 The impact of internationalization on SMEs innovation performance

Pursuing business activities in new and unknown environments is a difficult and challenging task for SMEs. A foreign market is not simply an unseized opportunity but also means greater competition for the internationalizing SME. In order to penetrate foreign markets, it must have some significant competitive advantage over the prevailing competition. This competitive advantage is often generated through highly innovative products and services and/or innovative processes and procedures (Bertschek, 1995). On the contrary, it can also be argued that the internationalizing SME is gaining access to new knowledge from the foreign markets and that such knowledge would not be available solely in domestic ones.

Blind and Jungmittag (2004) found in their study on more than 2,000 German companies, that domestic firms that started to import and export reported an increase in product and process innovations. Foreign products can be associated with foreign production technology and foreign production knowledge. Such technology needs to be transferred and is impacting the domestic firm by creating technology spillovers. The same effects were also reported after the companies undertook foreign direct investments (FDI). Here again, production and process technologies need to be transferred, stimulating both, the firms' domestic and foreign innovation capacity (Blind and Jungmittag, 2004). An SME that is importing and exporting its products and services as well as one undertaking FDI's is forced to incorporate the foreign business partner's knowledge about its product and processes. This knowledge is gained and fostered through processes observing its foreign partners (Banerjee et al., 2005) and intensified learning (Genc et al., 2019). Not only business partners but the foreign customer itself, whether private or business, can become a driving force for innovation (Cloodt et al.,

2006). The access to foreign knowledge can also be utilized to produce higher-quality innovations (Salomon and Shaver, 2005). Additionally, an internationalizing SME can also relocate its R&D to where it is most cost effective and productive (Kafourous and Buckley, 2008).

However, most research on the impact of internationalization on innovation was performed with large or medium-large sized firms. Genc et al. (2019) drew attention to the fact that so far, the relationship has not yet been extensively studied in the context of SMEs. Among the few studies existing on behalf of SMEs we find Frey et al. (2013) study on 300 Italian SMEs operating in sustainable economic sectors. They found support for positive effects from SMEs "level of internationalization" on their innovation capacity and effective innovations. Genc et al. (2019) studied the underlying mechanism of the internationalization innovation relationship and did also find a positive relationship between DoI and Innovation. In addition, they explored the nature of this relationship and found that it is mediated through Market orientation and EO. Ren et al. (2015) also found a positive relationship between internationalization and innovation and investigated on moderating factors of this relationship. Nevertheless, before exploring any complex relationship patterns, we first aim to concentrate on the overall relationship between these two variables in the context of SMEs.

Thus:

Hypothesis 3: the degree of internationalization has a direct effect on SME innovation performance.

Altogether our model consists of entrepreneurial orientation (EO) as an independent variable, positively impacting the SMEs degree of internationalization (DoI) and its innovation performance, as well as DoI itself also impacting innovation performance. As depicted on Fig. 1 below, we thereby control for firm size and the firms' experience in international business.

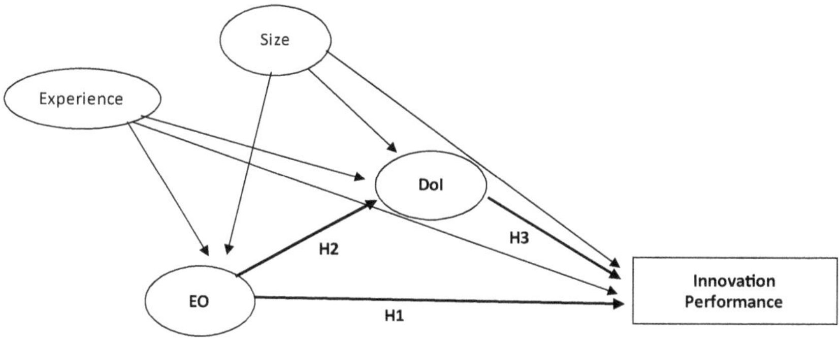

Fig. 1: The Interrelating Effects of EO, DoI and SME Innovation Performance

2. Method

2.1. The survey instruments

We chose internationalizing SMEs from the Swiss International Entrepreneurship Surveys (SIES) as our research setting. Given its relatively large population of highly innovative and internationalizing SMEs, Switzerland is providing an ideal setting for this type of data. The SIES examines the status of internationalizing behavior of Swiss SMEs and identifies current trends (Baldegger and Wild, 2019). Therefore, a comprehensive survey has been conducted five times respectively in a three-years interval from 2007 to 2019. The survey-team uses the EU definition of an SME as having fewer than 250 employees as their first sampling condition ("Bundesamt für Statistik," 2019; Muller et al., 2018). They also set a lower limit of annual foreign sales revenues of at least 5 % of total sales revenues to ensure international activity among the sampled firms (Brouthers et al., 2015; Brush, 2013). Data for the sampling procedure were ordered from the business data provider Bisnode D&B Ltd. According to the Federal Customs Administrations and the Federal Statistical Office, 7.8 % or approximately 45,000 SMEs export their goods and services ("Bundesamt für Statistik," 2019). The SMEs from the ordered dataset were categorized according to their distribution across the different linguistic and economic regions in Switzerland. In Switzerland, there is a main distinction between the German-speaking region bordering Germany and Austria, and the Latin region where a

French-speaking region is bordering France and a minor Italian-speaking part is bordering Italy. These three parts differ economically, as well as socially and culturally – representing well the diversity among SMEs – which is taken into account in this survey (Adler and Sinner, 2018). Subsequently, maintaining the relative weight of each category, 8,000 SMEs were randomly selected in this three-year interval and surveyed. They form almost 20 % of all exporting SMEs based in Switzerland. In each selected SME, only executive-level decision makers were targeted, since the choice of questions focuses specifically on high-level insights. By doing so, the survey team ensures that the respondents possess knowledge of innovation within the firm and that they are likely to have a wide-ranging view on the firm's strategic orientation and its internationalization activities (Genc et al., 2019). Finally, they confine the research sample to SMEs that are headquartered in Switzerland and included firm-level control variables, such as firm size, year of first exports and percentage of total sales revenues generated in foreign markets as of the end of the year prior the survey in order to purge the potential disturbance caused by a group affiliation or infrequently exporting SMEs (Deng and Sinkovics, 2018). A total of between 350 and 850 valid responses were achieved at the end of each survey, yielding a response rate of between 4.5 % and 10.5 %.

2.2. Sample description

The sample frame comprises internationalizing SMEs headquartered in one of the major economic regions in Switzerland. The overall sample frame consists of 1,519 firms, of which 607 firms were from the survey in 2010, 601 firms from the survey in 2016 and 311 firms in the survey of 2019. In each of these three specific surveys, a set of questions about the impact of internationalization on the SME's innovative strength was tested.

Tab. 1: The sample composition

Sample composition		
Category	n	%
Firm size		
1–9 employees (micro)	607	40.0 %
10–49 employees (small)	601	39.6 %
50–249 employees (medium)	311	20.5 %
Firm age		
< 10 years	80	4.9 %
11–20 years	341	20.8 %
20–30 years	379	23.2 %
30–40 years	236	14.4 %
40–50 years	133	8.1 %
More than 50 years	376	23.0 %
Industry of firm		
Mechanical engineering, electrical and metal industry	456	29.5 %
Chemistry, medical technology, pharmaceutical industry, cosmetics	142	9.2 %
Rest of manufacturing industry	195	12.7 %
Trade	239	15.5 %
Services	512	33.2 %
Respondent		
Founder & CEO	652	42.2 %
CEO	701	45.4 %
Senior management	191	12.4 %

As shown in Tab. 1, the sample represents SMEs from various industries and of various size and age. The largest share of the sample has so-called micro-sized firms with up to 9 employees (607 firms; 40 %) and small-sized ones with between 10 and 49 employees (601 firms; 19.6 %) as measured in full-time equivalents. Medium-sized firms with between 50 and 249 employees account for around one fifth of the sample. Half of the sample firms, 793 SMEs respectively 51.4 %, are active in manufacturing industries such as Mechanical and electrical engineering, chemistry as well as medical and pharmaceutical industries. The other half is divided into trade (239; 15.5 %) and services (512; 33.2 %). In addition, it should be noted that 87.6 % of the respondents were either owner and CEO (42.2 %) or CEO of the firm (45.4 %). 12.4 % belong to other high-level functions of the senior management.

2.3. Sample bias testing

In order to assess any possible bias between the respondent firms from the different surveys, non-bias tests were carried out. It reflected differences in selected firmographic and the independent variable DoI, which was calculated as the standardized product of FSTS and the number of countries, and was performed according to the non-response bias test from Armstrong and Overton (1977). We compared the firmographic variable size and FSTS as well as the independent variable DoI (product of FSTS, the number of countries and the number of continents) of the SME from each of the three surveys. The t-tests performed on firm size, FSTS and DoI between the first and the second, the first and the third as well as the second and the third group revealed no statistically significant difference ($p > 0.05$).

Tab. 2: Sample bias testing with student's t-test

Variable		**N**	**Mean**	**Std. Deviation**	**Mean difference Sample 1 Sample 2**	**Mean Difference Sample 1 Sample 3**	**Mean Difference Sample 2 Sample 3**
FSTS	Sample 1	509	56.14	35.47	4.82	9.53	-
	Sample 2	515	51.32	35.74	4.82	-	4.71
	Sample 3	234	46.61	37.20	-	9.53	4.71
Firm size	Sample 1	514	27.18	41.48	2.28	1.40	-
	Sample 2	581	24.90	40.46	2.28	-	-0.88
	Sample 3	309	25.78	44.80	-	1.40	-0.88
DoI	Sample 1	457	168.945	9351	-248.30	-74.326	-
	Sample 2	288	417.245	9298	-248.30	-	173.974
	Sample 3	183	243.271	2488	-	-74.326	173.974

*Significant at the 0.05 level (two-tailed); **significant at the 0.01 level (two-tailed); ***significant at the 0.001 level (two tailed);

2.4. Measures

The dependent variable in the model is labelled innovation-performance. It is measured through a reflective measure combining four items. The surveyed SMEs had to assess their companies' innovative capacity based on a self-evaluation. The four-items included (1) the number of patents generated by the firm, (2) new services and products developed, (3) new organizational developments, and (4) skilled personnel. In several studies, the number of patents owned is selected as the only measure of a firms' innovation performance (Brunnermeier and Cohen, 2003; Hsu et al., 2015; Genc et al., 2019). The uses of other constructs to measure a company's innovativeness are less common. Freeman and Soete (1997) refer to the rate of introduction of new products and devices as well as new processes in order to measure innovative performance in a "narrower sense" (Hagedoorn and Cloodt, 2003). In the same vein, Hitt et al. (1996) measures the degree to which new product announcements were made by companies in order to estimate their innovation performance. However, this measure alone causes problems since they are simply accepted because companies identify them as new. Nelson and Winter (1982) define a firm's innovation power considering their R&D efforts and inputs as part of their routines in managing R&D, their R&D expenditures and the skills that companies develop in creating an R&D strategy with a stable set of long term projects (Hagedoorn, 1989).

The first independent variable in the model is degree of internationalization (DoI). Multiple dimensions can be used in order to assess the progress of firm's internationalization process (Ramaswamy et al., 1996; Sullivan, 1994, 1996). We aimed to measure internationalization as comprehensively as possible by using a two-item construct using the following two factors: First, we measured the percentage of sales in foreign markets to total firm sales (Knight and Cavusgil, 2004; Lu and Beamish, 2006; McDougall and Oviatt, 1996). On average the surveyed SMEs generated 43.45 % of their total sales in foreign markets (standard deviation of 37.78). Second, we took stock of the number of foreign countries from which a firm is generating turnover. This measure has been used by numerous scholars beforehand (Stopford and Wells, 1972; Sullivan, 1994; Vernon, 1972).

The second independent variable in the model is entrepreneurial orientation (EO). It is consisting of nine items based on three dimensions: innovation, proactiveness, and risk-taking. The scale is based on Miller and Friesen's (1983) conceptualization of entrepreneurship and was further developed by Covin and Slevin (1989) in order to measure a firm's strategic posture. Covin and Slevin (1989) development concerned Miller and Friesen's (1983) and Khandwalla's (1977) items 1, 2, 3, 7, and 8, whereas the items 4, 5, 6, and 9 have remained unchanged ever since. Modern literature on entrepreneurship and firm performance uses this measure consistently (Lumpkin and Dess, 1996, 2001; Rauch et al., 2009; Wiklund and

Shepherd, 2003). The items are of the forced-choice type, the first three assessing the firm's tendency toward innovation, the second three its proactive orientation, and the third three its risk-taking propensity. A seven-point scale divides pairs of opposite statements. The respondents characterized their firms' strategic posture on the basis of this Likert scale: the higher their overall score, the more entrepreneurial the firm's strategic posture (Covin and Slevin, 1989). The mean score per item ranged from 3.82 to 4.62, with an overall mean of 4.25 and a standard deviation of 1.57.

We controlled for some variables that might impact the SME innovation performance in order to isolate the impact of the variables on the tested relationship in the model. Several scholars highlighted the differences between the SMEs size and its age and experience on the constructs such as EO (Tang et al., 2013; Eshima and Anderson, 2017; Wales et al., 2013) innovation performance (Wadhwa and Kotha, 2006; Genc et al., 2019) and the degree of internationalization (Meschi et al., 2017; Garcia-Garcia et al., 2017). Whereas the experience is measured in years since the SME started its first international activities (in general by starting to export), we measure the size through the number of employees as indicated in full-time equivalents (FTE).

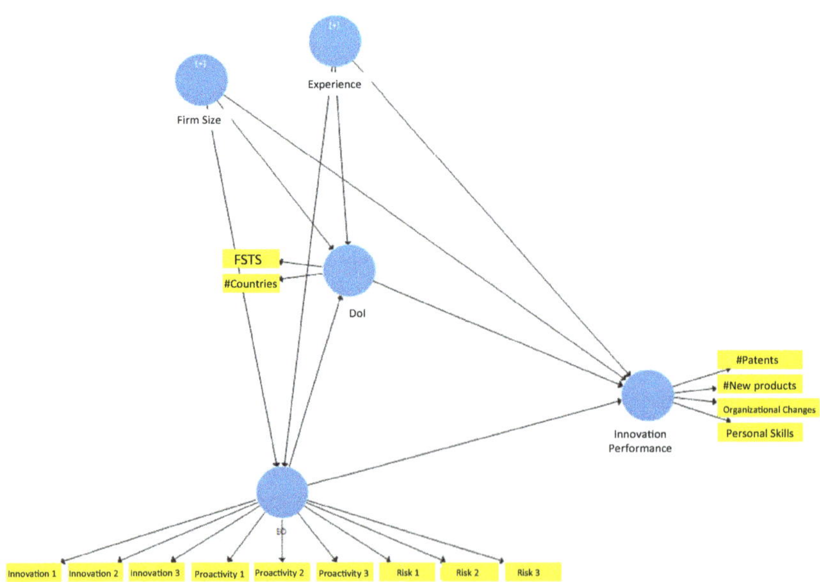

Fig. 2: The Research Model and Measurement Constructs

2.5. Model estimation

Since we are investigating on the nature of the relationship between various-item-constructs such as EO, DoI and Innovation-Impact, our model and research setting can be considered as complex and explorative. Therefore, we had to select an analysis method that seemed robust and enables the simultaneous analysis of path and measurement models of reflective constructs (Chin et al., 2008; Genc et al., 2019).

By applying the smart PLS 3 software (Hair et al., 2017), we used a partial least squares (PLS) technique in order to validate and test the conceptual model as depicted in Fig. 2. The PLS approach is a variance-based structural equation modelling technique aimed to test and validate structural measurement models in explorative types of research.

Since it is avoiding some of the restrictive assumptions usually enforced by covariance-based models, it is considered as a rather robust technique. In this sense it allows, among others, for non-normal distribution, high degrees of model complexity such as constructs with varying numbers of items and missing values (Ringle et al., 2005; Ringle et al., 2012; Baldegger et al., 2021; Hair et al., 2017).

The analysis is conducted and, in the following, presented in two steps. First, the adequacy of the measurement model was evaluated by inspecting the reliability of each item, their internal consistency when expected to measure the same construct, and the discriminant validity between the constructs. Secondly, the resulting model coefficients were interpreted.

3. Findings

3.1. Assessing the reflective measurement model

In order to determine the individual item validity and reliability, the loadings of each measure on their corresponding constructs was examined. Therefore, we calculated Cronbach's α of each item (Hulland, 1999). The dependent variable "Innovation performance" includes four items, the Cronbach's α for this construct amounts to 0.922. The independent variable "Entrepreneurial Orientation (EO)" is constructed with nine items, it's Cronbach's α is 0.747. the second independent variable "Degree of Internationalization (DoI)" is constructed with two items, its Cronbach's α is 0.456 and thus on the edge of the acceptable but still considered in the sufficient range starting with 0.45 (Taber, 2017). In the original DoI construct, the years of internationalization was added to FSTS and number of countries. Due to insufficiently high factor loadings this item then was excluded for further analyses. However, we kept the remaining two items considering that, next to an acceptable Cronbach's alpha, the values for composite reliability and the average variance extracted was above the recommended cut-off level (Genc et al., 2017; Hair et al., 2017). For all variables in the model, the composite reliability value is above the cut-off value of 0.7 and thus acceptable (Hair et al., 2017).

Next, we examined the discriminant validity. The discriminant validity ensures that each construct used is distinctive. In order to count as a reflective measurement model, the indicators must be highly correlated (Hulland, 1999). Discriminant validity was assessed by analyzing the item loadings and by evaluating average variance extracted (AVE) according to the Fornell-Larcker criterion. By considering Tab. 3 we can state that the factor-loading indicators are greater on the indicated constructs than all loadings of the other constructs (Hair et al., 2017). This is true for the dependent variable Innovation Performance as well as for the other two independent variables. Tab. 3 displays the square root of the AVE of each construct on the diagonal and the variances shared with other constructs. As required, all elements on the diagonal are greater than all other entries in the corresponding rows and columns (Hair et al., 2017; Baldegger et al., 2021). Consequently, we conclude that our measurement model is robust in terms of their internal consistency and reliability.

Tab. 3: Item reliability of the research model

Construct	**Number of items**	**Cronbach's α**	**Composite realiability**	**AVE**
Innovation performance	4	0.922	0.945	0.811
Entrepreneurial orientation	9	0.546	0.765	0.628
Degree of Internationalization	2	0.747	0.810	0.329
Size	1	1	1	1
Age	1	1	1	1

3.2. Structural model and hypothesis testing

We tested the relations in our structural model as suggested in our hypotheses by looking at significant path coefficients. A two-tailed bootstrapping sampling method with replacement was applied therefore. Since the original sample size is already fairly large, we computed 500 bootstrapping runs as recommended by Chin (1998). Several authors actually recommend that there should be a minimum of 20 times as many observations as variables to be tested in the model (Chin, 1998; Genc et al., 2017). In our original model and before dismissing some inconsistent items we counted around 20 variables. Therefore, it would be resulting in a minimum sample size of 400 observations, which is by far exceeded. The results are presented in Fig. 3.

First, we tested our basic model with EO as an independent variable influencing DoI and Innovation Impact as well as DoI influencing Innovation Impact as well, while controlling for the SMEs international experience in years and firm size. The path between DoI and Innovation performance is significant on the $p < 0.05$ level but rather weak ($\beta = 0.043$). Similarly, we found a significant but weak path from EO to DoI ($\beta = 0.057$, $p < 0.05$). EO's impact on Innovation performance was found to be stronger and highly significant ($\beta = 0.304$, $p < 0.001$). International experience as a control variable was found to have a mediocre positive but significant impact on DoI ($\beta = 0.125$, $p < 0.01$) and a weak negative impact on EO ($\beta = -0.067$, $p < 0.05$). No path could be confirmed between International Experience and Innovation Performance. Similarly, Firm size was found to be positively and highly significant related to DoI ($\beta = 0.128$, $p < 0.001$) and EO ($\beta = 0.151$, $p < 0.001$) but not to Innovation performance. This model results in weak R2 statistics (Chin, 1998): R2 = 0.046 for DoI and R2 = 0.094 for Innovation Performance (see Fig. 3). Thus, the variance explained in the endogenous constructs is rather low. Now, we tested for moderating effects of DoI on the EO – Innovation Performance relationship and moderating effects of EO on the DoI – Innovation Performance relationship. Both effects were found to be insignificant. Then, we tested quadratic effect of both independent variables DoI and EO on Innovation Performance as dependent variable. Here again, we found no quadratic effect from DoI on Innovation Performance. However, the positive effect from EO on Innovation Performance was found negatively quadratic on Innovation Performance ($\beta = -0.173$, $p < 0.001$). Here again, we also found a significant positive effect of firm size DoI (ß = 0.175, p <0.001) and EO (ß = 0.131, p < 0.001). In this model, R2 statistics for EO and Innovation performance could be slightly improved and the model is explaining more variance of these two variables: R2 = 0.033 for DoI, R2 = 0.073 for EO, and R2 = 0.132 for Innovation Performance.

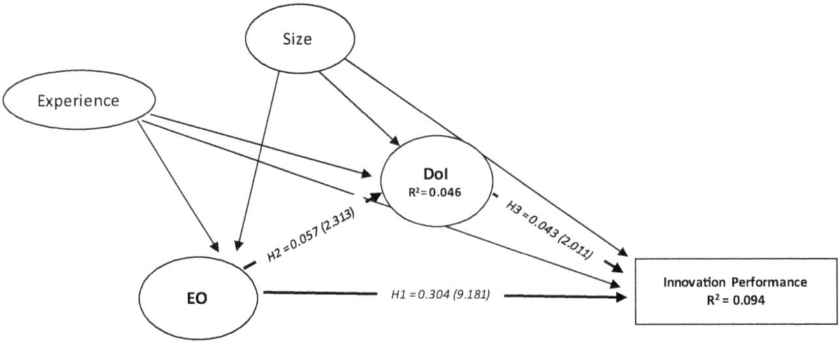

Fig. 3: PLS Results with Path Coefficients and T-Statistics for the Overall Model (linear effects)

3.3. Further analyses on the firm size

Since we observed a significant positive path relationship between the control variable Firm size and the explaining variables DoI and EO, we wanted to explore this relationship more in-depth. In particular the difference. Of particular interest were the differences between micro and medium-sized enterprises. We thus tested both models independently for micro-sized firms with up to 9 FTE and medium-sized ones with between 50 and 249 FTE. The PLS Results with path coefficients and T-statistics are depicted in Fig. 4. Our tests on micro-sized firms revealed insignificant effects from EO on DoI and from DoI on Innovation Performance. The path between EO and Innovation Performance however was significant (ß = 0.131, p < 0.05, n = 607), so was the square effect of EO on DoI (ß = –0.184, p < 0.05). The control variable International Experience was reported being insignificant. When testing the same model for medium-sized firms, we found that the EO to DoI path was likewise insignificant, and so was the control variable International Experience on all the other tested variables in the model. However, whereas also the EO to Innovation Performance relation was reported insignificant, we now found a significant positive relationship from DoI on Innovation Performance ($\beta = 0.147$, $p < 0.05$, $n = 311$).

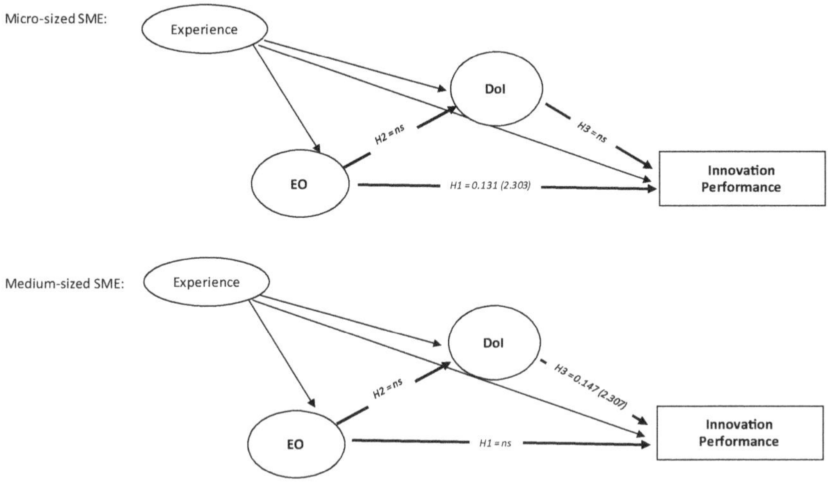

Fig. 4: PLS Results with Path Coefficients and T-Statistics for the two Sub-Samples

4. Discussion

This empirical contribution offers insights into the relationship among EO, DoI and Innovation Performance for internationalizing SMEs. Drawing on data from more than 1,500 internationalizing SMEs that we collected over a time period of 10 years, we aimed to explore this relationship in its depth. In the overall sample of SMEs, we found that SMEs Innovation Performance is significantly influenced by the Degree of Internationalization (DoI). This confirms the findings from scholars such as Wiklund and Sheperd (2003) and Salomon and Shaver (2005) demonstrating that an increase in international activities enhances the SMEs innovation capacity. Despite the significance of the result, it should be noted that only a very weak correlation was measured. On one hand, this could be explained by the highly heterogenous sample of internationalizing SMEs, spread over many industries and from various different backgrounds. Our study has not been conducted in a specific industry such as producing or trading industries solely and/or with SMEs that are part of a specific industry network such as in the case of many of previous publications in this field. In this regard, we can assume that this positive relationship between DoI and SME innovation performance exists in general traits. On the other hand, this result gives indications for other influencing variables, whether independent or contextual. Similarly to the DoI – Innovation performance relationship, the influence of Entrepreneurial Orientation (EO) on DoI was significant but weak. Although this also supports the many scholars who found a positive relationship between these two variables (Javalgi and Todd, 2011; Jantunen et al., 2005; Thanos et al., 2017), it also questions the extent to which this positive relationship needs to be further explored. Older publications described this relationship as being u-shaped (Geringer et al., 1989) whereas within newer streams of research, this relationship has also already been described as being inversely u-shaped (Capar and Kotabe, 2003; Ruigrok and Wagner, 2003). Being aware about the debate on the impact of EO on DoI, we tested these two variables for quadratic effects. According to our results, no quadratic relation could be confirmed, leading to the conclusion that this significant but weak relationship seems to be rather linear.

The path effect from EO on Innovation Performance, however, was reported being significantly positive and well stronger. This overall effect was even reported being negatively quadratic thus inversely u-shaped. It can be concluded from this, that there must be an optimum level of EO at which the innovative strength in the company is most strongly stimulated. The EO construct captures innovativeness with a set of three items (from a total of nine items). Certainly, this explains partially the positive and significant relationship between the SMEs EO and its innovation performance. But, as Kreiser and Davis (2010) are pointing out, also proactivity and being risk-prone, referring to the two remaining subdimensions of EO, have a strong effect on the SME's overall performance. Entering foreign markets is an undertaking that requires the firm to act proactive and involves an appetite for risk-taking, and only those firms who are particularly proactive and risk-taking are also likely to innovate. According to our results on the general sample, an innovative, proactive and risk-taking posture leads to a higher degree of internationalization and to a better innovation performance, but the latter is more influenced by the strategic posture (meaning EO) than by the degree of internationalization (DoI).

In contrast to the findings of Genc et al. (2019) we did not find moderating effects from EO on the DoI – Innovation performance relationship. Our result rather suggests that both, EO and DoI act as independent variables of which none is mediating the other and only EO slightly impacts DoI. When analyzing our results, it is important to consider that we used a new set of items in order to measure the SMEs innovation performance. Most studies use the number of patents (Genc et al., 2019) or general spendings in R&D in relation to the total number of employees (Hitt et al., 1997) in order to measure innovation performance. In our construct, the SMEs reported their innovation performance based on a self-evaluation comprising not just the number of new patents, but also new products, organizational changes and the improvements of employees' skills. The construct therefore does not refer to objective measures but to a self-evaluation. Altogether, it can be considered being more comprehensive than one of these single items.

According to our results, it can be assumed that EO does impact the SMEs innovation performance stronger than DoI does, and that this relationship is inversely u-shaped. Since firm size was reported having a significant impact on both variables explaining Innovation Performance, we decided to test the model for both opposite types of SMEs exclusively, namely micro- and medium-sized-firms. In analyzing these subsamples, we found that for micro-sized firms only EO has a positive effect on Innovation Performance whereas for medium-sized firms, Innovation Performance is affected solely by DoI and not by EO. Hence, the scope and intensity of international activities affects innovation performance solely in medium-sized firms of between 50 and 249 FTE. The strong impact from EO on micro-firm innovation performance can be explained by the importance of exogenous networks created through the entrepreneurial behavior of the firm-leaders. Several authors pointed out that high levels of EO among the team helps creating such networks and that the learning advantages through these networks stimulates innovation performance (Chesbrough, 2003; Wiklund and Sheperd, 2003; Salomon and Shaver, 2005). This can be assumed to be particularly true for internationally active micro-sized firms in which the mere intensity and scope of internationalization does not seem to be essential for innovativeness. In most cases, internationalization of microenterprises is generated through exports. Medium-sized firms, on the other hand, are able to internationalize through FDI. A wider scope and more intense collaboration with foreign partners allow the staff to access Their management and employees might benefit from the de-localization of internal business structures and from foreign collaborations. It can be assumed that a broader degree of internationalization allows their management and employees to benefit from a wider range of knowledge. Positive effects described as observing foreign partners (Banerjee et al., 2005; Genc et al., 2019) and customers (Cloodt et al., 2006), technology spillovers from knowledge transfers into and from foreign countries (Blind and Jungmittag, 2004) and the relocation of R&D to more cost effective and productive regions (Kafourous and Buckley, 2008) weigh more heavily on their innovation performance. In general, we can state that our results question the extent to which a construct on SME innovation performance can be applied to internationalizing SMEs in general. More specific research on innovation performance with regard to firm size need to be conducted will provide further insights.

5. Managerial implications

This study is not exempt from limitations. Different construct exists that measure our depended variable, the innovation performance of firms. Selecting a single measure item in order to measure innovation performance is common. In many cases, scholars have relied themselves on factually measurable indicators such as the number of patents, the number of new products created, or R&D spending, often even in relation to firm size. In our study, we rely on a self-evaluation of CEOs and senior management. On one hand, using a different measure allows for additional learnings about this explained variable. On the other hand, the reliability and objectivity of our innovation performance measure might therefore not be free of any bias.There are implications for practice within SMEs, whether they are micro-, small- or medium-sized, and for individual executives and their successors and offers them an opportunity to reflect.

According to our findings, both the degree of internationalization as well as the strategic posture as measured by EO are having a positive impact on the SMEs innovation performance. In particular for internationally active microenterprise with up to 10 employees, however, this does not mean that they have to intensify their international business as much as possible in order to generate positive effects on their innovation performance. Proactive and risk-taking behavior and a strong leadership-based culture that supports innovation seems to be far more effective than a mere dispersion of foreign clients across various countries. Firm leaders need to be aware of the extent to which their strategic stance strengthens the innovative power of their company.

Innovation in internationalizing micro-sized firms is triggered by other means than within medium-sized firms. In the course of the life-cycle of an SME, different impulses are therefore needed in order to ensure innovation power. For a medium-sized SME that is able to enter foreign business partnerships and to conduct foreign direct investments, keeping R&D efforts on home soil can be a hindrance for their future innovation performance.

Our study results do also include findings relevant for policy makers. They should be aware of the potential of having good framework conditions for internationalizing SMEs in order to promote the innovative strength of their economy. Since in many economies SME make out the large part of the total population of firms and employ more than half of the working population, the innovation power emanating from these companies must not be underestimated.

6. Limitations and future research

The measure of the degree of innovation, however, is often composed by a ratio of foreign sales to total sales (FSTS) and indications about the geographic scope. We aimed to rely on the number of geographic regions respectively on continents for our DoI measure too. Unfortunately, by adding this additional item the internal construct validity and reliability was no longer given and we had to exclude this item for further analysis. This was unfortunate as we did not have another metric for the distance between the SMEs home and focal markets. In particular the psychic distance to foreign markets, as generated through intercultural differences such differences in conducting a business and communicating as well as through different contextual and economic factors between home and focal market, is certainly playing a crucial role for innovation performance within internationalizing SMEs.

Further research regarding the impact of distance for SME innovation performance is certainly needed. Our test was conducted on a multi-sector analysis of SME with a fairly large sample of more than 1,500 SMEs. Although this is helpful for drawing general conclusions, it did not enable us to investigate about the specific conditions for internationalization and innovation in individual industries. We hope that this work motivates future researchers to further improve our understanding of the link between entrepreneurial orientation, internationalization and innovation.

References

Adler, T., & Sinner, L. (2018). La Suisse latine n'existe pas. Zürich/Lausanne: Avenir-Suisse.

Armstrong, J. S., & Overton, T. S. (1977). Estimating nonresponse bias in mail surveys. Journal of Marketing Research, 14(3), 396–402.

Baker, W. E., & Sinkula, J. M. (2009). The complementary effects of market orientation and entrepreneurial orientation on profitability in small businesses. Journal of Small Business Management, 47(4), 443–464.

Baldegger, R., & Wild, P. (2019). Swiss international entrepreneurship survey (SIES) 2019. Haute école de gestion Fribourg (HEG-FR), Haute école spécialisée de Suisse occidentale (HES-SO).

Baldegger, R., Wild, P., & Schueffel, P. (2021). The Effects of Entrepreneurial Orientation in a Digital and International Setting. Entrepreneurial Orientation: Epistemological, Theoretical, and Empirical Perspectives (Advances in Entrepreneurship, Firm Emergence and Growth, Vol. 22), Emerald Publishing Limited, 145–174.

Banerjee, S., Prabhu, J. C., & Chandy, R. K. (2015). Indirect learning: How emerging-market firms grow in developed markets. Journal of Marketing, 79(1), 10–28.

Bell, J., McNaughton, R., Young, S., & Crick, D. (2003). Towards an integrative model of small firm internationalisation. Journal of International Entrepreneurship, 1(4), 339–362.

Bertschek, I. (1995). Product and process innovation as a response to increasing imports and foreign direct investment. The Journal of Industrial Economics, 341–357.

Blind, K., & Jungmittag, A. (2004). Foreign direct investment, imports and innovations in the service industry. Review of Industrial Organization, 25(2), 205–227.

Brouthers, K. D., Nakos, G., & Dimitratos, P. (2015). SME entrepreneurial orientation, international performance, and the moderating role of strategic alliances. Entrepreneurship Theory and Practice, 39(5), 1161–1187.

Brouwer, E., & Kleinknecht, A. (1999). Innovative output, and a firm's propensity to patents: An exploration of CIS micro data. Research Policy, 28, 615–624.

Brunnermeier, S. B., & Cohen, M. A. (2003). Determinants of environmental innovation in US manufacturing industries. Journal of Environmental Economics and Management, 45(2), 278–293.

Bruque, S., & Moyano, J. (2007). Organisational determinants of information technology adoption and implementation in SMEs: The case of family and cooperative firms. Technovation, 27(5), 241–253.

Brush, C., Edelman, L., & Manolova, T. (2002). The impact of resources on small firm internationalization. Journal of Small Business Strategy, 13(1), 1–17.

Bundesamt für Statistik. (2019, September 8). Kleine und mittlere Unternehmen. Retrieved May 5, 2021 from https://www.bfs.admin.ch/bfs/de/home/statistiken/industrie-dienstleistungen/unternehmenbeschaeftigte/wirtschaftsstruktur-unternehmen/kmu.html

Che Senik, Z., Scott-Ladd, B., Entrekin, L., & Adham, K. A. (2011). Networking and internationalization of SMEs in emerging economies. Journal of International Entrepreneurship, 9(4), 259–281.

Chesbrough, H. (2003). Open innovation: The new imperative for creating and profiting from technology. Harvard Business School Press, Boston.

Chin, W. W. (1998). The partial least squares approach to structural equation modeling. Modern methods for business research, 295(2), 295–336

Chin, W. W., Peterson, R. A., & Brown, S. P. (2008). Structural equation modeling in marketing: Some practical reminders. Journal of Marketing Theory and Practice, 16(4), 287–298.

Cloodt, M., Hagedoorn, J., & Van Kranenburg, H. (2006). Mergers and acquisitions: Their effect on the innovative performance of companies in high-tech industries. Research Policy, 35(5), 642–654.

Coviello, N. E., & Munro, H. J. (1995). Growing the entrepreneurial firm: Networking for international market development. European Journal of Marketing, 29 (7), 49–61.

Covin, J. G., & Slevin, D. P. (1989). Strategic management of small firms in hostile and benign environments. Strategic Management Journal, 10(1), 75–87.

Deng, Z., & Sinkovics, R. R. (2018). Rapid expansion of international new ventures across institutional distance. Journal of International Business Studies, 49(8), 1010–1032.

Eshima, Y., & Anderson, B. S. (2017). Firm growth, adaptive capability, and entrepreneurial orientation. Strategic Management Journal, 38(3), 770–779.

Freeman, C., & Soete, L. (1997). The Economics of Industrial Innovation. MIT Press, Cambridge, MA.

Frey, M., Iraldo, F., & Testa, F. (2013). The determinants of innovation in green supply chains: Evidence from an Italian sectoral study. R&D Management, 43(4), 352–364.

Fujita, M. (1998). The Transnational Activities of Small and Medium-sized Enterprises.Kluwer Academic Publisher, Boston.

Gabrielsson, P., Gabrielsson, M., & Gabrielsson, H. (2008). International advertising campaigns in fast-moving consumer goods companies originating from a SMOPEC country. International Business Review, 17(6), 714–728.

Genc, E., Dayan, M., & Genc, O. F. (2019). The impact of SME internationalization on innovation: The mediating role of market and entrepreneurial orientation. Industrial Marketing Management, 82, 253–264.

Geroski, P., Machin, S., & Van Reenen, J. (1993). The profitability of innovating firms. The RAND Journal of Economics, 24(2), 198–211.

Hagedoorn, J. (1989). The Dynamic Analysis of Innovation and Diffusion. Pinter, London.

Hagedoorn, J., & Cloodt, M. (2003). Measuring innovative performance: Is there an advantage in using multiple indicators? Research Policy, 32(8), 1365.

Hair, J. F., Hult, G. T. M., Ringle, C. M., & Sarstedt, M. (2017). A Primer on Partial Least Squares Structural Equation Modeling (PLS-SEM), 2nd ed. Sage, Thousand Oaks, CA.

Hitt, M. A., Hoskisson, R. E., Johnson, R. A., & Moesel, D. D. (1996). The market for corporate control and firm innovation. Academy of Management Journal, 39(5), 1084–1119.

Hsu, C.-W., Lien, Y.-C., & Chen, H. (2013). International ambidexterity and firm performance in small emerging economies. Journal of World Business, 48, 58–67.

Hsu, C. W., Lien, Y. C., & Chen, H. (2015). R&D internationalization and innovation performance. International Business Review, 24(2), 187–195.

Jantunen, A., Puumalainen, K., Saarenketo, S., & Kyläheiko, K. (2005). Entrepreneurial orientation, dynamic capabilities and international performance. Journal of International Entrepreneurship, 3(3), 223–243.

Javalgi, R. R. G., & Todd, P. R. (2011). Entrepreneurial orientation, management commitment, and human capital: The internationalization of SMEs in India. Journal of Business Research, 64(9), 1004–1010.

Johanson, J., & Vahlne, J. E. (1977). The internationalization process of the firm – a model of knowledge development and increasing foreign market commitments. Journal of International Business Studies, 8(1), 23–33.

Johanson, J., & Vahlne, J. E. (1990). The mechanism of internationalisation. International Marketing Review, 7(4), 11–24

Kafouros, M. I., & Buckley, P. J. (2008). Under what conditions do firms benefit from the research efforts of other organizations?. Research Policy, 37(2), 225–239.

Khandwalla, P. N. (1977). The Design of Organizations. Harcourt Brace Jovanovich, New York, NY.

Knight, G. A., & Cavusgil, S. T. (2004). Innovation, organizational capabilities, and the born-global firm. Journal of international business studies, 35(2), 124–141.

Lee, C., Lee, K., & Pennings, J. M. (2001). Internal capabilities, external networks, and performance: A study on technology-based ventures. Strategic Management Journal, 22(6–7), 615–640.

Lu, J. W., & Beamish, P. W. (2006). SME internationalization and performance: Growth vs. profitability. Journal of International Entrepreneurship, 4(1), 27–48.

Lumpkin, G. T., & Dess, G. G. (1996). Clarifying the entrepreneurial orientation construct and linking it to performance. Academy of Management Review, 21(1), 135–172.

Lumpkin, G. T., & Dess, G. G. (2001). Linking two dimensions of entrepreneurial orientation to firm performance: The moderating role of environment and industry life cycle. Journal of Business Venturing, 16(5), 429–451.

McDougall, P. P., Shane, S., & Oviatt, B. M. (1994). Explaining the formation of international new ventures: The limits of theories from international business research. Journal of Business Venturing, 9(6), 469–487.

McDougall–Covin, P., Jones, M. V., & Serapio, M. G. (2014). High–potential concepts, phenomena, and theories for the advancement of international entrepreneurship research. Entrepreneurship Theory and Practice, 38(1), 1–10.

Meschi, P. X., Ricard, A., & Moore, E. T. (2017). Fast and furious or slow and cautious? The joint impact of age at internationalization, speed, and risk diversity on the survival of exporting firms. Journal of International Management, 23(3), 279–291.

Miller, D., & Friesen, P. H. (1983). The correlates of entrepreneurship in three types of firms. Management Science, 29(7), 770–791.

Mostafa, R. H., Wheeler, C., & Jones, M. V. (2005). Entrepreneurial orientation, commitment to the Internet and export performance in small and medium sized exporting firms. Journal of International Entrepreneurship, 3(4), 291–302.

Muller, P., Mattes, A., Klitou, D., Lonkeu, O., Ramada, P., Ruiz, F. A., ... & Steigertahl, I. (2018). Annual Report on European SMEs 2017/2018. The 10th Anniversary of the Small Business Act. Brussels, European Commission.

Nelson, R. R., & Winter, S. G. (1982). The Schumpeterian tradeoff revisited. The American Economic Review, 72(1), 114–132.

Nelson, R., & Winter, S. (1982). An Evolutionary Theory of Economic Change. Harvard University Press, Cambridge, MA.

Neubert, M. (2016). Significance of the speed of internationalisation for born global firms-a multiple case study approach. International Journal of Teaching and Case Studies, 7(1), 66–81.

OECD (2013). Fostering SME's Participation in Global Markets, Final Report, Paris.

Ojala, A., & Tyrväinen, P. (2009). Impact of psychic distance to the internationalization behavior of knowledge-intensive SMEs. European Business Review, 21(3), 263–277

Paul, J., Parthasarathy, S., & Gupta, P. (2017). Exporting challenges of SMEs: A review and future research agenda. Journal of World Business, 52(3), 327–342.

Penner-Hahn, J., & Shaver, J. M. (2005). Does international research and development increase patent output? An analysis of Japanese pharmaceutical firms. Strategic Management Journal, 26(2), 121–140.

Ramaswamy, K., Kroeck, K. G., & Renforth, W. (1996). Measuring the degree of internationalization of a firm: A comment. Journal of International Business Studies, 27(1), 11.

Régnier, P., & Wild, P. (2018). SME internationalisation and the role of global cities: A tentative conceptualisation. International Journal of Export Marketing, 2(3), 158–179.

Ren, S., Eisingerich, A. B., & Tsai, H. T. (2015). How do marketing, research and development capabilities, and degree of internationalization synergistically affect the innovation performance of small and medium-sized enterprises (SMEs)? A panel data study of Chinese SMEs. International Business Review, 24(4), 642–651.

Rialp, A., & Rialp, J. (2001). Conceptual frameworks on SMEs' internationalization: Past, present and future trends of research. In Reassesing the Internationalization of the Firm. Emerald Group Publishing Limited, Somerville, MA.

Ringle, C. M., Sarstedt, M., & Straub, D. W. (2012). Editor's comments: A critical look at the use of PLS-SEM in" MIS Quarterly". MIS Quarterly, 36(1), iii–xiv.

Ringle, C. M., Wende, S., & Will, A. (2005). SmartPLS 2.0 (beta).University of Hamburg, Hamburg.

Rosenbusch, N., Brinckmann, J., & Bausch, A. (2011). Is innovation always beneficial? A meta-analysis of the relationship between innovation and performance in SMEs. Journal of Business Venturing, 26(4), 441–457.

Ruzzier, M., Hisrich, R. D., & Antoncic, B. (2006). SME internationalization research: past, present, and future. Journal of Small Business and Enterprise Development, 13(4), 476–497

Salomon, R., & Shaver, J. (2005). Learning by exporting: New insights from examining firm innovation. Journal of Economics & Management Strategy, 14, 431–460.

Schueffel, P. E., & Baldegger, R. J. (2008). The Process Model of Internationalization and the International New Venture Framework. Growth Publisher, Liebefeld/Bern.

Schwens, C., Zapkau, F. B., Bierwerth, M., Isidor, R., Knight, G., & Kabst, R. (2018). International entrepreneurship: A meta–analysis on the internationalization and performance relationship. Entrepreneurship Theory and Practice, 42(5), 734–768.

Shane, S. (2009). Technology strategy for managers and entrepreneurs. Pearson Education India, Delhi, NCR, Noida.

Shi, D., DiStefano, C., McDaniel, H. L., & Jiang, Z. (2018). Examining chi-square test statistics under conditions of large model size and ordinal data. Structural Equation Modeling: A Multidisciplinary Journal, 25(6), 924–945.

Stopford, J. M., & Wells, L. T. (1972). Managing the multinational enterprise. Basic Books, New York, NY.

Sullivan, D. (1994). Measuring the degree of internationalization of a firm. Journal of International Business Studies, 25(2), 18.

Sullivan, D. (1996). Measuring the degree of internationalization of a firm: A reply. Journal of International Business Studies, 27(1), 14.

Taber, K. S. (2018). The use of Cronbach's alpha when developing and reporting research instruments in science education. Research in Science Education, 48(6), 1273–1296.

Tang, J., Tang, Z., & Cowden, B. J. (2017). Exploring the relationship between entrepreneurial orientation, CEO dual values, and SME performance in state-owned vs. nonstate-owned enterprises in China. Entrepreneurship Theory and Practice, 41(6), 883–908.

Thanos, I. C., Dimitratos, P., & Sapouna, P. (2017). The implications of international entrepreneurial orientation, politicization, and hostility upon SME international performance. International Small Business Journal, 35(4), 495–514.

Vernon, R. (1972). Economic and political consequence of multi-national enterprise. Division of Research, Graduate School of Business Administration, Harvard University, Boston, MA.

Wadhwa, A., & Kotha, S. (2006). Knowledge creation through external venturing: Evidence from the telecommunications equipment manufacturing industry. Academy of Management Journal, 49(4), 819–835.

Wales, W., Gupta, V. K., Marino, L., & Shirokova, G. (2019). Entrepreneurial orientation: International, global and cross-cultural research. International Small Business Journal, 37(2), 95–104.

Wales, W. J., Gupta, V. K., & Mousa, F. T. (2013). Empirical research on entrepreneurial orientation: An assessment and suggestions for future research. International Small Business Journal, 31(4), 357–383.

Wiklund, J., & Shepherd, D. (2003). Knowledge-based resources, entrepreneurial orientation, and the performance of small and medium-sized businesses. Strategic Management Journal, 24(13), 1307–1314.

Wiklund, J., & Shepherd, D. A. (2011). Where to from here? EO-as-experimentation, failure, and distribution of outcomes. Entrepreneurship Theory and Practice, 35(5), 925–946.

Zahra, S. A., & George, G. (2002). Absorptive capacity: A review, reconceptualization, and extension. Academy of Management Review, 27(2), 185–203.

Zahra, S. A., Korri, J. S., & Yu, J. (2005). Cognition and international entrepreneurship: Implications for research on international opportunity recognition and exploitation. International Business Review, 14(2), 129–146.

Zucchella, A., Maccarini, M. E., & Scabini, P. (2007). Entrepreneurial capabilities in MNEs subsidiaries: The case of the dialysis industry. International Journal of Entrepreneurship and Small Business, 4(3), 305–324.

Zucchella, A., & Scabini, P. (2007). A theoretical model for international entrepreneurship. In International Entrepreneurship (pp. 99–136). Palgrave Macmillan, London.

Chapter 2

Enhancing innovativeness through internationalization

Jean-Paul David and Jean-Christophe Gessler

Introduction

Internationalization and innovation are mutually evolving dynamics (Golovko and Valentini, 2011; Filippetti et al., 2011). On the one hand, a company's assets in terms of innovation as well as its innovative capabilities would promote its development in the global marketplace. Moreover, a company entering a foreign market is faced with many differences and stumbling blocks, compelling it to adapt its offering as well as its organization to the realities of new countries (Freixanet, 2014). Thanks to increased sales volume, crossing borders allows a company to achieve economies of scale as well as to amortize its R&D investments. But adaptation or localization is sometimes not enough, so much so that the company is forced to revisit its products, its processes as well as its strategies.

On the other hand, the company's experiences in the conduct of activities in foreign markets also contribute to the development of its innovative capabilities, both in terms of products or processes. As such, the company's gains in terms of know-how and technological upgrades as part of its activities in foreign markets would help make it more innovative (Cassiman and Golovko, 2011; Love and Mansury, 2009) and maintain a competitive edge in the marketplace, both internationally and domestically.

1. Innovation via internationalization

This chapter addresses this second relationship, that is the increased innovativeness of the company induced by the conduct of its international activities. According to Kiriyama (2012), the innovative capacity of the company arises in many different ways in an international setting: access to technologies through imports, foreign direct investment and technology transfer; incentives to promote innovation; and exports in that such entry strategy offers many learning opportunities, notably related to upgrading the offering.

The case of Bélanger Laminés, the largest manufacturer of post-formed products in Canada, provides a good illustration of this phenomenon. In 2016, the company explored options to expand its business beyond North America, to other developed markets, only to find out that in addition to seizing new growth opportunities, doing international business allowed the company to innovate not only in terms of products and marketing but also in terms of manufacturing processes. Thanks to its international experience, and therefore to its innovative developments, notably in developed markets, Bélanger Laminés was able to consolidate its leading position both in the Canadian and the American markets.

2. The effect of developed markets as countries of destination

In a study of 258 exporters, Vacek (2010) observed that the country of destination of the exports has an important effect on the extent and the nature of the innovation gains. Interestingly, the study shows higher innovative benefits for companies exporting to developed countries such as those of the European Union. The need to adapt the products in order to comply with a stringent regulatory environment provides innovation gains to the company. Furthermore, customers in developed countries would set higher standards, forcing their suppliers to upgrade or to revisit their products and processes. Innovation gains are achieved as exporters acquire know-how, practices and processes that are not readily available in their domestic market.

Demers Ambulances, a Canadian developer of ambulances provides a case in point. The company has been active internationally for a few decades. However, because of the standards for this type of vehicle (in particular with regard to its frame), the only possible markets for Demers Ambulances, beyond North America where the company has a strong presence, are the Middle-East and North of Africa. Thus far, Demers' growth strategy has been external, that is through acquisitions, a strategy that allows for gains in terms of know-how as well as for immediate access to local markets and networks.

The pressure to innovate in Demers' case stems more from its competitors in the international markets (target markets and other foreign markets), more so than from the local demand. World class rivals make use of cutting-edge technologies in the manufacturing processes. They also strive to take advantage of cross-fertilization opportunities in their innovation projects.

Furthermore, thanks to an incoming flow of business intelligence, which is ensured by its representatives' active participation in industry shows and events (prior to the Covid-19 pandemic) and its market monitoring system, Demers manages to stay abreast of the threats and opportunities, so that it can act or react in a timely manner. According to Demers' top managers, the company's experience in the development of its foreign markets allowed to upgrade its business processes and products and sustain or increase its innovativeness edge, hence its competitive posture, as far as in their domestic market.

3. The effect of emerging markets as countries of destination

Likewise, emerging markets may also foster innovation gains for companies active in these countries, particularly through reverse innovation, also named trickle-up or frugal innovation. Defined as a process by which a company from a developed country imports, in its home market, products or processes initially developed in large emerging markets (Nunes and Breene, 2011), reverse innovation favors innovativeness. When warranted by the size of the markets, although less fortunate, companies invest in products' reengineering and spread the costs over a very large sales volume, and thereafter redeploy the innovations in developed markets. Although traditionally exploited by large companies (e.g. GE, Nestlé, Coca-Cola), this strategy may serve as well SMEs according to Immelt, Govindarajan and Trimble (2009).

It has been the case for Alphard Group, a Canadian SME specialized in multidisciplinary projects related notably to professional engineering, environmental performance, project management advice and services tailored to its customers' needs. Due to the distribution of its customers around the world, including in many emerging countries, Alphard has undertaken to revisit its leak detection service in order to remotely monitor the events, and by the same token, allow its distant customers to benefit from an automated service with timely support and access to economical and efficient solutions. Traditionally, this service used to be provided via physical presence of engineers at the clients work sites. The new system allows Alphard to reach a significantly larger number of customers around the world in hard-to-reach areas as well as many more in its home market, that is Canada whose geographic scope is immense. To achieve this, an official R&D project was launched. The transition from the service to a digital product was made possible thanks to the involvement of an expert in leak detection, an engineer in automation and a programmer.

Govindarajan and Trimble (2012) demonstrated that reverse innovation would result from five types of gap that can be observed between a developed market and an emerging market.

1. The performance gap: Consumers in emerging countries generally have lower demands and expectations than those in developed markets. To promote sales in markets with limited purchasing power, a price reduction is often practiced, but this is usually accompanied by reduced performance or the elimination of certain features of the product. In such case, however, the reduction in the level of performance is never as marked as (or proportional to) that of the price. To achieve this, the innovation effort is devoted to the overhaul of a number of elements such as materials and design with the aim of offering products of respectable performance and at competitive prices.
2. The infrastructure gap: In countries where facilities, systems and services to the wider society are inadequate or lacking, companies wishing to do business there often have to innovate to fill these gaps (smaller product design, portability, autonomy, virtual delivery, Etc).
3. The environmental gap: Emerging countries are increasingly turning to alternative sources that require less energy. Often grappling with serious pollution problems, a number of these economies are more likely to welcome and encourage innovations in this respect.
4. The regulatory gap: Most emerging markets impose less (or little) "barriers to innovation", such as bureaucratic or regulatory constraints which are more prevalent in developed economies.

Companies therefore enjoy greater freedom in the development of new products or processes.

5. The preference gap: It is a question here of the divergence of tastes linked essentially to the culture and lifestyles of consumers. Companies doing business in these markets are led to discover many new facets of the profile and the buying process of consumers. Companies would thus develop a greater ability to detect opportunities even in their domestic market.

According to Miranda et al. (2013), reverse innovation starts with unlearning, a strategy that requires internal resources and capabilities that are not abundant in SMEs. These companies are less endowed than multinational enterprises with regard to financial and human resources. In addition, SMEs often lack the necessary know-how on international markets (trends, attitudes, clients' purchasing criteria and decision process, etc.) which is imperative to achieving a reverse innovation strategy. SMEs face both external and internal barriers to innovation as described hereafter (Tab. 1). Miranda et al. (2013) argue that appreciating and overcoming these barriers is utmost important to their success with this strategy.

Tab. 1: SMEs' barriers to innovation

Internal Barriers	External Barriers
• Intellectual Property Management • Project Management • Internationalization • Conceptualization of innovative products Marketing	• Financial constraints • Availability of Skilled Labor • Bureaucratic Hurdles • Difficulties in cooperations / partnerships

That being said, developing countries may represent a springboard for innovation enhancement insofar as companies first adopt a market orientation, that is to say a culture that seeks to go beyond a simple stripping of products for these emerging markets.

4. The effect of market orientation and entrepreneurial orientation

In a recent study carried out with SMEs in the United Arab Emirates, Genc et al. (2019) have not only confirmed the positive effect of internationalization on innovation but they also showed that two factors allow for this result: entrepreneurial orientation and market orientation. The simultaneous presence of these two factors would favor positive innovative performance in the context of internationalization. These findings have also been previously verified by other researchers (Piperopoulos et al., 2018; Küster and Villa, 2011) who have shown that market-oriented companies are more likely to innovate because they seek to respond to different and constantly evolving expectations and needs. Several argue (O'Grady and Lane, 1996; Baker and Sinkula, 2009; Merrilees et al., 2011) that it is the synergistic effect of market orientation and entrepreneurial orientation that arouses the innovative capacity of the SME. Entrepreneurial orientation, on the other hand, is defined by an increased ability to take risks, an essential asset in R&D.

More specifically, the impact of market orientation would turn out to be particularly apparent in the context of industrial marketing where the learning of suppliers would be stimulated by the close relationship they maintain with their prime contractors, a common case in the joint development of new products (Eggers et al., 2014).

For Automatech-Robotik, the international adventure allowed for a spectacular leap in innovativeness. This Canadian developer and supplier of automated solutions for wood manufacturers explains that, "just by staying abreast of the latest developments in technologies through the participation in industry trade exhibitions like LIGNA[1] in Germany as well as meetings with major European players, the Company could appreciate the technological gaps between its European and North American competitors and import new practices and processes to improve its competitive posture in North America."

But, unlike Demers Ambulances, discussed earlier, it is above all its market orientation, that is its openness and endeavor to understand the realities and characteristics of the foreign markets, that enabled Automatech-Robotik to improve its innovation capabilities. Moreover, this interest in the specificities of the market combined with the entrepreneurial mindset of the management team drew the attention of one of its main European competitors with whom a strategic alliance was formed.

1 LIGNA is the world's leading trade fair for woodworking and wood processing plant, machinery and tools.

According to this agreement, joint innovation projects will be carried out to create solutions that would be impossible to develop individually.

Conclusion

Internationalization and innovation are two realities that mutually influence each other. The company's innovation capacity promotes internationalization. Likewise, according to the companies discussed above and to a number of authors, the conduct of activities in foreign markets enables the company to experience gains in terms of innovative capability, which is reflected in upgrades in know-how, technologies, as well as in processes, products and services. The level of development of target countries appears to be one factor inducing innovation benefits for enterprises as part of their internationalization journey. Merely having to comply with more stringent rules or to adapt the product's offering to a more sophisticated demand in a developed country promotes innovativeness. But carrying out activities in an emerging market also contributes to further gains in terms of innovation and is notably illustrated in the form of reverse innovation. It is also interesting to observe that many SMEs would possess at least one of the two factors that would contribute to innovation: entrepreneurial orientation (the other being market orientation).

These observations provide for a better grasp of the value appreciation of the company as part of its international journey. Beyond the financial gains resulting from a greater turnover, innovation gains induced by the international activities represent another source of value creation that deserves further investigation. Beyond the experiences of the Canadian cases aforementioned, it would be most insightful to study these observations with companies from different business sectors and that would carry out activities in countries with different levels of development.

References

Baker, W. E., & Sinkula, J. M. (2009). The complementary effects of market orientation and entrepreneurial orientation on profitability in small businesses. Journal of Small Business Management, 47(4), 443–464.

Cassiman, B., & Golovko, E. (2011). Innovation and internationalization through exports. Journal of International Business Studies, 42(1), 56–75.

Ebru Genc, Mumin Dayan, & Omer Faruk Genc, (2019). The impact of SME internationalization on innovation: The mediating role of market and entrepreneurial orientation. Industrial Marketing Management, 82, 253–264.

Filippetti, Andrea, Frenz, Marion, & Jetto-Gillies, Grazia, July (2011). Are Innovation and Internationalization Related? An Analysis of European Countries Article in Industry and Innovation. DOI: 10.1080/13662716.2011, 583461.

Freixanet, Joan, Innovation and internationalization relationship and implications for management and public policy. (2014). International Journal of Entrepreneurial Knowledge Issue, 2 57(2/2014). DOI: 10.1515/ijek-2015-0006.

Garcia Miranda, Garcia, Duran Heras, Duncan, & Casado, Giraldo Casado, (2013). Application of reverse innovation in SMEs, 7th International Conference on Industrial Engineering and Industrial Management, Valladolid, July 10–12, 2013.

Golovko, E., & Valentini, G. (2011). Exploring the complementarity between innovation and export for SMEs' growth. Journal of International Business Studies, 42(3), 362–380.

Govindarajan V., Trimble C., & Nooyi I. K. (2012). Reverse innovation: Create far from home, win everywhere. Harvard Business Review Press. ISBN 978-1-4221-5764-0.

Immelt, Jeffrey R., Vijay Govindarajan, Vijay, & Trimble, Chris Trimble, (October, 2009). How GE is Disrupting Itself. Harvard Business Review, 11 pages.

Kiriyama, N. (2012). Trade and innovation: synthesis report, OECD Trade Policy Papers, 135.

Küster, I., & Vila, N. (2011). Successful SME web design through consumer focus groups. International Journal of Quality & Reliability Management, 28(2), 32–154.

Love, J. H., & Mansury, M. A. (2009). Exporting and productivity in business services: Evidence from the United States. International Business Review, 18(6), 630–642.

Merrilees, B., Rundle-Thiele, S., & Lye, A. (2011). Marketing capabilities: Antecedents and implications for B2B SME performance. Industrial Marketing Management, 40, 368–375.

Nunes, Paul, & Breene, Tim (2011). Jumping the S-Curve. Boston, MA: Harvard Business Review Press.

O'Grady, S., & Lane, H. (1996). The psychic distance paradox. Journal of International Business Studies, 27(2), 309–333.

Vacek, Pavel (2010), Productivity gains from exporting: Do Export destinations matter?, IES Working Paper, No. 18/2010, Charles University in Prague, Institute of Economic Studies (IES), Prague.

Chapter 3

Towards a joint approach of supporting innovation and export: Proposal of a decision-making tool

Daniel Galvez, Camila Muñoz, Manon Enjolras, and Mauricio Camargo

Introduction

The high level of competitiveness in the market forces companies to develop their capabilities in order to gain advantages. The innovation capability has been a source of interest for companies to develop competitive advantages. This industrial interest has led different organizations and researches to seek to establish guidelines and models for innovation capability management. Since the late 1990s, it has been established that the best way to study innovation in organizations is by identifying good practices, as shown, for example, in the Oslo manual (OECD et Eurostat, 2005). One of the first models of innovation management based on good practices was proposed by Chiesa et al. (1996), opening an area of research worked by several authors (Guan, 2006; Boly et al., 2013; Galvez et al., 2013). These models have made it possible to better characterize and understand the activities and practices that support the innovation capability of companies. Recently, the management of innovation capability has been reinforced by the creation of the ISO standard (ISO 56002, 2019).

Export capability has also gained much relevance in recent years. Globalization has pushed a number of companies to go beyond their country's borders. Similarly, to innovation, several authors have studied the factors and practices that characterize the export capability of companies. In this way, it has also been possible to establish models for evaluating the export capability of companies. The proposal of these models has revealed several common factors between innovation and export. Intellectual property, networking with other organizations, strategic vision and technological vigilance are some of the common points between innovation and export.

In both capabilities, management models are very useful because they allow diagnosing the company's performance, and also, thanks to the identification of good practices, they allow establishing improvement strategies. However, limited resources are a major barrier, especially for SMEs, to the implementation of these improvement strategies. In the search to optimize the use of resources, the following questions arise: Is it possible to take advantage of the similarity between innovation and export to generate joint strategies? Is it possible to establish a management model based on the existing synergies between innovation and export? Is it possible to enhance innovation capability from resources used in export capability and vice versa?

In this chapter, we propose a joint management model based on the similarity and complementarity between the innovation and export capability of the companies in order to determine improvement plans by exploiting existing synergies.

1. The relationship between innovation and export: Towards a paradigm shift

Innovation and export are important growth factors for companies of all sizes, and this is particularly true for SMEs. If one activity or the other separately opens up interesting opportunities, it would seem that innovation and export are also intrinsically linked in the development of companies. Indeed, if we look at the Europe-wide figures for recent years, European SMEs which are internationally active are three times more likely to introduce new products or services than their purely domestic counterparts and they grow more than twice as fast (OECD, 2009). From 2012 to 2014, exporting SMEs introduced twice as many product and process innovations as non-exporting SMEs (OECD, 2018). In 2015, faster-growing SMEs (52 %) were almost twice as likely to export as SMEs that were in decline or static (28 %) (FedEx corp. 2015). Finally, in 2019, European exporting SMEs were more likely to engage in innovation (European Commission, 2019). So, the link between innovation and export seems to be clearly highlighted by the figures.

This is why the study of the link between innovation and export is generating a growing interest in the academic world, and the number of related scientific publications is constantly increasing.

1.1. A long-standing causal approach

The majority of the studies carried out by researchers aim to identify how these two activities impact each other in order to construct cause-and-effect relationships explaining the link between innovation and export. The different theories can be modeled in the shape of a virtuous circle including different causal and directional relations (Fig. 1).

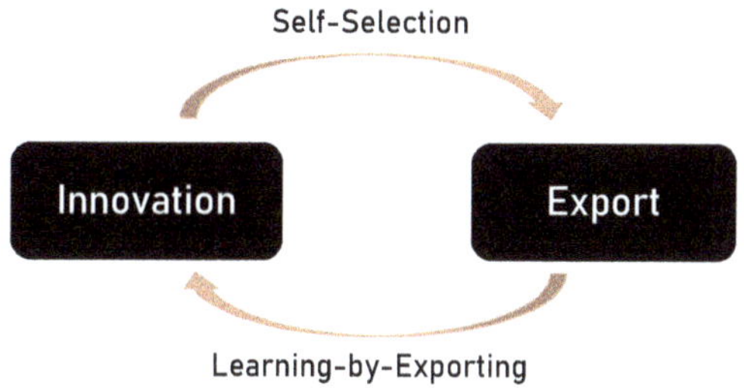

Fig. 1: Innovation/Export causal relations

First, the self-selection theory considers that innovation has a positive impact on export, by giving the company a competitive advantage which allows it to improve its performance in foreign markets (Boso et al., 2013; Dai et al., 2019; Monreal-Pérez, Aragón-Sánchez, and Sánchez-Marín, 2012; Ribau et al., 2019; Roper and Love, 2002). This directed relation supports the hypothesis that innovation has a positive impact on exporting activities because it increases the company's performance in a general way. Only the most competitive companies are able to reach a foreign market. On the contrary, the second theory called "learning by exporting" considers that the knowledge and experience acquired on international markets feed the innovation capacity of companies (Di Cintio et al., 2019; Fassio, 2018; Golovko and Valentini, 2014; Kafouros et al., 2008). This relation favors the direction according to which international activities can represent opportunities to develop innovation projects, as a continuous source of inspiration.

These two theories represent respectively opposite causal relations in this virtuous circle and it is interesting to see that the researchers confront each other with theoretical and empirical studies aiming to prove or refute one or the other of these theoretical in different contexts. Even if they are oppositely oriented, these relations can coexist in this virtuous circle in the form of sequences, but there is no real consensus and they seem to be very dependent on the context in which companies operate. Differentiating factors such as the sector of activity, the size of the company, the cultural distance from the foreign market and the type of innovation proposed appear and potentially modify the identified sequences. For example, the learning-by-exporting effect is limited by the cultural distance with the foreign market. Exporting to a country that is close in terms of habits and culture is not so beneficial in terms of innovation outputs, because the learning process is low. Moreover, exporting activities seem to be particularly fostered by product innovation compared to process innovation. This result can be explained by the fact that product innovation allows for strong differentiation from competitors in foreign markets as well as for better product quality, which provides a greater competitive advantage than process innovation, which is aimed more at reducing costs.

These controversial results highlight the complexity of the relationship between innovation and export (Love and Roper, 2015; Golovko and Valentini, 2011). Moreover, Ayllon and Radicic (2019) found that while a relationship between innovation and exports exists, it remains only through contemporaneous effects. Their results suggest no support for a causal link from past product and process innovations to current export activities. Based on this assumption, the innovation/export relationship shifts from a causal impact-related point of view to a complementarity paradigm, including a temporal aspect.

1.2. Towards a synergistic vision:

Some studies indeed propose considering that innovation and export are complementary activities. This theory is supported by some researchers who wish to overcome the causal confrontation that is predominantly adopted in the scientific literature. It means that if a commitment is made in one of these activities, it facilitates the commitment in the other one simultaneously. As an illustration, the results of Golovko and Valentini (2011) show that Spanish manufacturing SMEs who invest in innovation and export at the same time enjoy better growth than those who invest either in innovation or in exports or neither. The return on investment of one activity increases with the performance level of the other activity.

Following this complementarity-oriented vision, some factors have been recognized in the literature as joint facilitators, enabling to explain the complementarity between innovation and export. For example, human resources management appear as a crucial factor both for innovation and export because it relates to the ability of people to develop competencies, to work in teams and to accept changes (Love and Roper, 2015; Wheeler et al., 2008; Enjolras et al., 2016). Customer consideration and involvement are also strong facilitators that enable an easier access to both domestic and foreign market by identifying and fitting as best as possible the customer needs (Love and Roper, 2015; Enjolras et al., 2016). This source of information has then to be exploited through a structured process of product design (MacPherson, 2000; Flor and Oltra, 2005; Rodil et al., 2016) or R&D (Harris and Moffat, 2011; Guan and Ma, 2003) in order to transform it into a value proposition activity. Networking and collaboration are considered as an important source of knowledge (Jones and Craven, 2001; Haahti et al., 2005; Boso et al., 2013) to be exploited through a strong ability to implement a continuous learning process (Guan and Ma, 2003) supported by absorptive capacity (Gkypali et al., 2018). Finally, all these factors have to be supported by a strong organizational structure, an important founding capacity (Ughetto, 2008; Bellone et al., 2010) and a dedicated leadership (Wheeler et al., 2008) aiming to spread the company strategy (Guan and Ma, 2003; Enjolras et al., 2016) both in term of innovation and international development.

Based on these joint facilitators coming from the academic literature, it seems that the causal vision of the innovation/export relationship can be questioned in favor of a systemic and synergistic vision enabling to highlight best practices that could be implemented within companies to foster the emergence of joint benefits both for innovation and export activities.

1.3. What contributions for the support of SMEs?

Coming back to the companies' world and considering the practices of the support bodies, this synergistic vision is progressively adopted by these structures. The European Commission has put forward a trend in 2007 aimed at coupling innovation and export support mechanisms, but according to a benchmarking performed by Enjolras et al. (2015) at the global level, the joint mechanisms are rather scarce. So, there is still a lot of work to be done on this point because innovation and export are still mostly handled separately by different organizations specialized respectively in innovation or in international support.

For example, innovation and export do appear as priorities for action at the European level, but they remain separate initiatives. From one side, the INTERREG strategy[1], from 2014 to 2020 dedicated a whole axis to increasing the cross-border competitiveness of SMEs. From the other side, the H2020 strategy[2] focused on an innovation support program for SMEs. But the link between innovation and cross-border or international activities was not really addressed. More recently, export does not seem to be a priority anymore. Looking at the Horizon Europe[3] strategy, a whole pillar is dedicated to innovation, with some initiatives encouraging international collaborations, but in the context of technological research projects. It does not really consider the international competitiveness of companies.

Thus, despite a consensus that synergies are possible between these two activities and a trend to encourage the coupling of the support offered to companies, the link between innovation and export seems difficult to implement on the ground. As a matter, considering innovation or export within a company, and even within an SME with 10 employees, usually requires getting in touch with different departments and different people. Traditionally, export is managed by the sales department and innovation by the technical or R&D department. The business leader generally has a global vision of these two activities, but not always an operational one, and it is intellectually very difficult to describe the functioning of a company from the point of view of both innovation and export. So, implementing a joint innovation/export action plan within a company requires to embrace the complexity of the innovation/export relationship while remaining aware of the operational and structural difficulties that may hinder the creation of synergies in the daily routine practices of the company.

---

1 https://www.interregeurope.eu/

2 https://ec.europa.eu/programmes/horizon2020/

3 https://ec.europa.eu/info/research-and-innovation/funding/funding-opportunities/funding-programmes-and-open-calls/horizon-europe_en

1.4. Our conceptual approach

To move away from the cause-and-effect view that is prevalent in the scientific literature, while taking into account the operational difficulties that SMEs may face in their daily work, this research work assumes the existence of a common space between innovation and export activities (Fig. 2). Looking at the internal processes of companies, an innovation space could be identified, represented by practices related to the generation of ideas, the development of novelties, etc., Additionally, an export space could also be considered, including the mastery of foreign languages or customs formalities… Finally, at the intersection of these two spaces, a common space could be identified, composed of joint practices both related to innovation and to export. They are routines that potentially benefit these two activities.

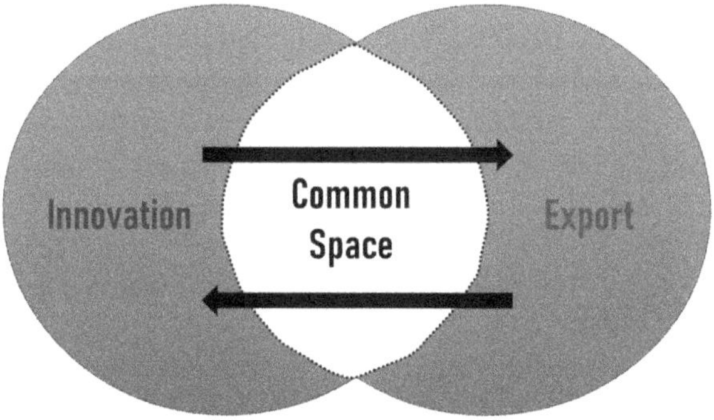

Fig. 2: Conceptual approach

By encouraging SMEs to act on this common space, we finally activate one single lever, which has a simultaneous impact on innovation and export. Through the prism of the common space, we can identify which innovation practices could be pillars on which the company could rely to facilitate its international development or, on the contrary, which elements could slow down this development. It is thus possible to make targeted recommendations according to the chosen strategy. So, in the particular context of SMEs where resources are limited, this seems to make sense because it reduces the effort associated with the joint improvement of their innovation and export capabilities.

As an illustration, consider a company that, from an innovation point of view, is very efficient and that particularly masters one of the joint innovation/export facilitators related to information gathering. Imagine that the R&D department already defined axes of technological watch, stores and shares this information with all the departments concerned and has adopted a digital business intelligence tool. On the other hand, regarding exports, its monitoring is rather limited. The company works on an opportunity basis and has not defined a precise information gathering axis on its targeted markets. Based on the hypothesis that the defined common space can act as a bridge between innovation and export activities, we can then suggest to the company to transfer practices from its innovation management system to its export management system. For example, the company may consider extending the digital tool already used for the technological watch to the sales or export department, to facilitate the commercial monitoring activity. Moreover, maybe some joint strategic research axes could be defined between its foreign and domestic markets in order to exploit synergies. This way, we achieve our real ambition: proposing an operationalization of the link between innovation and export by proposing a joint action plan. The goal is to optimize the resources used company's practices, by relying on what it already masters for one or the other activity.

2. Methodology

In order to meet the objective of eliciting a model to generate strategies to take advantage of the common space between innovation capability and export capability, the following methodology is proposed (Fig. 3).

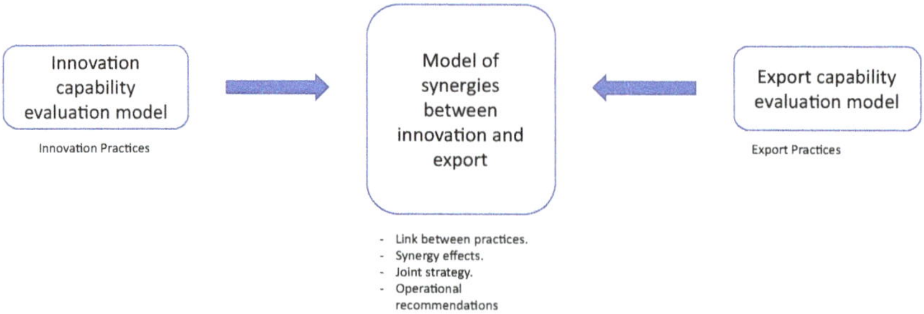

Fig. 3: Methodological approach

Given that both innovation and export capabilities have tested and validated evaluation models, first, the reference models for each capability are selected. The selection of the models should be driven by the following requirements: The models must have been both theoretically and empirically tested. In addition, the two models must address the same type of company. In this case we will work with SMEs, therefore, the models must be valid for this type of company. Finally, the models must be compatible, they must have a similar structure, be based on good practices and share the same operating principles.

Once the models have been selected, the work focuses on determining the complementarity between them. Based on the best practices of each model, existing links are established in order to identify potential synergies between innovation and export. Based on the bibliographic analysis and the experience of a group of experts, the common space between both capabilities is established by identifying the innovation practices that share some use of resources (equipment, knowledge, etc.) with some export practice.

A relational model is built on this common space to generate common strategies to improve the innovation capability based on the resources currently used in the export capability and vice versa. This relational model acts on the level of performance that firms can achieve in innovation and export practices. The objective is to use synergy effects to increase the level of performance of the related practices with less effort by leveraging resources currently used by the firm.

Finally, the model provides a series of actions to be taken to improve one or both of the capabilities involved. The operating principle of the model is based on the current level of performance that the company has individually in innovation and export practices. Considering this input and the existing relationships between the use of resources of the practices, the actions that allow taking better advantage of the synergies for the profile and the particular preferences of the company are defined, prioritizing the recommendations that generate a greater impact on the company's performance.

3. Model for the generation of joint strategies between innovation and export

3.1. Innovation and export assessment models selection

The structure of the proposed model is based on the individual evaluation of the innovation and export capabilities of the companies in order to subsequently work on the common space and establish joint improvement strategies. The increase in research on management models and evaluation of innovation and export capabilities in companies presents a wide variety of alternative models to use as a reference. In order to select relevant models, preference is given to models that are adapted to the characteristics of SMEs and that have been validated both theoretically and empirically. In addition, the models chosen should make it possible to exploit the complementarity between innovation and exports.

In this line, the work of the ERPI laboratory of the University of Lorraine is specialized in the creation of indicators and models for the management of internal processes of companies, especially SMEs. Fig. 4 shows a summary of the main models proposed by the ERPI laboratory.

Research work began in 2000 with the first studies of an innovation capability management model based on the identification of good internal practices. This model allowed the development of one of the laboratory's main lines of research centered on a model for evaluating the innovation capability of companies, called the Potential Innovation Index (PII) (Boly et al., 2013; Galvez et al., 2013). This model has evolved, allowing in the first instance the evaluation of the innovation capability of SMEs based on the use of maturity grids as an evaluation method and the use of multi-criteria methods for the calculation. The latest versions of the PII allow the generation of recommendations to improve the innovation capability of companies. The assessment and subsequent innovation capability improvement strategy allows the creation of a spin-off, innovation-way.com, for companies to diagnose and manage their innovation potential on the basis of an online questionnaire.

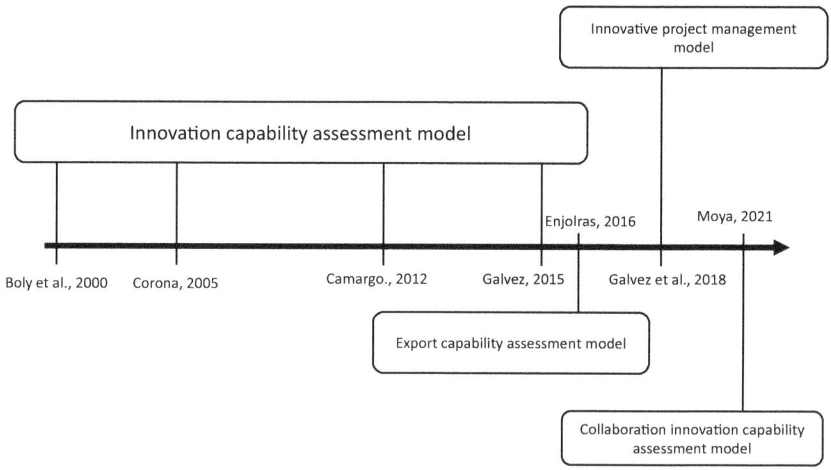

Fig. 4: ERPI laboratory models (University of Lorraine)

In recent years, the ERPI laboratory has developed other models for managing capabilities and processes associated with innovation, such as a model for managing innovation projects, a model for managing open innovation or collaborative innovation, and a model for assessing the export capability of SMEs (PEI). In particular, the export capability model is built following the same principles of the PII, basing its structure on a multi-criteria method and its evaluation on maturity grids.

Both the PII and PEI have been tested in several European and Latin American companies, showing a good response to the reality of companies, particularly SMEs. Its multi-criteria structure makes it possible to identify and group the processes and practices that characterize each of the capabilities and allows the calculation of a global index, making it possible to perform an analysis both at the global level (index) and at the process level (practices) (Fig. 5). In addition, the use of an evaluation method such as the maturity grid allows to clearly define performance levels that the company can achieve in the different practices, improving the accuracy of the evaluation and also providing guidelines on improvement strategies. Therefore, it is decided that the reference models used to individually evaluate innovation capability and export capability will be the PII and PEI, respectively.

Fig. 5: Potential Innovation Index (PII) and Potential Export Index (PEI)

3.2. Practices in the common space between innovation and export

Each capability assessment model is composed of internal company practices. In order to identify the practices of the common space between innovation and export, the following three stages are established:

1. Comparison of practices: Based on the global definition of each practice, a theoretical relationship is established between the practices that make up the innovation capability assessment model and the practices of the export capability model. This relationship is based on the similarity of the practices focused on whether they use the same type of resource (knowledge, competence, equipment, etc.).
2. Maturity grid comparison: The relationships established in the previous stage are studied in greater detail based on the defined

maturity grid. In this way, it is established specifically how each common resource impacts the level of performance that the company can have in the common practices. A resource X may allow the development of an innovation practice at a medium level; if this resource is common to exports, this same resource could help to increase the performance of an export practice, taking advantage of the synergy of the common space. To establish more clearly the similarity by level, a matrix is constructed as shown in Fig. 6.

E / I		P1					P2			P3				P4			P5			P6	
		A1	A2	A3	A4	A5	A1	A2	A3	A1	A2	A3	A4	A1	A2	A3	A1	A2	A3	A1	A2
P1	A1	X	X	X	X	X			X	X						X			X		
	A2		X	X				X	X												
	A3	X	X		X																
	A4	X				X			X	X											
P2	A1	X	X	X		X		X	X	X			X								
	A2		X	X				X													
	A3	X	X			X			X									X			
P3	A1	X		X			X	X		X	X	X	X								
	A2	X						X				X						X			
	A3	X			X							X									
	A4		X					X													
P4	A1	X													X						
	A2	X		X										X							
	A3	X			X									X		X					
	A4	X											X								
	A5																				
P5	A1																				
	A2																		X		
	A3	X	X												X				X		X
P6	A1	X				X								X							X
	A2													X							
	A3																		X	X	X

Fig. 6: Comparison between innovation and export practices

3. Expert validation: In order to confirm the defined relationships, a panel of experts from the ERPI laboratory, who have participated in the PII and PEI studies, is interviewed. The experts validate the relationships using the same concept of similarity in the use of resources.

3.3. Model implementation

The model is implemented considering four stages (Fig. 7):

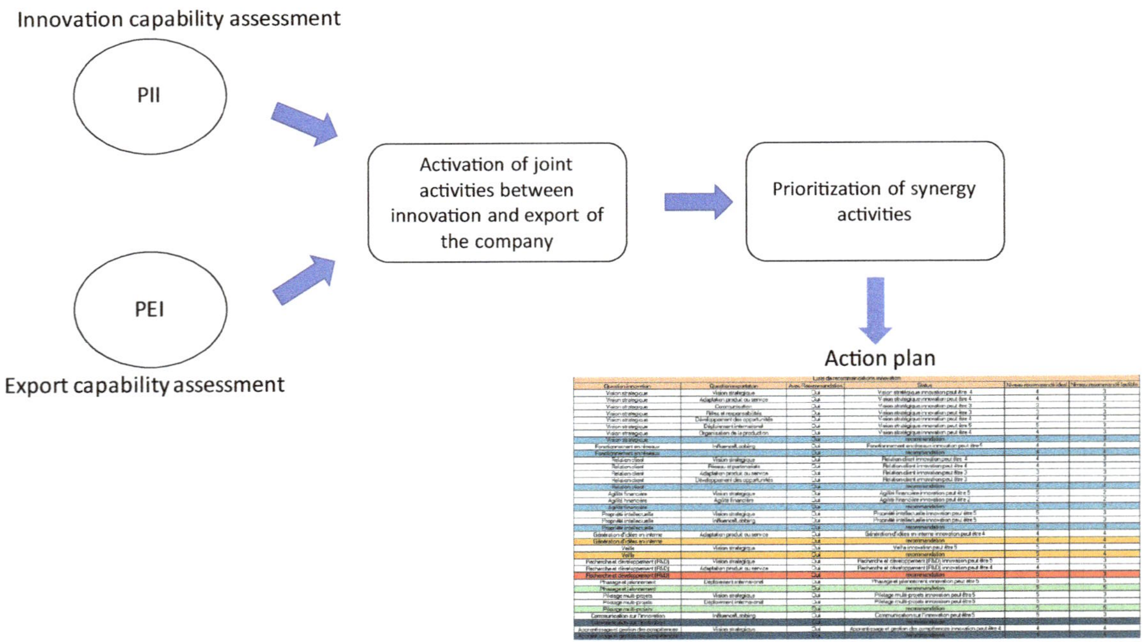

Fig. 7: Model implementation phases

The first stage seeks to individually evaluate the company's innovation and export capabilities. This allows defining the company's profile and establishes a diagnosis of its innovation and export practices.

In the second stage, conditional equations are used to automatically identify the practices in which the company has used resources that are common to innovation and export. In other words, the model establishes a comparison of all the potential relationships identified between innovation and export with the company's evaluation to identify which relationships the company can exploit to generate synergy effects.

In the third stage, the practices that have the greatest impact on the company's performance are identified: the practices that are strengths of the company and generate a great synergy benefit (drivers) and the practices that are weak and limit the development of the company's capabilities (brakes). Based on these definitions, the prioritization of innovation and/or export practices is established.

Finally, based on the identification of the practices to be improved, an action plan is established, defining the concrete actions that will allow obtaining the required level of performance in each practice. Priority is given to the strategy of improving one of the capabilities by leveraging on the current performance in the other capability, which is complemented by improving the practices that impact both capabilities by investing in new resources.

4. Application Case

In order to test the proposed model in a real context, a case study has been realized within a French wine SME from the Burgundy region. The steps presented in section 3.3 has been performed in order to assess the innovation and export capabilities of this company and to provide a customized improvement plan relying on synergistic effects.

4.1. The French wine context: The case of the Burgundy region

The French wine industry is structured around three federations:

- Trading companies do not carry out any production or winemaking activities, they buy either grapes, must, or wine already produced to take over the commercial activity.
- The wineries produce their own grapes and wine and sell them through different distribution channels
- Cooperative wineries bring together several producers and provide the opportunity to mutualize the winemaking tools and the commercial process within the same structure.

The industry is structured by territory because this corresponds to the appellations and historical operating modes. These territories do not necessarily correspond to the French administrative regions. The sector is mainly composed of SMEs.

Regarding international activity, the Burgundy region sells one in two bottles of wine for export. This region has more than 84 different wine appellations[4]. This complicates the visibility for export as it is difficult for a foreign customer to distinguish between them. This is why, for international sales, it is progressively the grape variety that is put forward rather than the geographical appellation. Although this transition provokes reticence on the part of the historical regions, because they adopt a "terroir" strategy, it allows them to adapt to the knowledge of the foreign customer and to make the commercial offer more legible.

Both at the regional and national levels, French wine companies are facing strong competition from emerging wine-producing countries (Rousset, 2004) such as Chile, which is adopting an offensive export strategy. The local economic context is indeed very favorable for Chilean wineries, and wine is integrated into every agreement concluded in terms of international trade. On the other hand, the export markets for French wines are concentrated around seven or eight countries. Some of these target markets are therefore rapidly saturated and require strong differentiation, which is not always easy in the face of international competition.

As a general rule, the term innovation is not really internalized, due to the rather conservative nature of the sector. The vision of innovation is generally not very product-oriented, in favor of a process-oriented vision. This can be explained by the fact that many wines have a Protected

---

[4] https://www.vins-bourgogne.fr/nos-vins-nos-terroirs/la-bourgogne-et-ses-appellations/la-bourgogne-une-localisation-privilegiee,2377,9170.html?

Designation of Origin (PDO), which limits innovation on the product itself. However, product innovation is possible on the proposed format/container (packaging, bag-in-box...) and a trend appears concerning the reduction of the alcohol content. Innovation is also reflected in the sustainable development factor, which is an important issue for the sector (Kockmann, 2007). The notion of innovation in this sense is currently widely valued. The issues linked to crop dieback and climatic hazards are also sources of innovation favored by the sector, the securing of the volume of supply being an omnipresent problem for producers.

4.2. Presentation of the company

The company we are studying is a group of cooperative wineries located in the Burgundy region. It mainly exploits the Pinot Noir and Chardonnay grape varieties and has a turnover of approximately 30 million euros for 2019.

The company has a Management Board of 18 members representing the associated wineries, a CEO and an Executive Committee. The company has about 20 employees. It relies on a sales team that manages the marketing of the entire range of wines from the involved wineries. For the upstream/production part, however, each range is managed by a dedicated operations manager.

Strongly committed to sustainable development, the associated wineries are engaged in respecting a set of specifications that labels them "Winegrowers committed to sustainable development". They are also committed to projects aimed at promoting soil conservation, better understanding the impact of packaging, reducing energy consumption and limiting the carbon footprint, for example through the use of eco-designed glass bottles.

Based on these experiences, the company shows an innovation profile oriented towards openness (networking, customer relations), R&D, digital integration, learning and knowledge management (Fig. 8). Although the company's innovation capability remains limited, it seems to rely on these strengths to carry out innovation projects, oriented towards its commitment to sustainable development. However, it has certain weaknesses, mainly related to the definition of a strategic vision, support for innovation among its employees and suppliers, communication and the ability to stand back from actions carried out (feedback and continuous improvement).

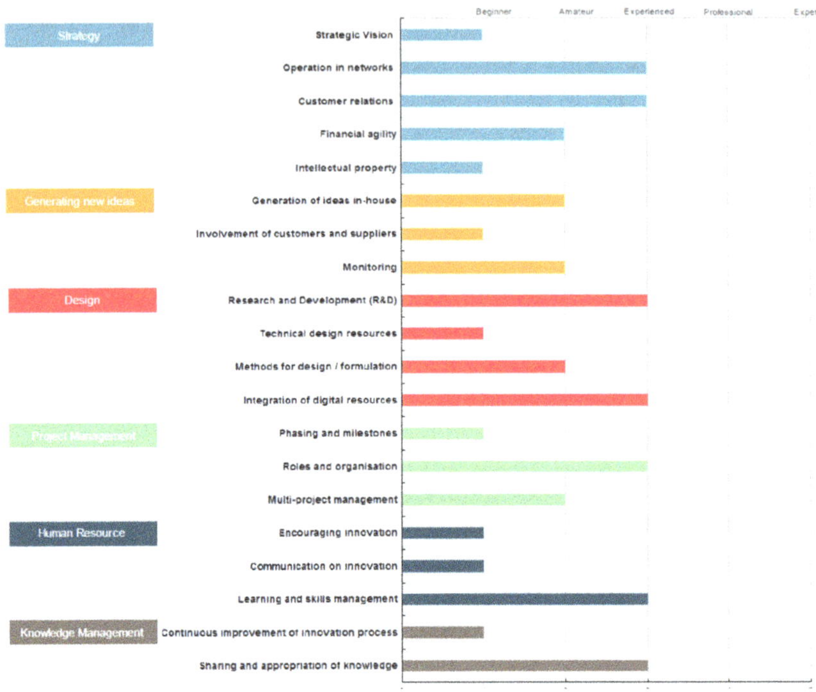

Fig. 8: Innovation profile – source: *www.innovation-way.com*

For all these reasons, it adopts a reactive attitude to innovation. It means that its attitude regarding to the future and the potential disturbances of its environment can be considered as adaptative (Godet, 1997; Rejeb et al., 2008). The priority of this company is then to react to these disturbances by implementing changes in its daily operations, instead of considering the possibility of an anticipative strategy (Galvez et al., 2013).

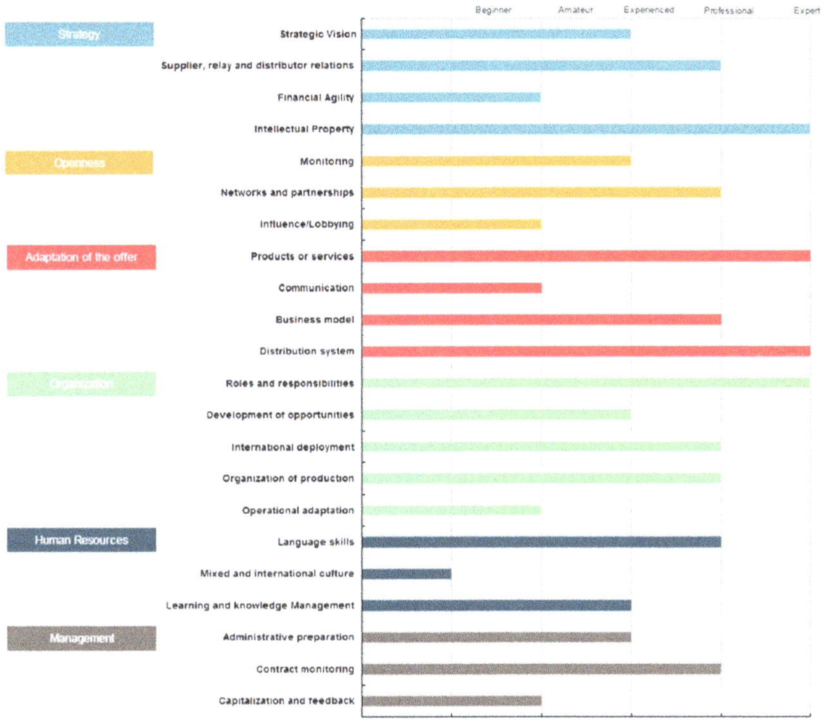

Fig. 9: Export profile – source: *www.innovation-way.com*

Regarding export, the company shows a higher level in terms of maturity (Fig. 9). Because of its strong workforce involved in the sales and marketing processes, the company reach a strong level of mastery regarding its products and services adaptation for international markets, as well as its valorization in terms of intellectual property. The company is able to define the most suitable business model and distribution channel to reach foreign targeted markets (exclusively B2B oriented). For that purpose, it cultivates strong relationships with its foreign distributors and partners. In organizational and administrative terms, it has built up a formalized process enabling it to monitor contracts with foreign customers, to structure and pilot its export process and to prioritize the most promising markets. In a similar way to innovation, it lacks communication abilities, influence within the industry and the capacity to take a step back to improve the processes in place.

4.3. Recommendations identified and potential synergies

4.3.1. From export to innovation

As the company's export profile is more mature than its innovation profile, the first recommendations identified by the model are aimed at exploiting the strengths of the company's export capability, to make them pillars on which it could rely to strengthen its innovation activity. The aim is to transfer good practices implemented in the context of the company's international activities, in order to exploit the synergies that these could create in terms of structuring the innovation process.

Thus, according to the model, the company could, first of all, rely on its maturity in terms of international deployment.

Its ability to evaluate and prioritize international market deployment opportunities relying on a strategic vision and using various operational criteria (potential financial gains, logistical constraints, production capacity, cultural remoteness.) could be a strong basis to improve its maturity in terms of innovation strategy, project management and prioritization. The company is currently involved in several projects related to sustainable development and by exploiting mechanisms and procedures used by its commercial department to manage its international activities for the benefit of these projects, it could be able to define evaluation criteria in terms of risks, generated value or commercial potential in a similar way as it could for foreign markets. This is a transfer of competence from export to innovation. In the same way, the definition of these evaluation criteria could be associated with the construction of a longer-term strategy, for which it would then be able to prioritize its development projects on the basis of the criteria it has defined as relevant. In this way, it would be part of a more regular innovation dynamic supported by a vision that is both technical and commercial.

On the other hand, the company's ability to carry out a commercial watch for its foreign markets could also be transposed to its innovation dynamics. In the same way that the company is able to follow technological and commercial developments related to its industry, suppliers and competitors, it could also be able to implement the same information-gathering techniques for the benefit of monitoring activities related to its innovation projects. Furthermore, its ability to identify the main trends and user habits in its international market could be an opportunity to propose adaptations of its products or processes to be implemented both for its domestic or foreign markets, via the dissemination of identified user needs and trends to all departments of the company, as a source of inspiration and improvement for innovation projects. This ability to find information and to monitor the company's strategic development axes could also lead to an improvement in the management of the company's intellectual property applied to the development of new products/ processes. Indeed, if this practice is well mastered for the aspects linked to the company's international commercial activities, it is also a point to be considered as a means of enhancing the company's innovation activities. Monitoring is an important lever to be mobilized for this purpose.

Finally, the company's ability to adapt its business model to foreign markets, and in particular its ability to build a suitable price positioning as well as a brand image adapted to each market, can be particularly useful in feeding the company's strategic vision in terms of developing innovation projects. Because of its great adaptability, it is able to adjust and evolve its offer by listening to the market. This is an important asset for building its innovation strategy in the long term. Thus, the adaptability of the company from a commercial point of view can lead to the emergence of a synergy to be built, so as to orientate its product and process development process.

In view of the recommendations identified, the company's export capability represents an important pillar of the company, enabling it to transfer and adapt practices carried out within its international activities to the management of its innovation activities (Tab. 1). The aim is to build a bridge between export and innovation by mobilizing elements already mastered in one context to adapt them to another. Export therefore appears to be a potential innovation driver for the company.

Tab. 1: Export practices supporting the company's innovation capability improvement

Innovation practice to be improved	Supporting export practice
Innovation Strategic vision	International deployment
Phasing and millstones	
Multi-project management	
Intellectual property	International Monitoring
Customers involvement	
Innovation monitoring	
Innovation strategic vision	Business model adaptation
Methods for product/process design	

4.3.2. Towards the identification of synergies

If the company shows a weaker profile in terms of innovation capability than that associated with its export dynamics, it can nonetheless highlight certain synergies to be mobilized in order to gain maturity in both aspects (Tab. 2). The model has therefore identified several recommendations.

Indeed, one of the company's strong points in terms of innovation concerns its ability to manage skills and create a learning dynamic among its employees. This capacity can be a real asset to address a point of vigilance identified both in terms of innovation and export: the capitalization of knowledge and experience sharing. Indeed, the notion of learning is closely linked to the implementation of feedback and the transfer of knowledge and know-how. Thus, the implementation of time dedicated to this sharing and feedback could be an added value that would benefit both the innovation and export activities of the company. This is a synergy to be exploited in order to progress simultaneously on both activities by pooling resources. In this case, it is a question of exploiting an impulse given by the company in terms of innovation to help it grow and evolve towards a joint and transverse practice.

Tab. 2: Joint practices to be improved relying on synergistic effects

Joint Practice to be improved	Synergies to be implemented (coming from innovation)
Capitalization and experience sharing	Learning and Knowledge management
	Sharing and appropriation of knowledge

Discussions and conclusion

This research work aims to exploit the strong relationship between innovation and export activities through the proposal of a joint model based on synergy effects. Through this model, our objective was to highlight the interest of coupling support to SMEs in these two areas, proposing recommendations for joint improvement.

By focusing on the specific context of SMEs, the proposed model aims to optimize the exploitation of SMEs' internal resources by allowing them to act simultaneously on their innovation and export capabilities, without putting themselves in difficulty. To do this, the model relies on the company's "drivers" (in terms of innovation or export), to serve as a solid basis for the dissemination and transferability of good practices from one activity to another.

From a separate evaluation of innovation and export practices within a company, the model then proposes a joint vision of these two evaluations, through the exploitation of synergy effects in the recommendations proposed to companies to move towards a joint action plan.

Through an application case carried out in the French wine sector, we were able to illustrate the potential contributions of this model for an SME with about twenty employees. Depending on the company's predisposition for export or innovation, the aim is to identify the practices that can be considered as drivers facilitating the rise in performance in one or other of these activities. In the same way, synergistic practices can be identified, which have a beneficial effect on both activities and make it possible to mutualize resources and reduce the effort associated with improving the company's performance.

However, from an operational point of view, certain implementation difficulties have been raised. On the one hand, although the model appears to be a representation tool that can initiate dialogue between different departments, the transfer or sharing of good practices between these departments must be supported and encouraged at an operational level and by top management. Without this fertile ground, the disruptions associated with the implementation of this joint strategy cannot be overcome and the actions put in place will not be sustained.

On the other hand, in its current state of development, the model identifies avenues for improvement without reaching the stage of proposing operational actions to be implemented. To reach this stage, it seems necessary to call upon business support organizations whose job it is to propose action plans to businesses based on their practical experience. Thus, the proposed model is positioned as a potential diagnostic and decision support tool for business advisors, as a facilitating device for the construction of a joint innovation/export and personalized advice.

Finally, the prioritization of the recommendations proposed to the company is a significant issue to be studied, in order to build a realistic action plan for an SME that potentially has difficulty mobilizing significant resources. This prioritization is currently carried out by choosing to rely on the company's levers with the greatest potential impact on the organization in terms of the number of synergies to be exploited. The number of practices impacted is therefore given priority in the prioritization of recommendations. However, other factors could be integrated in order to propose a more adapted and targeted action for the companies. For example: to act in priority on the weak points of a company, to favor the practices considered as critical in view of the context in which the company evolves or of its strategy, or to personalize the recommendations according to the sector of activity, the size, or the geographical area. This represents the main improvement paths of this research work in order to adopt a stronger operational and customized perspective of the joint challenge of innovation and export within SMEs.

References

Ayllon, S., and Radicic D. 2019. "Product Innovation, Process Innovation and Export Propensity: Persistence, Complementarities and Feedback Effects in Spanish Firms." Applied Economics 51 (33): 3650–64. https://doi.org/10.1080/00036846.2019.1584376.

Bellone F., Musso F., Nesta L., and Schiavo S. 2010. "Financial Constraints and Firm Export Behaviour." World Economy 33 (3): 347–73. https://doi.org/10.1111/j.1467-9701.2010.01259.x.

Boly, V., Morel, L., Assielou, G., and et Camargo, M. (2013). "Evaluating innovative processes in french firms: Methodological proposition for firm innovation capacity evaluation." Research Policy 43 (3): 608–622

Boso, N., Story V. M., J. W. Cadogan J. W., Micevski M., and Kadić-Maglajlić S. 2013. "Firm Innovativeness and Export Performance: Environmental, Networking, and Structural Contingencies." Journal of International Marketing 21 (4): 62–87. https://doi.org/10.1509/jim.13.0052.

Chiesa, V., Coughlan, P., and et Voss, C. A. 1996. Development of a technical innovation audit. Journal of Product Innovation Management 13, 105–136.

Dai M., Liu H., and Lin L. 2019. "How Innovation Impacts Firms' Export Survival: Does Export Mode Matter?" World Economy 43 (1): 81–113. https://doi.org/10.1111/twec.12847.

Di Cintio M., Ghosh S., and Grassi E. 2019. "Direct or Indirect Exports: What Matters for Firms' Innovation Activities?" Applied Economics Letters 27(2), 93–103. https://doi.org/10.1080/13504851.2019.1610693.

Enjolras M., Camargo M., and Schmitt C. 2016. "SMEs' Innovation and Export Capabilities: Identification and Characterization of a Common Space Using Data Spatialization." Journal of Technology Management & Innovation 11 (2): 56–69. https://doi.org/10.4067/S0718-27242016000200006.

Enjolras M., Camargo M., Schmitt C, and Morel L. 2015. "Comparatif Des Dispositifs de Soutien à l'internationalisation Des PME : Les Apports de La Prise En Compte de l'innovation." In 6ème Rencontre Du Groupe de Recherche Thématique "Innovation" de l'AIMS. Strasbourg France.

European Commission. 2018. "Annual Report on European SMEs 2017/2018 : Special Background Document on the Internationalisation of SMEs." SME Performance Review 2017/2018. https://publications.europa.eu/en/publication-detail/-/publication/a435b6ed-e888-11e8-b690-01aa75ed71a1/language-en/format-PDF.

European Commission. 2018. 2019. Annual report on European SMEs 2019/2020. LU: Publications Office of the European Union. https://data.europa.eu/doi/10.2826/603707.

Fassio, C. 2018. "Export-Led Innovation: The Role of Export Destinations." Industrial and Corporate Change 27 (1): 149–71. https://doi.org/10.1093/icc/dtx028.

FedEx corp. 2015. "European SME Export Report – Export /Import Trends and Behaviours of SMEs in Europe." FedEx Express. http://www.fedex.com/gb/small-business/sme-europe.html.

Flor M., and Oltra M. J. 2005. "The Influence of Firms' Technological Capabilities on Export Performance in Supplier-Dominated Industries: The Case of Ceramic Tiles Firms." R&D Management 35 (3): 333–47. https://doi.org/10.1111/j.1467-9310.2005.00393.x.

Galvez D., Camargo M., Rodriguez J., and Morel L. 2013. "PII- Potential Innovation Index: A Tool to Benchmark Innovation Capabilities in International Context." Journal of Technology Management & Innovation 8 (4): 36–45.

Gkypali A., Arvanitis S., and Tsekouras K. 2018. "Absorptive Capacity, Exporting Activities, Innovation Openness and Innovation Performance: A SEM Approach towards a Unifying Framework." Technological Forecasting and Social Change 132 (July): 143–55. https://doi.org/10.1016/j.techfore.2018.01.025.

Godet, M. 1997. Manuel de prospective stratégique. Paris: Dunod.

Golovko E., and Valentini G. 2011. "Exploring the Complementarity between Innovation and Export for SMEs Growth." Journal of International Business Studies 42 (3): 362–80.

Golovko E., and Valentini G. 2014. "Selective Learning-by-Exporting: Firm Size and Product Versus Process Innovation." Global Strategy Journal 4 (3): 161–80. https://doi.org/10.1002/gsj.1080.

Guan, J., and N. Ma. 2003. "Innovative Capability and Export Performance of Chinese Firms." Technovation 23 (9): 737–47. https://doi.org/10.1016/S0166-4972(02)00013-5.

Haahti A., Madupu V., Yavas U., and Babakus E. 2005. "Cooperative Strategy, Knowledge Intensity and Export Performance of Small and Medium Sized Enterprises." Journal of World Business 40 (2): 124–38. https://doi.org/10.1016/j.jwb.2005.02.003.

Harris R.C., and Smith J. 2011. "R&D, Innovation and Exporting." SERC Discussion Papers 0073, Spatial Economics Research Centre, LSE.

ISO 56002:2019 – Innovation Management System.

Jones O., and Craven M. 2001. "Beyond the Routine: Innovation Management and the Teaching Company Scheme." Technovation 21 (5): 267–79. https://doi.org/10.1016/S0166-4972(00)00042-0.

Kafouros M. I., Buckley P. J., Sharp J.A., and Wang C., 2008. "The Role of Internationalization in Explaining Innovation Performance." Technovation 28 (1–2): 63–74. https://doi.org/10.1016/j.technovation.2007.07.009.

Kockmann F. 2007. "L'agriculture Interrogée Par Le Développement Durable : Une Expérience En Saône-et-Loire." Le Courrier de l'environnement de l'INRA 54 (54): 65–79.

Love J. H, and Roper S. 2015. "SME Innovation, Exporting and Growth: A Review of Existing Evidence." International Small Business Journal 33 (1): 28–48. https://doi.org/10.1177/0266242614550190.

MacPherson A. 2000. "The Role of International Design Orientation and Market Intelligence in the Export Performance of US Machine Tool Companies." R&D Management 30 (2): 167–76. https://doi.org/10.1111/1467-9310.00166.

Monreal-Pérez J., Aragón-Sánchez A., and Sánchez-Marín G. 2012. "A Longitudinal Study of the Relationship between Export Activity and Innovation in the Spanish Firm: The Moderating Role of Productivity." International Business Review 21 (5): 862–77. https://doi.org/10.1016/j.ibusrev.2011.09.010.

OECD and Eurostat. 2005. Oslo Manual (Organisation for Economic Co-operation and Development).

OECD. 2009. "Top Barriers and Drivers to SME Internationalisation." Working Party on SMEs and Entrepreneurship. http://www.oecd.org/cfe/smes/43357832.pdf.

Rejeb, H., Morel-Guimarães L., Boly V., and Assiélou G. 2008. "Measuring Innovation Best Practices: Improvement of an Innovation Index Integrating Threshold and Synergy Effects." Technovation 28 (12): 838–54. https://doi.org/10.1016/j.technovation.2008.08.005.

Ribau C. P., Moreira A. C., and Raposo M. 2019. "The Role of Exploitative and Exploratory Innovation in Export Performance: An Analysis of Plastics Industry SMEs." European Journal of International Management 13 (2): 224–46. https://doi.org/10.1504/EJIM.2019.098149.

Rodil Ó., Vence X., and Sánchez M. C. 2016. "The Relationship between Innovation and Export Behaviour: The Case of Galician Firms." Technological Forecasting and Social Change 113 (December): 248–65. https://doi.org/10.1016/j.techfore.2015.09.002.

Roper S., and Love J. H. 2002. "Innovation and Export Performance: Evidence from the UK and German Manufacturing Plants." Research Policy 31 (7): 1087–1102. https://doi.org/10.1016/S0048-7333(01)00175-5.

Rousset S. 2004. "Qualité et coordination économique dans les industries agroalimentaires. Analyse institutionnelle comparée de l'industrie du vin en Bourgogne, Californie et Nouvelle-Zélande." PhD thesis, Université de Bourgogne. https://tel.archives-ouvertes.fr/tel-00089184.

Ughetto, E. 2008. "Does Internal Finance Matter for R&D? New Evidence from a Panel of Italian Firms." Cambridge Journal of Economics 32 (6): 907–25.

Wheeler C., Ibeh K., and Dimitratos P. 2008. "UK Export Performance Research: Review and Implications." International Small Business Journal 26 (2): 207–39. https://doi.org/10.1177/0266242607086574.

Chapter 4

A business model taxonomy for international SMEs in traditional manufacturing industries

Germán Benito-Sarriá, José Pla-Barber, and Cristina Villar

Introduction

Small and medium-sized enterprises (SMEs), and specifically those that operate in traditional manufacturing industrial sectors, are essential for the local economies and society. However, these SMEs have significant difficulties surviving in the global market due to constraints derived from their size, home location, and industry technological level. Compared to large firms, SMEs face poorer survival prospects (Freeman et al., 1983). This inequality, known as "the liability of smallness" (Aldrich and Auster, 1986), is explained by the limitation that small size generates in terms of resources and capabilities and the possibilities of reacting to environmental disruptions (Guercini and Milanesi, 2016). In addition, SMEs can suffer significant barriers to internationalization due to the lack of different knowledge and skills (Crick and Barr, 2007) and barriers to innovation (Teece, 1996; Madrid-Guijarro et al., 2009). Second, European companies in manufacturing industries have specific difficulties competing internationally (Pla-Barber et al., 2020). Aspects such as the possible saturation of their domestic markets, high labour costs, or problems accessing raw materials affect their prospects for survival. Additionally, there is a widespread belief that only those organizations dedicated to R&D or high technology create employment and wealth in Western economies (Hirsch-Kreinsen, 2008). Finally, low/medium-tech firms may have difficulties finding highly qualified workers and support from institutions or society in general. For these reasons, European traditional manufacturing SMEs do not seem to have the best internal characteristics or compete in the best environment to support their success in the local market and certainly not in their international expansion.

Despite this unfavourable situation, we can still find some European manufacturing SMEs in international markets that have been able to cope with the competition of multinational firms. Such companies have designed a business model that is a source of competitive advantage internationally (Villar et al., 2020). Rather than imitating the strategies of large companies, successful exporting SMEs develops their own rules, focusing on aspects such as flexibility and proximity to the customer. For this reason, the objective of this work is to increase our knowledge about these resilient companies through the business model framework. To achieve this objective, we propose a taxonomy of the business model of traditional manufacturing exporting SMEs, explaining how they have managed to compete, survive and succeed in international markets.

In the last two decades, the interest of management researchers in the business model has not stopped growing (Foss and Saebi, 2017; Massa et al., 2017; Cosenz and Noto, 2018). The business model is defined as "how the enterprise creates and delivers value to customers, and then converts payments received to profits" (Teece, 2010; p. 173). The business model perspective allows us to have a global vision of the firm's businesses; they play an essential role in explaining the performance of companies (Zott et al., 2011) because companies compete through their business models (Casadesus-Masanell and Ricart, 2010). As such, the business model perspective offers excellent opportunities for management researchers (Tallman, Luo and Buckley, 2018). However, it is rarely applied accurately, leading to great confusion around this concept (Klang et al., 2014). The main issue is the absence of precise measurements or scales (Child et al., 2017), and consequently, the operationalization of the business model is still a challenge for researchers. Some authors have already defined different business models through various methodologies and tools (e.g., Weill et al., 2005; Camisón and Villar-López, 2010; McQuillan and Scottt, 2015; Child et al., 2017; Pels and Sheth, 2017). These works have also used a very heterogeneous description of the elements involved in the business model and various grouping tools.

This study aims to clarify the business model concept and facilitate its use in future research by providing a complete description of the components that define a business model. We describe the business models through 34 questions that compile the main theoretical and empirical works on business models. In this case, the description is adapted to the nature of manufacturing companies. It also includes aspects of internationalization as the international dimension is rarely considered in the business model definition (Onetti et al., 2012).

The chapter is structured as follows. First, we review the theoretical framework, paying particular attention to the components that define an export manufacturing business model. Second, we describe the methodology used and present the results obtained. In the discussion section, we describe the identified business models and their common characteristics. Finally, we conclude with the implications for academia and practitioners and propose avenues for further research.

1. Theoretical framework

Traditionally, management researchers have classified organizations into groups to identify patterns of behaviour and common characteristics and simplify the complex business reality. A group of organizations could be classified through common sense, prior theoretical knowledge, or through an empirical process based on similarities and contrasts (Warriner, 1984). The latter is an inductive procedure known as "taxonomy" (Rich, 1992; Baden-Fuller and Morgan, 2010).

In our analysis, the business model is the subject of taxonomy. Many works have focused on analyzing the particular business models of a firm. The cases of IKEA (Jonsson and Foss, 2011) or ING direct (Dunford et al., 2010) are good examples of studies dedicated to a specific firm. However, at a more general level of granularity (foundational level), the same model can capture the essence of the businesses of several firms (Morris et al., 2005). In this work, we use an empirical method to classify firms at a business model level.

Business model logic provides the opportunity to have a global vision of various areas of the organization, composed of different components that offer complementary information about the business. Still, these components of business models are not considered in isolation; they are developed as an interconnected system. For instance, Onetti et al. (2012) state that the business model logic connects different characteristics of organizations based on their competitive strategy.

At the theoretical level, the multifaceted nature of business models can be analyzed through complementary theoretical perspectives (DaSilva and Trkman, 2014; Child et al., 2017). From the lenses of the Resource-Based View (Grant, 1996), the business model shows aspects of the SMEs (i.e., their resources and capabilities) that can create their source of competitive advantage. From a Relational perspective (Andersson et al., 2002; Obadia et al., 2017), this literature introduces links with other external actors, including network links and transactional channels. SMEs have different endowments of resources and capabilities – including those resources and competencies obtained through network links – that define different ways of operating internationally (Child et al., 2017), thus leading to various configurations of international SMEs and business model patterns.

In this vein, international entrepreneurship research has also explored the business model characteristics useful in early internationalization. In fact, Hennart (2014) proposes the business model framework as an explanation for the International new venture / Born global (Oviatt and McDougall, 1994; McDougall and Oviatt, 2000; Cavusgil and Knight, 2015; Coviello, 2015). According to this approach, some companies do not require any extra effort to create, deliver and capture value from a foreign customer compared to a national one. This business model pattern is based on offering distinctive products to niche markets, the standardization of both the marketing mix and the transactions, and an expert industrial customer profile. Such a theoretical pattern facilitates and speeds up the internationalization of firms; nonetheless, the best models to achieve high international performance might differ.

Many conceptual and empirical works have corroborated aspects of the business model associated with the success of international entrepreneurial companies. An example of these characteristics widely associated with international entrepreneurial business models is offering a high-quality product addressed to a niche market (e.g., Kraus et al., 2017; Autio, 2017).

Another aspect suggested by this literature is the importance of the relationships with external actors such as suppliers and clients (e.g., Sainio et al., 2011). Based on the multifactorial nature of the business model and the characteristics of the industry, Child et al. (2017) identified in manufacturing firms from the clothing industry a successful business model grounded mainly on the direct delivery to retailers or international trading houses, the close relationship with suppliers and the flexibility to adapt to consumer requirements. However, other aspects of the internationalization strategy are less evident in the literature. For example, the choice of the foreign operation mode, the decision to focus on a global offer or the adaptation to different markets have been widely addressed by the international business literature, yet from different perspectives and inconclusive results.

Business models components in exporter manufacturing SMEs

The study of the business model as an element of analysis may be confusing due to the diversity of definitions in the literature (DaSilva and Trkman, 2014; Massa et al., 2017). The Business Model Canvas (Osterwalder and Pigneur, 2010) is the most used tool to describe business models for managers. However, there is no consensus on the combination of components that make up a business model for academics (Morris et al., 2005; Shafer et al., 2005; Osterwalder, Pigneur and Tucci, 2005; Wirtz et al., 2016; Massa et al., 2017). From a value-based perspective (Teece, 2010), the business model components should allow us to answer three questions: *What is the value proposition? How is value created and distributed? and How is value captured?* (Richardson, 2008; Landau et al., 2016).

The *Value proposition* generally includes aspects regarding what the company offers and to whom. In other words, it is crucial to define the characteristics of the products and the features of the client/target markets to know the reasons why the client values the company's offer.

In addition to this, we incorporate two other aspects that sometimes are forgotten by empirical studies under the business model logic. On the one hand, we consider the "*customer perceived value*" or "*customer value proposition*" (CVP): the "*consumer's overall assessment of the utility of a product (or service) based on perceptions of what is received and what is given*" (Zeithaml, 1988; p. 14). This aspect is critical for understanding the business model definition (Payne et al., 2017). On the other hand, while traditional theories of value creation and value delivery assume that value is only created by producers (Priem, 2007), the business model approach considers that value can also be created on the demand side (Massa et al., 2017). Therefore, this framework needs to include the possibility that the value could be co-created with the client (Ngo and O'Cass, 2009; O'Cass and Ngo, 2011). Consequently, we begin the business model description with three constructs: the offering characteristics – including the possibility that the product is created in collaboration with the customer –, the CVP and the market characteristics.

Besides, the firm will need to *adapt* the value proposition to changes in conditions across markets (Tallman et al., 2018). International companies can strategically develop a marketing mix that is global or specially adapted to target markets (Powers and Loyka, 2010). As discussed earlier, this is a business model aspect that affects the time of internationalization of companies (Hennart, 2014). The more changes needed in the model, the greater the effort that firms should make to expand. Therefore, understanding what marketing elements should be adopted internationally and which ones are globalized is essential when describing the business model of an exporting company.

Furthermore, the business model shows how value emerges through the firm's interaction with customers and other actors (Ehret et al., 2013; Massa et al., 2017). This *interaction with actors* outside the boundaries of the firm occurs in two different modes: the delivery of the value to consumers occurs through customer relational channels and transactional channels (Osterwalder et al., 2005) and the company's relationship with other actors in the market, such as clients, suppliers or competitors, and other non-market actors, such as research institutes or local governments and institutions (Andersson et al., 2002; Child et al., 2017).

Firms create value through competences that can be internal or external. External competences derive from partner relationships, but internal ones result from the firm's unique combination of resources. Therefore, knowing which are the main *internal competences* of the firm is essential to understand how it creates value and, thus, to define its business model (Morris et al., 2005; Child et al., 2017). For this reason, we identify the main internal competences as another fundamental component of the business model.

Finally, we must include aspects of *value capture*. The revenue and cost structure are important aspects of the business model (Osterwalder et al., 2005; Morris et al., 2005; Richardson, 2008; Teece, 2010), and thus it is required to include information about the company's sources of income and other financial data in the business model description.

According to our literature review, we propose eight blocks to analyze business models: offering characteristics, market characteristics, VCP, adaptation to foreign markets, transactional channels, internal competencies, key partners and economic factor. Tab. 1 presents the eight theoretical blocks (constructs) of the business model and, for each block, a list of similar concepts used by other works and a list of different items to measure the constructs.

Tab. 1: Theoretical constructs in International business models (Source: own elaboration)

Construct	Constructs used in other works with similar definitions	Items
Offering characteristics	Artefacts (Mason and Spring, 2011), Offering (Morris et al., 2005; Richardson, 2008), Products (Landau et al., 2016), Value proposition (Osterwalder et al., 2005), etc.	Broad line of products Deep lines of products Highly customized products Co-created with the client
Market characteristics	Customer (Magretta, 2002), Market factor (Morris et al., 2005), Market segment (Chesbrough and Rosenbloom, 2002), Target customer (Osterwalder et al., 2005; Richardson, 2008; Landau et al., 2016), etc.	B-to-b market Niche market
Value customer proposition	Customer value (Magretta, 2002), Offering (Landau et al., 2016), Value (Mason and Spring, 2011), Value proposition (Chesbrough and Rosenbloom, 2002; Boons and Ludeke-Freund, 2012), etc.	High quality Low price or cost-saving High affective value Social status
Adaptation to foreign markets	Marketing mix adaptations (Hennart, 2014).	Product adaptation Promotion methods adaptation Distribution methods adaptation Price adaptation
Transactional channels	Customer interface (Boons and Ludeke-Freund, 2012), Relationship (Osterwalder et al., 2005), Distribution channel (Osterwalder et al., 2005), Transactional channels to foreign markets (Child et al., 2017), etc.	Impersonal customer contact channels Indirect export Direct export

Continued

Tab. 1: Continued

Construct	Constructs used in other works with similar definitions	Items
Internal competences	Core competency (Osterwalder et al., 2005), Core competency strengths (Child et al., 2017), Competences (Demil and Lecocq, 2010), Internal capability factors (Morris et al., 2005), Resources and capabilities (Richardson, 2008), etc.	Production/operating system Selling/marketing Information management Technology/R&D/innovation Financial Supply chain management Networking/resource leveraging
Key partners	Key external network links (Child et al., 2017), Partner network (Osterwalder et al., 2005), Position in the value network (Richardson, 2008), etc.	Client Supplier Competitors Local authorities/governments Research institutes/universities Sector associations
Economic factors	Cost structure (Chesbrough and Rosenbloom, 2002; Osterwalder et al., 2005), Economic factors (Morris et al., 2005), Economics of the business (Richardson, 2008), Financial model (Boons and Ludeke-Freund, 2012), Revenue and Costs (Landau et al., 2016), Revenue model (Osterwalder et al., 2005), etc.	High volumes High margins High operating leverage Price is fixed

2. Methods

The methodology used in this work is shown below, including the research design, the measures for the business model, and the statistical analysis characteristics. Fig. 1 shows the steps followed in this work.

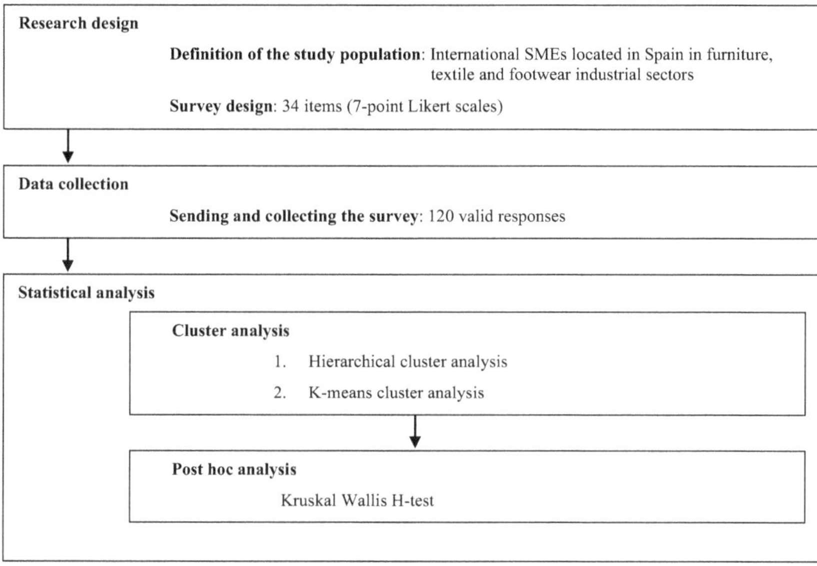

Fig. 1: Methods (Source: own elaboration)

2.1. Research design

The sample population was obtained from the ORBIS database by Bureau van Dijk. We included exporting SMEs with less than 250 employees (European Union) located in Spain and included in the NACE 2009 codes of 13, 15 or 31 (furniture, textile and footwear manufacturing industries).

The data collection was carried out in 2019 through a survey questionnaire. This method allows us to obtain non-financial data necessary to answer our research question. The questionnaire was pretested by academic and professional experts (Collins, 2003). In this process, we considered Podsakoff et al. (2003) recommendations to avoid ex-ante common method bias.

We obtained 120 valid responses. This number of observations is sufficient to ensure statistical power in the social sciences (Cohen, 1992). Although firms belong to different sectors, the sample composition is relatively balanced, in that 25.0 % of our firms belong to the furniture industry, 35.8 % are in the textile industry and 39.2 % in footwear. Firms in our sample differ in the number of employees, age, international experience, or level of exports, accounting for the heterogeneous profiles of firms competing in these industrial sectors.

2.2. Business model measurement

The business model has been described through 34 7-point Likert scales that measure the respondent's degree of agreement or disagreement concerning each item (1 being totally disagreed and 7 being totally agreed). Based on the theory and our description of the business model components, already described in Tab. 1, items are grouped in eight blocks to facilitate their understanding and subsequent discussion of the results: offering characteristics (Morris et al., 2005), CVP (Sweeney and Soutar, 2001), market characteristics (Morris et al., 2005; Hennart, 2014), marketing mix adaptation (Lages et al., 2009), transactional channels, main partners, main competences (Morris et al., 2005) and economic factors (Morris et al., 2005).

2.3. Statistical analysis

We test our framework using cluster analysis (Punj and Stewart, 1983; Hair et al., 1998). Cluster analysis is a technique widely used by strategy researchers to define taxonomies (Hagen et al., 2012). In our case, we have applied a traditional protocol consisting of two steps. In the first step, we carried out a hierarchical cluster analysis to identify the number of groups present in the sample. In the second step, we have carried out a K-means analysis (non-hierarchical cluster analysis) to identify each cluster and assign each firm its permanence cluster. Ward's method minimizes the within-cluster differences and avoids problems associated with other clustering methods (Aldenderfer and Blashfield, 1984). Subsequently, we performed a post-hoc analysis. We also verified the validity of the cluster analysis and the results obtained through the Kruskal-Wallis H-test.

3. Results

Hierarchical cluster analysis permits the identification of the number of clusters present in our sample. As shown in Tab. 2 there is a great distance between the agglomeration coefficients of 3-clusters and 2-clusters solutions; hence we considered grouping the firms into 3 clusters as the most appropriate solution.

Tab. 2: Hierarchical cluster analysis (Source: own elaboration)

Number of Clusters	Agglomeration Coefficient	Change in Agglomeration Coefficient
2	8696.384	869.019
3	**8054.400**	**641.848**
4	7676.237	378.227
5	7386.989	289.284
6	7110.403	276.586

Note: Bold values refer to selected number of clusters and relative agglomeration coefficients.

Additionally, we performed a post-hoc analysis through Kruskal-Wallis H-test to check if each item's individual distribution between clusters is sufficiently different. Kruskal-Wallis H-test shows that the 3 clusters differed significantly for 31 items ($p < 0.05$) and do not find significant differences in 3 items. First, we do not find statistically significant differences in the value of product quality between the clusters. $H(2) = 2.326$, $p = 0.313$. Second, we do not find statistically significant differences in the value of clients as main partners between the different models. $H(2) = 3.815$, $p = 0.148$. There are also no statistically significant differences in the value of the providers as main partners between the groups. $H(2) = 1.108$, $p = 0.575$. These three items have not been removed from the cluster analysis because even though they do not show significant differences between clusters, they intervene when defining the three clusters (Hair at al., 1998).

Tab. 3: Cluster means (Source: own elaboration)

BM Block	Item	Cluster 1 (N=51)	Cluster 2 (N=47)	Cluster 3 (N=22)	Overall mean
Offering characteristics	Broad line of products	4.22	**3.70**	5.27	4.21
	Deep lines of products	**4.04**	4.91	5.00	4.56
	Highly customized products	4.75	5.51	**4.18**	4.94
	Co-created with the client	**3.96**	5.00	4.09	4.39
Customer value proposition	High quality*	5.84	6.28	5.41	5.93
	Low price or cost saving	**3.86**	4.77	4.68	4.37
	High affective value	**4.00**	5.62	5.14	4.84
	Social status	**3.55**	5.81	4.73	4.65
Market characteristics	B-to-b market	4.82	5.36	**3.77**	4.84
	Niche market	**4.31**	5.28	4.50	4.73
International Adaptation	Product	**2.86**	4.11	3.59	3.48
	Promotion methods	**2.14**	4.30	4.14	3.35
	Distribution methods	**2.35**	4.21	4.27	3.43
	Price	**2.90**	4.68	5.14	4.01
Channels	Impersonal customer contact channels	**1.65**	1.98	2.05	1.85
	Indirect export	3.53	**2.40**	5.45	3.44
	Direct export	4.27	5.19	**2.41**	4.29
Main partners	Client*	6.25	6.55	6.27	6.37
	Supplier*	5.90	6.28	6.00	6.07
	Competitors	**4.00**	5.04	4.68	4.53
	Local authorities and / or governments	**2.39**	3.89	3.14	3.12
	Research institutes and universities	**2.22**	3.53	3.41	2.95
	Sector associations	**2.59**	3.68	3.82	3.24
Main internal competences	Production/operating system	5.00	5.72	**4.77**	5.24
	Selling/marketing	**4.59**	5.36	5.27	5.02
	Information management	**4.63**	5.26	4.91	4.93
	Technology/R&D/creative or innovative	**4.14**	5.68	5.23	4.94
	Financial	**4.39**	4.89	5.32	4.76
	Supply chain management	**4.65**	5.26	5.14	4.97
	Networking/resource leveraging	**4.45**	5.36	4.77	4.87
Economics factors	High volumes	**4.25**	5.21	5.32	4.82
	High margins	**3.49**	4.85	4.00	4.12
	High operating leverage	**3.86**	5.21	4.50	4.51
	Price is fixed	**3.55**	3.57	5.09	3.84

*Note: Shaded values refer to highest values and the bold values refer to lowest values. * There are no statistically significant differences between the clusters.*

4. Discussion

The taxonomy of traditional manufacturing SMEs reveals three types of export business model. Each type of model or pattern is grouping together companies whose business model present some common characteristics. These characteristics define a coherent model; that is, the characteristics of a pattern are aligned with each other under the same strategic approach. Consequently, we renamed each type of business model for the strategic approach from which it derives. Hence, the taxonomy of exporting manufacturing SMEs is defined by three business models: the traditional business model, customer-oriented business model, and product-oriented business model. Tab. 4 summarizes the main characteristics of the three business models.

Tab. 4: International business models in traditional manufacturing SMEs (Source: own elaboration)

	Traditional business model	**Customer-oriented business model**	**Product-oriented business model**
Value proposition	- Medium customization and low customer intervention - High quality - Lower value - Global marketing mix	- Customization and co-creation - High quality - Higher value - Niche market - B-to-B - International adaptation	- Standardization - Variety - High quality - B-to-C - International adaptation
Value creation	- Production/operations system as main competence - Lower competences - Value chain networks - Few collaboration networks outside the value chain	- Highest competences - Value chain networks - Greater collaboration with local authorities/ governments and research organizations - Coopetition	- Financing as main competence - Value chain networks - Greater collaboration with sector associations

Continued

Tab. 4: Continued

	Traditional business model	Customer-oriented business model	Product-oriented business model
Value delivery	– Traditional channels to contact new clients – Direct and indirect exports	– Traditional channels to contact new clients – Direct exports	– Traditional channels to contact new clients – Moderate use of impersonal/generic channels – Indirect exports
Value capture	– Sales of medium volumes – Negotiable price	– Sale of large volumes – Negotiable price – High margins – High operating leverage	– Sale of large volumes – Fix price

4.1. Business model 1: Traditional business model

The Traditional business model focuses on the production of high-quality products. It is a more independent and isolated model than the other two, although it does present the companies involved in its value chain as key partners. Its international configuration seems a natural extension of its national model since no significant adaptations to the foreign market are identified. It is a classic or traditional model in the manufacturing industries (Villar et al., 2020); in fact, it is the business model that most firms apply.

Value proposition: this pattern defines a simple offering covered by an average number of product lines with a low depth. The product presents a medium level of customization to the customer and low adaptation to the characteristics of the different international markets. The offer is created with a low intervention of the client. In general terms, this pattern offers a lower value to the client than the rest of the business models. At the market level, the product is provided more to businesses than to final consumers, and the market tends to be more general as compared to the two other models.

Value creation: the main internal competence of this model are the production and the operations system, displaying lower values in the rest of the internal competences. Regarding its main partners, this model relies mainly on its value chain (clients and suppliers) and presents a collaborative relationship with its competitors lower than the other models. The relationships with other potential partners for innovation and international expansion are not significant.

Value delivery: this model contacts its new customers through traditional channels, such as fairs or sales agents. This model relies less on the new channels which are more general and impersonal, i.e., the internet, advertisements in the media or social networks. In addition, it operates abroad through a mix of indirect and direct export.

Value capture: this business model does not sell large volumes of product. It also does not present high margins and operating leverage compared to the other two models; the product's price is mainly negotiable since it presents a low fixed price level.

4.2. Business model 2: Customer-oriented business model

This business model seems to derive from a strategic customer orientation. This model's value proposition is characterized by maximizing consumer satisfaction and focusing on a market niche. These firms focus on understanding the client and satisfying their needs better than the competition through personalization, international adaptation, co-creation with the client and closeness.

Value proposition: customer-oriented business model offers a small variety of products but with high customization and a great co-creation with the client. This model delivers the most outstanding value to the consumer regarding quality, economic value, affective value and social status. The target market is very narrow or specific and is largely made up of other businesses. Regarding international markets, the model presents a great adaptation of its marketing plan to the particularities of each foreign market, being the adaptation of the product and the adaptation of promotion methods outstanding.

Value creation: this model has the highest level in most internal competences, including networks. In this case, the cooperative relationship with competitors stands out. This relationship of coopetition with other companies helps the expansion of the firm (Brandenburger and Nalebuff, 2011). These firms compete in some activities while also cooperating in aspects such as compensating for host market failures; share suppliers or distribution channels or finding industrial clusters (Luo, 2007). The relationship with local authorities and research institutes or universities is greater than the rest of the competition models, although it is still low.

Value delivery: due to the need to have a closer relationship with the customer, this business model mainly uses direct export as a foreign operations mode.

Value capture: firms in this model sell high volumes of product at a reasonably negotiable price. This group has higher margins than the rest of the models and higher fixed costs, so this pattern requires more resources for its implementation.

4.3. Business model 3: Product-oriented business model

Our third and final business model appears to derive from a strategic product orientation. The value proposition is quite varied and seems to be focused on expanding the product range. This model shows high competence in technology, innovation and creativity. These qualities are typical of companies focused on differentiation (Bamiatzi and Kirchmaier, 2014). This model is the least common in our sample.

Value proposition: Their value proposition is very varied, with wide and deep product lines but minimal customization. Quality is the principal value of the product, followed by affective value. The value proposition is generally addressed to consumers more than to other companies. Far from being a passive internationalization, these companies adapt aspects such as distribution methods and prices to their different foreign markets.

Value creation: the product-oriented model has the least competition in the production and activity system of the three business models. This model shows the highest value in obtaining financing, sales and marketing capacity, and innovation and technological capacity. As regards their networks, the customer and the provider are also the main partners. The role of industry associations must also be highlighted; even though they play a moderate role, these are more relevant than in the other two models.

Value delivery: this model features the highest levels of generic and impersonal customer contact channels, products being distributed internationally through indirect export.

Value capture: this business model has medium operating leverage and average margin levels. With this pattern, very high volumes of product are sold at a previously set price.

4.4. Common characteristics to manufacturing SMEs that compete internationally

The three business models present important differences between them, in that they derive from different strategic approaches. However, they share the same orientation towards internationalization. In addition to expanding beyond their domestic markets, these business models show two fundamental common characteristics: the high quality of the product and the importance of its partners in the value chain. Focusing on more specific or niche markets through high-quality products is a competitive positioning associated with higher levels of international sales in SMEs (Hennart et al., 2019) and better export performance (Namiki, 1988). Also, according to Zucchella and Siano (2014), the partnerships with customers and suppliers are also positively related to the export performance of traditional SMEs (Zucchella and Siano, 2014). Therefore, both characteristics appear to be associated with the competitiveness of manufacturing SMEs. Figs. 2, 3, 4 and 5 graphically compare the main features of these business models described above.

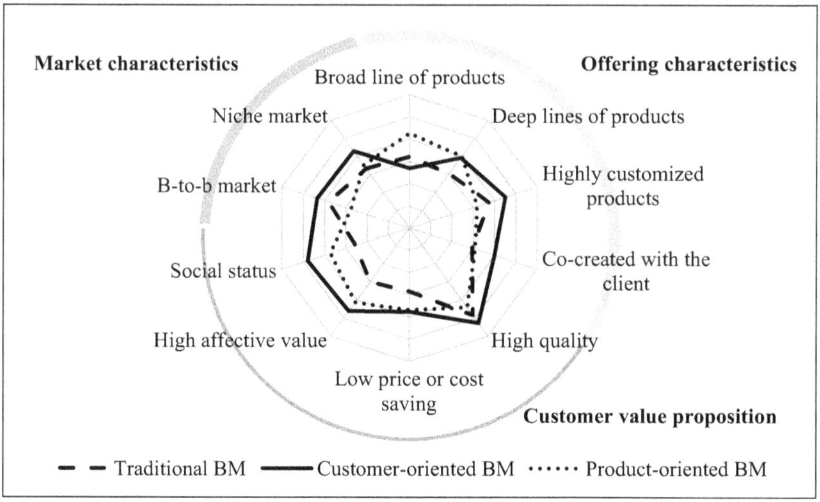

Fig. 2: Value proposition of exporting manufacturing SMEs (Source: own elaboration)

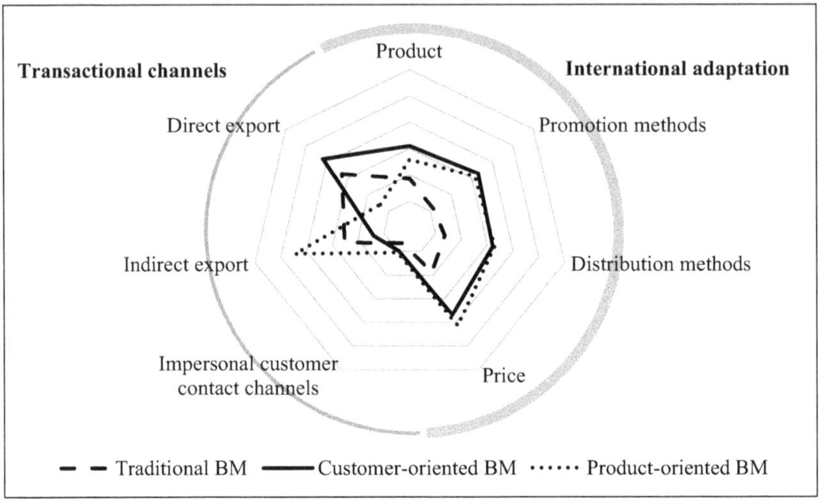

Fig. 3: International Adaptation and transactional channels of exporting manufacturing SMEs (Source: own elaboration)

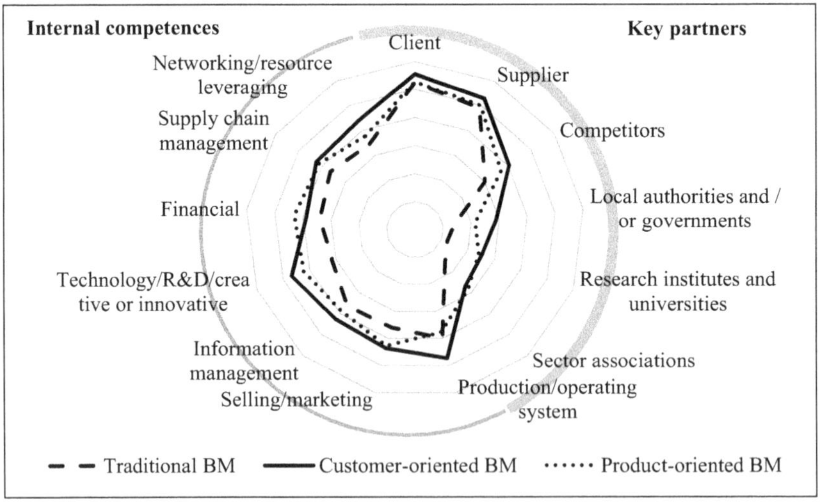

Fig. 4: Value creation of exporting manufacturing SMEs (Source: own elaboration)

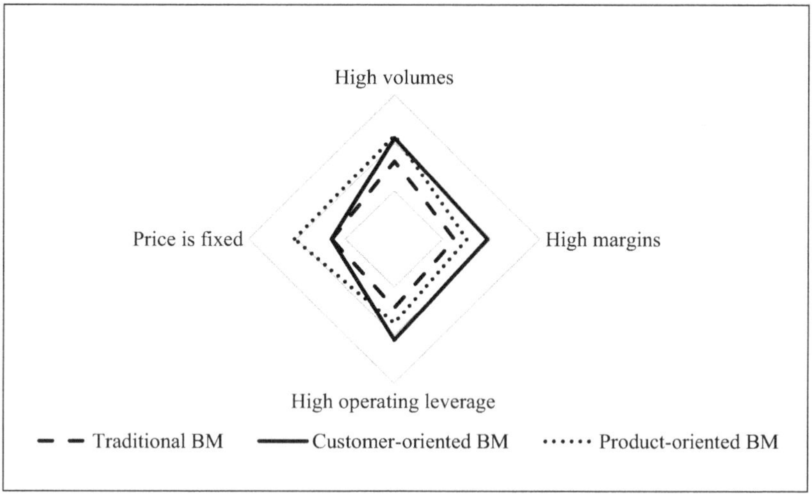

Fig. 5: Value capture of exporting manufacturing SMEs (Source: own elaboration)

Conclusions

In this work, we have identified three models: the traditional business model, this being the most widely used model with characteristics similar to the classic models of traditional manufacturing sectors; the customer-oriented business model, a model that seeks to satisfy customer needs through personalization and closeness to the customer, and the product-oriented model: the least used model that is based on selling innovative and high-quality products, in the international consumer market, through indirect export. Despite the differences between these archetypes, we find many shared characteristics in exporting manufacturing SMEs, such as offering a high-quality product or the great importance of customer and supplier.

We believe these results provide meaningful contributions to the literature at the intersection of business models and international business management. On the one hand, the taxonomy of business models and the identification of common characteristics associated with international success represent an advance in the understanding of the international competitiveness of European manufacturing SMEs. Due to the important role these companies play in nations' economic and social development and the difficulties they confront, we can affirm that academic research focused on improving their survival expectations is pertinent and necessary.

On the other hand, this work responds to the lack of clarity in business model research (Klang et al., 2014), offering a list of items grouped in blocks for improving the business model description. This list has been developed by a rigorous review of major business model research and is relatively comprehensive and precise. In addition, this list is adapted to manufacturing companies and includes aspects of the internationalization of firms. As such, we consider this work offers a helpful tool for operationalizing and promoting the business model study in future academic research.

Furthermore, our study not only contributes to academia but also has implications for practitioners. First, SMEs must be aware of important decisions for internationalization, e.g., the choice of entry modes, or the adaptation/standardization of the international offer, which are not isolated decisions; they must be part of the overall business model design. Our study shows the existence of business model design patterns and that, consequently, successful companies have attained an alignment in the components of their business model. The strategy of replicating some decisions previously made by other organizations should be questioned. The success of these actions is marked by exogenous factors, such as the industry or the market, and the available resources and the alignment of both elements. All business model design options must be consistent with the value proposition that the company has strategically defined.

Second, regarding the particular context of traditional manufacturing SMEs, our study shows some guidelines that may be useful for designing or redesigning their companies' business models, seeking to achieve higher performance. Finally, these results can also be helpful for politicians since they can design public policies that allow SMEs to improve their business models. Aspects such as the inclusion of SMEs in global value chains, the promotion of innovation towards higher quality products or facilitating access to financing can be practical measures for these companies.

However, this study is not without limitations. We acknowledge limitations in terms of sample size and data, limiting the number of business archetypes. These results refer to a single context of a single country of origin and three non-knowledge-intensive industries. Likewise, we do not have a reference group made up of local non-international companies. Although our variables are based on perceptual measures, which can amplify part of the phenomenon, the cross-sectional nature of the data also represents a limitation, restricting the possibility of studying the evolution of business models.

Further research could analyze other companies' profiles regarding home country, industry, and level of internationalization to test if the same patterns are consistent. It would also be interesting to analyze larger samples to look for more detailed models that show the equifinality of the business models in such a way that different business models that pursue the same strategic approach could be identified. Finally, introducing qualitative methodologies would also be an appropriate way to delve into the links between the design of the model and the characteristics of the environment and current issues such as industry 4.0 or sustainability in traditional manufacturing SMEs.

References

Aldenderfer, M. S., and Blashfield, R. K. (1984). A review of clustering methods. In Cluster analysis (pp. 33–61). London: SAGE research methods.

Aldrich, H., and Auster, E. R. (1986). Even dwarfs started small: Liabilities of age and size and their strategic implications. Research in Organizational Behaviour, 8, 165–198.

Andersson, U., Forsgren, M., and Holm, U. (2002). The strategic impact of external networks: Subsidiary performance and competence development in the multinational corporation. Strategic Management Journal, 23(11), 979–996.

Autio, E. (2017). Strategic entrepreneurial internationalization: A normative framework. Strategic Entrepreneurship Journal, 11(3), 211–227.

Baden-Fuller, C., and Morgan, M. S. (2010). Business models as models. Long Range Planning, 43(2–3), 156–171.

Bamiatzi, V. C., and Kirchmaier, T. (2014). Strategies for superior performance under adverse conditions: A focus on small and medium-sized high-growth firms. International Small Business Journal, 32(3), 259–284.

Boons, F., and Lüdeke-Freund, F. (2013). Business models for sustainable innovation: state-of-the-art and steps towards a research agenda. Journal of Cleaner production, 45, 9–19.

Brandenburger, A. M., and Nalebuff, B. J. (2011). Co-opetition. Currency. New York: Bantam Doubleday Dell Publishing Group, Inc.

Camisón, C., and Villar-López, A. (2010). Business models in Spanish industry: A taxonomy-based efficacy analysis. M@ n@ gement, 13(4), 298–317.

Casadesus-Masanell, R., and Ricart, J. E. (2010). From strategy to business models and onto tactics. Long Range Planning, 43(2–3), 195–215.

Cavusgil, S. T., and Knight, G. (2015). The born global firm: An entrepreneurial and capabilities perspective on early and rapid internationalization. Journal of International Business Studies, 46(1), 3–16.

Chesbrough, H., and Rosenbloom, R. S. (2002). The role of the business model in capturing value from innovation: Evidence from Xerox Corporation's technology spin-off companies. Industrial and corporate change, 11(3), 529–555.

Child, J., Hsieh, L., Elbanna, S., Karmowska, J., Marinova, S., Puthusserry, P., Tsai, T., Narooz, R., and Zhang, Y. (2017). SME international business models: The role of context and experience. Journal of World Business, 52(5), 664–679.

Cohen, J. (1992). Statistical power analysis. Current Directions in Psychological Science, 1(3), 98–101.

Collins, D. (2003). Pretesting survey instruments: An overview of cognitive methods. Quality of Life Research, 12(3), 229–238.

Cosenz, F., and Noto, G. (2018). A dynamic business modelling approach to design and experiment new business venture strategies. Long Range Planning, 51(1), 127–140.

Coviello, N. (2015). Re-thinking research on born globals. Journal of International Business Studies, 46(1), 17–26.

Crick, D., and Barr, P. (2007). SMEs' barriers towards internationalization and assistance requirements in the UK: Differences between exporters and firms employing multiple modes of market entry. Journal of Small Business & Entrepreneurship, 20(3), 233–244.

DaSilva, C. M., and Trkman, P. (2014). Business model: What it is and what it is not. Long Range Planning, 47(6), 379–389.

Demil, B., and Lecocq, X. (2010). Business model evolution: In search of dynamic consistency. Long Range Planning, 43(2–3), 227–246.

Dunford, R., Palmer, I., and Benveniste, J. (2010). Business model replication for early and rapid internationalization: The ING direct experience. Long Range Planning, 43(5–6), 655–674.

Ehret, M., Kashyap, V., and Wirtz, J. (2013). Business models: Impact on business markets and opportunities for marketing research. Industrial Marketing Management, 42(5), 649–655.

European Union (2003). Official Journal of the European Union L 124, p. 36 of 20 May 2003. (2).

Foss, N. J., and Saebi, T. (2017). Fifteen years of research on business model innovation: How far have we come, and where should we go? Journal of Management, 43(1), 200–227.

Freeman, J., Carroll, G. R., and Hannan, M. T. (1983). The liability of newness: Age dependence in organizational death rates. American Sociological Review, 48(5), 692–710.

Grant, R. M. (1996). Toward a knowledge-based theory of the firm. Strategic Management Journal, 17(S2), 109–122.

Guercini, S., and Milanesi, M. (2016). Interaction approach and liabilities: A case analysis of start-up firms. Journal of Business-to-Business Marketing, 23(4), 293–309.

Hagen, B., Zucchella, A., Cerchiello, P., and De Giovanni, N. (2012). International strategy and performance – Clustering strategic types of SMEs. International Business Review, 21(3), 369–382.

Hair, J., Andersson, R., Tatham, R., and Black, W. (1998). Multivariate Data Analysis. Upper Saddle River, NJ: Prentice Hall.

Hennart, J. F. (2014). The accidental internationalists: A theory of born globals. Entrepreneurship Theory and Practice, 38(1), 117–135.

Hennart, J. F., Majocchi, A., and Forlani, E. (2019). The myth of the stay-at-home family firm: How family-managed SMEs can overcome their internationalization limitations. Journal of International Business Studies, 50(5), 758–782.

Hirsch-Kreinsen, H. (2008). "Low-tech" innovations. Industry and Innovation, 15(1), 19–43.

Jonsson, A., and Foss, N. J. (2011). International expansion through flexible replication: Learning from the internationalization experience of IKEA. Journal of International Business Studies, 42(9), 1079–1102.

Klang, D., Wallnöfer, M., and Hacklin, F. (2014). The business model paradox: A systematic review and exploration of antecedents. International Journal of Management Reviews, 16(4), 454–478.

Kraus, S., Brem, A., Schuessler, M., Schuessler, F., and Niemand, T. (2017). Innovative born globals: Investigating the influence of their business models on international performance. International Journal of Innovation Management, 21(1), 1750005.

Lages, L. F., Abrantes, J. L., and Lages, C. R. (2008). The STRATADAPT scale: A measure of marketing strategy adaptation to international business markets. International Marketing Review, 25(5), 584–600.

Landau, C., Karna, A., and Sailer, M. (2016). Business model adaptation for emerging markets: A case study of a German automobile manufacturer in India. R&D Management, 46(3), 480–503.

Luo, Y. (2007). A coopetition perspective of global competition. Journal of World Business, 42(2), 129–144.

Madrid-Guijarro, A., Garcia, D., and Van Auken, H. (2009). Barriers to innovation among Spanish manufacturing SMEs. Journal of Small Business Management, 47(4), 465–488.

Magretta, J. (2002). Why business models matter. Harvard Business Review, 80(5), 86–92.

Mason, K., and Spring, M. (2011). The sites and practices of business models. Industrial Marketing Management, 40(6), 1032–1041.

Massa, L., Tucci, C. L., and Afuah, A. (2017). A critical assessment of business model research. Academy of Management Annals, 11(1), 73–104.

McDougall, P. P., and Oviatt, B. M. (2000). International entrepreneurship: The intersection of two research paths. Academy of Management Journal, 43(5), 902–906.

McQuillan, D., and Scott, P. S. (2015). Models of Internationalization: A business model approach to professional service firm internationalization. In Business Models and Modelling (Advances in Strategic Management. Volume 33) (pp. 309–345). Emerald Group Publishing Limited, Bingley UK.

Morris, M., Schindehutte, M., and Allen, J. (2005). The entrepreneur's business model: Toward a unified perspective. Journal of Business Research, 58(6), 726–735.

Namiki, N. (1988). Export strategy for small business. Journal of Small Business Management, 26(2), 21–37.

Ngo, L. V., and O'Cass, A. (2009). Creating value offerings via operant resource-based capabilities. Industrial Marketing Management, 38(1), 45–59.

O'Cass, A., and Ngo, L. V. (2011). Examining the firm's value creation process: A managerial perspective of the firm's value offering strategy and performance. British Journal of Management, 22(4), 646–671.

Obadia, C., Vida, I., and Pla-Barber, J. (2017). Differential effects of bilateral norms on SMEs' export relationships: A dynamic perspective. Journal of International Marketing, 25(3), 21–41.

Onetti, A., Zucchella, A., Jones, M. V., and McDougall-Covin, P. P. (2012). Internationalization, innovation and entrepreneurship: Business models for new technology-based firms. Journal of Management & Governance, 16(3), 337–368.

Osterwalder, A., and Pigneur, Y. (2010). Business Model Generation: A Handbook for Visionaries, Game Changers, and Challengers. John Wiley & Sons, Hoboken, New Jersey, USA.

Osterwalder, A., Pigneur, Y., and Tucci, C. L. (2005). Clarifying business models: Origins, present, and future of the concept. Communications of the Association for Information Systems (CAIS), 16(1), 1–25.

Oviatt, B. M., and McDougall, P. P. (1994). Toward a theory of international new ventures. Journal of International Business Studies, 25(1), 45–64.

Payne, A., Frow, P., and Eggert, A. (2017). The customer value proposition: Evolution, development, and application in marketing. Journal of the Academy of Marketing Science, 45(4), 467–489.

Pels, J., and Sheth, J. N. (2017). Business models to serve low-income consumers in emerging markets. Marketing Theory, 17(3), 373–391.

Pla-Barber, J., Villar, C., and Benito-Sarriá, G. (2020). Configurational theory in traditional manufacturing industries: A new model of high-performing small and medium-sized enterprises. Sustainability, 12(17), 6818.

Podsakoff, P. M., MacKenzie, S. B., Lee, J. Y., and Podsakoff, N. P. (2003). Common method biases in behavioral research: A critical review of the literature and recommended remedies. Journal of Applied Psychology, 88(5), 879.

Powers, T. L., and Loyka, J. J. (2010). adaptation of marketing mix elements in international markets. Journal of Global Marketing, 23(1), 65–79.

Priem, R. L. (2007). A consumer perspective on value creation. Academy of Management Review, 32(1), 219–235.

Punj, G., and Stewart, D. W. (1983). Cluster analysis in marketing research: Review and suggestions for application. Journal of Marketing Research, 20(2), 134–148.

Rich, P. (1992). The organizational taxonomy: Definition and design. Academy of Management Review, 17(4), 758–781.

Richardson, J. E. (2008). The business model: An integrative framework for strategy execution. Strategic Change, 17(5–6), 133–144.

Sainio, L. M., Saarenketo, S., Nummela, N., and Eriksson, T. (2011). Value creation of an internationalizing entrepreneurial firm: The business model perspective. Journal of Small Business and Enterprise Development, 18(3), 556–570.

Shafer, S. M., Smith, H. J., and Linder, J. C. (2005). The power of business models. Business horizons, 48(3), 199–207.

Sweeney, J. C., and Soutar, G. N. (2001). Consumer perceived value: The development of a multiple item scale. Journal of Retailing, 77(2), 203–220.

Tallman, S., Luo, Y., and Buckley, P. J. (2018). Business models in global competition. Global Strategy Journal, 8(4), 517–535.

Teece, D. J. (1996). Firm organization, industrial structure, and technological innovation. Journal of Economic Behavior & Organization, 31(2), 193–224.

Teece, D. J. (2010). Business models, business strategy and innovation. Long Range Planning, 43(2–3), 172–194.

Villar, C., Pla-Barber, J., and Ghauri, P. (2020). Learning from foreign operation modes: The virtuous path for innovation. BRQ Business Research Quarterly, 23(2), 159–171.

Warriner, C. K. (1984). Organizations and their environments: Essays in the sociology of organizations. Greenwich, CT: JAI Press.

Weill, P., Malone, T. W., D'Urso, V. T., Herman, G., and Woerner, S. (2005). Do some business models perform better than others? A study of the 1000 largest US firms. MIT Center for coordination science working paper, 226.

Wirtz, B. W., Pistoia, A., Ullrich, S., and Göttel, V. (2016). Business models: Origin, development and future research perspectives. Long Range Planning, 49(1), 36–54.

Zeithaml, V. A. (1988). Consumer perceptions of price, quality and value: A means-end model and synthesis of evidence. Journal of Marketing, 52(3), 2–22.

Zott, C., Amit, R., and Massa, L. (2011). The business model: Recent developments and future research. Journal of Management, 37(4), 1019–1042.

Zucchella, A., and Siano, A. (2014). Internationalization and innovation as resources for SME growth in foreign markets: A focus on textile and clothing firms in the Campania Region. International Studies of Management & Organization, 44(1), 21–41.

Chapter 5

Characterizing exporting SMEs in Costa Rica: A current overview

Susan Arce, Margie Faith, and José Martínez

Introduction

SMEs in Costa Rica and around the globe greatly impact the economy, contributing to the Gross Domestic Product (GDP) and employment rates. However, although authorities have set up aid and support programs for this sector, high mortality rates plague SMEs during their first five years.

SMEs is an umbrella term that includes micro, small, and medium enterprises. In Costa Rica, one way to classify them is according to their number of employees; micro enterprises (1–5); small ones (6–30) and medium enterprises (31–100).

Regarding SME's internationalization process, one of the main disadvantages is their size, as they lack the resources and capabilities compared to large enterprises. This has also been observed in Costa Rican SMEs, whose exporting processes are unstable throughout the years.

The Costa Rican Foreign Trade Promoter (PROCOMER) is the Costa Rican institution that oversees and assists companies with their exporting processes. Data obtained from SMEs' detailed exporting records are used to calculate an index that measures each company's export performance annually, through their Export Performance Index (EPI). This index is expressed as a digit between one and ten, where one is the lowest exporting performance and ten is the highest. To calculate the index, they consider an SME's exporting continuity, exporting dynamism, market diversification, and market access conditions.

It is noted that company's indexes are unsteady through the years, oscillating between a great index and a poor one. High-performance companies continue exporting because their main activity is exporting, while others only export when a foreign client demands it.

For the last eight years, we have been studying the impact of the export performance index on different aspects of SMEs in Costa Rica. To date, we have analyzed four different functional areas. For each one, we started with a qualitative research approach by conducting in-depth interviews and then surveyed the companies to measure the influence statistically. The specific method will be further presented for each study.

We defined a critical path to carry out the research steps. The first field studied was finance, followed by strategy, innovation, and digital marketing. The last field is currently in the data collection process.

In this chapter, we will share our experience to date, as well as some of our findings on each of the functional areas studied.

1. Finance

We analyzed the impact of financial management on the export performance of SMEs in Costa Rica, along with other variables that might be affected, given that managers should have a better understanding of financial management to improve their decision-making processes.

The results were obtained from a sample of 302 SMEs, by conducting telephone surveys with a structured questionnaire including five sections (interviewee characteristics, business characteristics, financial management, financial planning and demographics), as shown in Tab. 1.

Tab. 1: Methodology used for the finance study

Aspects	Methodology
Research approach	Quantitative study
Sample	302
Participant	SME's owner, CEO or accountant
Data collection instrument	Structured questionnaire
Analysis	Hypothesis testing and correlations

To evaluate the financial management, we considered financial activities such as accounting reports, financial reports, financial analysis, interpretation of financial information, financial planning, budgeting, capital budgeting, accounts receivable, and accounts payable management, as well as the company's financial order.

Regarding how often companies carry out various financial-accounting activities, the most frequent ones are related to the base of financial management and accounting – among these, accounting reports, financial reports, analysis, interpretation, and decision making based on financial information – while, for activities that require the use of financial models, it was found that most of the companies do not perform them.

Furthermore, it was noted that companies use technological tools to perform these financial-accounting activities, making it vital for financial undertakings.

It is important to point out that only in 26.5 % of the SMEs studied the owner is also the administrator; in the remaining companies, the owner's involvement is minimal or null, with the analyzed activities falling on an administrator.

The main financial reports carried out by exporting SMEs are balance sheet, income statement, and cash flow. We also found that financial analysis is rare and can be summarized into vertical, horizontal, and financial ratio analysis.

Concerning financial planning, the most common budgets are cash flow, master budget, and capital budget, in that order. In addition, these budgets are based mainly on the company's historical data and experience. Finally, only a very small percentage used cash management theories to construct their budget.

Regarding capital budgeting, some companies use a financial model to prepare them – most commonly the recovery period and Internal Rate of Return (IRR), followed by Net Present Value (NPV) – while the remaining companies base the analysis solely on experience.

On the other hand, the most used technological resources are accounting systems, accounting reports, payroll control, asset management, and cash flow control. Accounts receivable are managed utilizing different models, such as supervision, setting standards, and selecting credit standards.

The results revealed that there is no significant difference between the Export Performance Index and how often companies perform financial-accounting activities. However, there is a relationship between some specific activities and the EPI, specifically the financial report preparation, financial analysis, and decision-making based on financial information.

We conclude that the financial management of Costa Rican exporting SMEs is still at very basic levels. In addition, finances are solely managed as per the Direct Taxation national regulation, given that the most commonly performed financial reports are the statement of financial position (balance sheet) and the income statement, both required by the Costa Rican Ministry of Treasury (Ministerio de Hacienda).

2. Strategy

Environmental factors can affect the export performance of both large and small companies disparately; internal factors, such as failure to apply good administrative practices and strategic planning, can have a greater impact on SMEs than on large companies because of the dissimilar resources and capabilities among them.

This section provides evidence of the possible relationship between the application of strategic management practices by SMEs and their export success.

Porter (1980) described three generic strategies that a company can use: cost leadership, differentiation, and focus. A cost leadership strategy consists of creating a competitive advantage, generating and maintaining low costs compared to the competition. Differentiation emphasizes on developing products and services that are recognized by consumers as unique. Finally, a focus strategy considers a particular group of consumers, geographic market or specific product line segment. We decided to take Porter's postulates as a basis to identify the dominant strategy in Costa Rican exporting SMEs and its influence on their performance.

We aimed to identify the key factors for exporting success and the relationship between strategy application and an SME's export performance. We gathered information from successful exporting SMEs according to their EPI, to understand the elements or key factors that helped the company have a high EPI, as well as to identify the SME's strategy and establish if it is a determining factor for the export performance. We delved into the way they differentiate their products or services to identify the generic strategy and its impact on the EPI. The methodology used for this study is summarized in Tab. 2.

Tab. 2: Methodology used for the strategy study

Aspects	**Methodology**
Research approach	Qualitative study
Sample	11
Participant	SME's CEO or person in charge of the company's exports
Data collection instrument	In-depth interview with semi structured questionnaire
Analysis	Coding with ATLAS.ti 6.2 software

The results revealed that most of the SMEs belong to the industry sector and that Central America is their main exporting market. We were able to identify three high export performance factors: quality-based strategy, communication with clients, and market knowledge, as shown in Tab. 3.

Sales, products, the company type, and quality are also elements that influence high export performance. Most companies mentioned that differentiation is the generic strategy related to their export performance, with quality as their main objective. In some cases, they mentioned price, but it was always accompanied by high quality.

Tab. 3: Number of mentions for each aspect by the interviewees

Aspect	**Mentions**
Quality-based strategy	15
Differentiation	6
Communication with clients	5
Market knowledge	3
A combination of quality and price	3

Considering that Costa Rica has a significantly higher salary cost structure than its Central American neighbors and that these countries are the main export destination for Costa Rican SMEs, it seems reasonable to recommend generic strategies leading to quality in this type of economies. On the other hand, cost-based strategies seemed more suitable for specific moments where the economy is either unstable or behaving erratically.

We also found that most of the companies lack formal strategic planning. Although the reasons are not readily identifiable, one possible explanation is that owners and managers lack formal education in business administration and management.

Finally, we noticed that these companies rarely have a defined strategy, basing strategic decisions on market requirements. Thus, in regard to exporting, they start the process upon request from a client or because they identify an opportunity and then continue exporting.

3. Innovation

We examined the influence of open innovation and strategic orientation on the innovation performance of SMEs in the Information and Communications Technology (ICT) sector.

Open innovation processes are understood as any new idea generated either outside the company, within it, or a combination of both. As such, it is essentially different from closed innovation in that it takes any innovation and applies it, allowing the organization to improve its products, services, or processes without necessarily controlling the innovative processes (Chesbrough, 2006).

Innovation performance is the degree of success achieved by companies in meeting their goals related to new products or services (Henard and Szymanski, 2001; Montoya-Weiss and Calantone, 1994). It can be measured in terms of new innovative products or services, a new product or service's degree of success, customer service, and financial success (Atuahene-Gima and Wei, 2011; Baker and Sinkula, 1999; Blazevic and Lievens, 2004; Im and Workman Jr, 2004; Salomo et al., 2008).

There is evidence of a positive correlation between the application of open innovation and the company's innovation performance.

It has been documented that SMEs can improve their productivity and economic development when incorporating innovation in their processes and integrating the positive influence of strategic orientation in innovation performance (Frohmann et al., 2016).

We used the scale developed by Chen and Huizingh (2014) to prove the existing relationships between open innovation processes, strategic orientation, and innovation performance, using a Partial Least Squares (PLS) path modeling, as shown in Fig. 1.

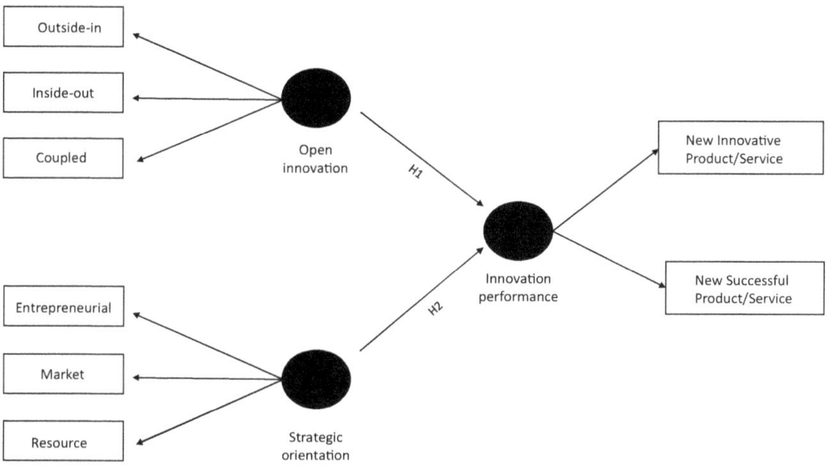

Fig. 1: Innovation performance conceptual framework

We developed a conceptual framework that includes all three types of open innovation activities: outside-in, inside-out, and coupled activities. It also considers the three aspects under which the strategic orientation can be observed: entrepreneurial, market, and resource orientation. The implementation of these strategic orientations is key to achieving superior and continuous business performance.

For this innovation study, we followed a mixed research approach, divided in two phases, as shown in Tab. 4. For the first phase, we collected the data through a structured questionnaire including five sections (interviewee characteristics, control variables, then innovation performance, strategic orientation and open innovation aspects). For the second qualitative phase, the semi structured questionnaire included questions based on the same five aspects evaluated.

Tab. 4: Methodology used for the innovation study

Aspects	Methodology	
	Phase I	**Phase II**
Research approach	Quantitative	Qualitative
Sample	70	15
Participant	SME's CEO or Dept. Manager	SME's CEO or Dept. Manager
Data collection instrument	Structured questionnaire	In-depth interview with semi structured questionnaire
Analysis	PLS path modeling	Coding with ATLAS.ti 8 software

The results revealed a moderately positive influence between both open innovation and innovation performance, and open innovation and strategic orientation. The data indicates item reliability, internal consistency, and convergent and discriminant validity between constructs. Fig. 2 shows each indicator factor loadings as well as the path coefficients.

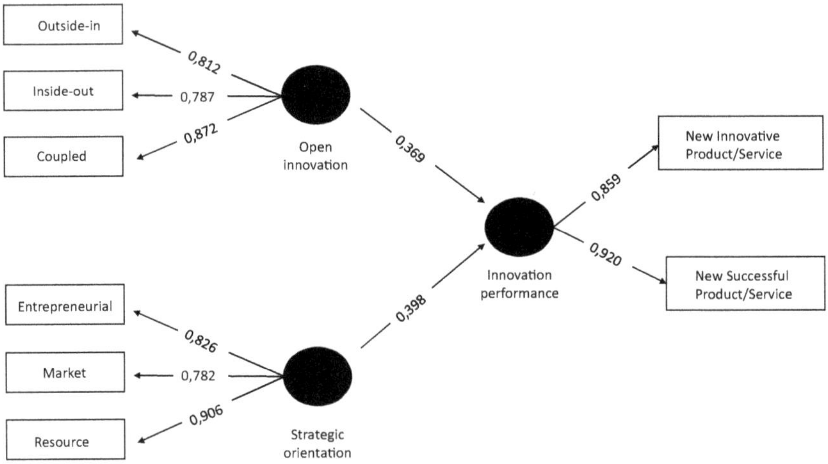

Fig. 2: Path model estimation

A complementary qualitative study showed that, although the SMEs studied have no innovation department, they do perform both inside-out and outside-in innovation, even though they usually have no system or culture involving innovation management. SMEs tend to focus on customer satisfaction and financial benefits to assess innovation success. Some of them also evaluate innovation performance and the success of the new product or service offered.

To improve the results obtained with innovation processes, SMEs enhance open innovation, considering their strategic orientation as a determining factor in these processes; the entrepreneurial and market orientation are the most common ones across the SMEs studied. Other SME sectors and variables that affect innovation processes should be studied in the future.

4. Digital marketing

The use of digital tools allows SMEs to improve their export performance and strengthen their growth and development, which in turn increases their international operations through exports (Murphy, 2008; Singh, 2009). In recent years, the use of communication technologies has become a competitive advantage (Ahmad et al., 2015).

This fact led us to conduct a study to identify SME insights on digital marketing as part of their business strategy and the tools utilized, as well as their perceptions on its positive impact on their companies, benefits for the suppliers and customers, and the new capabilities required to use digital marketing.

We analyzed the advantages that companies obtained from information on their competition, new customers, marketing strategies, products, distribution channels, and suppliers. The details for the methodology used are shown in Tab. 5.

Tab. 5: Methodology used for the digital marketing study

Aspects	Methodology
Research approach	Qualitative study
Sample	10
Participant	SME's owner or CMO
Data collection instrument	In-depth interview with semi structured questionnaire
Analysis	Coding with ATLAS.ti 8 software

The results indicate that companies know about digital marketing and perform some type of marketing action by using digital tools and platforms (Tab. 6). Some are starting to use digital tools, while others have been using them for over a decade. The most used platforms are social media and the corporate website. Regarding social media platforms, Facebook is a site in which all of them have corporate presence.

Tab. 6: Digital tools used by the interviewed companies

Digital Tools	Companies
Facebook	10/10
Website	9/10
Instagram	4/10
WhatsApp	2/10
Email	2/10

In terms of the benefits stemming from relationships with strategic allies and key aspects of the company, we identified that most of them do not perceive any benefit with their suppliers, whereas, regarding their customers, most of them find that digital marketing actions favor them.

We would like to point out that those companies with the highest export index in all variables acknowledge a favorable value on digital marketing.

Regarding the benefit of digital marketing data, most of the companies value positively obtaining information on their competition and its contribution to both strategy development and new customer generation. As to the distribution channels, it is companies with high EPI that identify it as beneficial.

Furthermore, we found that marketing activities in half of the SMEs are performed empirically by employees, who take them on as a secondary task to their main role in the company. The other half carry out these activities with external support either from an acquaintance, an agency, or trained staff dedicated solely to the digital marketing field.

Some of the SMEs do not perceive a relevant benefit from digital marketing management, specifically companies that handle these activities empirically, without proper training or external support.

Regarding digital marketing metrics management, although SMEs use tools such as Facebook and Google Analytics, most of them perform no analysis at all.

Most of the companies consider that executing any kind of digital marketing action demands new capabilities on their business management, and agree with the importance of training their staff, outsourcing the task or hiring someone prepared to conduct these activities.

In general, there is a clear understanding of the importance and necessity of digital marketing in their business management. However, only a few have organized processes according to their business goals, especially any in which they understand and use their competitive and comparative advantage provided by obtaining, analyzing, and utilizing the data.

Conclusion

We found that one of the main factors affecting an SME's export index stability is a lack of a clear export strategy. We noticed that SMEs overwhelmingly begin their exporting journey after being contacted by foreign clients.

This situation leads to limited knowledge on the impact that finance, strategy, innovation, and digital marketing could have on an SME's export performance.

Our attempt to characterize exporting SMEs in Costa Rica allowed us to determine that companies perform their financial analysis according to the demands of government institutions, without considering their impact on improving their export performance.

Regarding strategic orientation, the main conclusion is that, despite having no formal strategy, SMEs have a clear vision of their company's goals and how to achieve them, even if it applies to their general business strategy and is not focused on their export performance.

As to innovation, companies perform and actively seek to implement these activities, highlighting the importance and positive benefits of innovation in their business, even if they do not focus on improving these processes to directly impact their exports.

Furthermore, SMEs have a clear understanding of the necessity and influence that digital marketing has on their business management. The fact that it is a growing trend in recent years explains why we identified SMEs that are starting these activities and why others have had an organized digital marketing strategy for quite some time.

In 2017, the Costa Rican Ministry of Economy, Industry, and Commerce (Ministerio de Economía, Industria y Comercio) stated that SMEs represented 97.5 % of the total companies in the country, contributed 34.5 % to job creation, and account for 35.7 % of the Gross Domestic Product, a fact that highlights the importance of SMEs for the country and justifies this study's critical path.

Future lines of research include human talent studies focusing on areas such as entrepreneurship exporting, managerial attitudes towards exporting activities, and working together with SMEs in developing and improving their export activities.

References

Ahmad S. Z., Abu Bakar, A. R., Faziharudean, T. M., & Mohamad Zaki, T. A. (2015). An Empirical study of factors affecting e-commerce adoption among small and medium size enterprises in a developing country: Evidence from Malasya. Information Technology for Development 21(4): 555–5572. https://doi.org/10.1080/02681102.2014.899961

Atuahene-Gima, K., & Y. Wei. (2011). The vital role of problem-solving competence in new product success. Journal of Product Innovation Management 28: 81–98.

Baker, W. E., & J. M. Sinkula. (1999). The synergistic effect of market orientation and learning orientation on organizational performance. Journal of the Academy of Marketing Science 27: 411–27.

Blazevic, V., & A. Lievens. (2004). Learning during the new financial service innovation process: Antecedents and performance effects. Journal of Business Research 57: 374–91.

Cheng, C., & Huizingh, K. R. E. (2014). When is open innovation beneficial? The role of strategic orientation. The Journal of Product Innovation Management, 31(6), 1235–1253. https://doi.org/10.1111/jpim.12148

Chesbrough, H. (2006). The era of open innovation. Managing Innovation and Change, 127, 34–41.

Frohmann, A., Mulder, N., Olmos, X., & Urmeneta, R. (2016). Internacionalización de las pymes: innovación para exportar.

Henard, D., & D. Szymanski. (2001). Why some new products are more successful than others. Journal of Marketing Research 38: 362–75.

Im, S., & J. Workman. (2004). Market orientation, creativity, and new product performance in high-technology firms. Journal of Marketing 68: 114–32.

Montoya-Weiss, M. M., & R. Calantone. (1994). Determinants of new product performance: A review and meta-analysis. Journal of Product Innovation Management 11: 397–417.

Murphy, P. (2008). Exporting knitted apparel. A study of the determinants of exporting performance in the UK knitted apparel sector (Doctoral Thesis). University of Bradford. http://hdl.handle.net/10454/4292

Porter's (1980). Generic strategies as determinants of strategic group membership and organizational performance. Academy of Management Journal, 27 (3), 467–488.

Salomo, S., K. Talke, & N. Strecker. (2008). Innovation field orientation and its effect on innovativeness and firm performance. Journal of Product Innovation Management 25: 560–76.

Singh, D. (2009). Export performance of emerging market firms. International Business Review 18 (4): 321–330. https://doi.org/10.1016/j.ibusrev.2009.03.002

Chapter 6

Innovation and export capabilities: Toward a taxonomic approach of companies internal practices

Manon Enjolras, Mauricio Camargo, and Christophe Schmitt

Introduction

Innovation and export have been identified as two of the main drivers of economic growth Globalization changed the rules of the game for the competitiveness of all enterprises and forces them to adapt their own strategies and processes in order to get a competitive advantage in their markets. This is why innovation and export are usually considered within the scientific literature as activities having a strong relationship (Love and Roper, 2015). The high performance of innovative companies enables them to be also active on international markets, and exporting companies are able to exploit their experience and knowledge from the international markets to identify innovation opportunities. Although the nature of this relationship between innovation and export is not yet consensual in the academic literature, a trend is emerging for several years in the institutional and practitioner world to consider innovation and export jointly in order to exploit this relationship in the support provided to companies (European Commission, 2007).

Moreover, both innovation and export activities can be considered as phenomena implying disruptions within companies (Torrès and Julien, 2005). For example, innovation impacts the whole company and involves a large number of different actors who need to collaborate. Similarly, exporting requires the mobilization of additional and possibly significant resources, and requires the implementation of a learning process to be able to enter a foreign market. So, in order to overcome these changes, innovative and exporting companies have to change their organization and management methods, moving towards a formalization and structuring of their internal processes.

However, depending on the context in which companies operate, the way they are going to adapt their internal practices can vary. Relying on the contingency theory of Mintzberg (1979), the structure of an organization depends both on its own characteristics and on the nature of its environment. Thus, the internal practices of companies are as varied as the environment they have to deal with. In order to remove the constraints linked to its environment, the company must adjust its behavior, by taking strategic decisions that enable setting up a coherent and specific internal functioning. Regarding specifically innovation and export activities, some contingency factors are identified within the literature, as differentiating factors explaining specific behavior in terms of innovation and export management. They reflect both structural and contextual elements that may push companies to adopt certain behaviors.

Thus, this research work aims to draft distinctive profiles of innovative and exporting companies, adopting an explorative taxonomic approach. The objective of establishing a taxonomy is to have empirical evidence to group and classify elements in categories that share common features (de Jong and Marsili, 2006).

In order to propose a classification of companies according to their innovation and export management approach, we assess their maturity in terms of innovation and export internal practices, and consider additionally specific contingency factors that may have an impact on the way they implement these internal practices. We therefore elicit several companies' profiles representing their behavior as a function of internal, structural and contextual differentiating factors.

1. Conceptual framework

According to the scientific literature, the disruptive nature of innovation and export activities pushes companies to modify their organization to move towards greater structuring and deal with the induced disruptions. Moreover, in order to set up a suitable organization, companies must adapt to the context in which they operate. This will depend on specific contingency factors. To illustrate these statements, and to build the conceptual framework of this research, a literature review was carried on.

1.1. The innovation/export relationship

Around the world, researchers and practitioners are trying to identify and test the relationship between innovation and export to explain the competitiveness of firms. Research papers studying this link are plentiful and propose two dominant theories:

- Self-selection: innovation gives the company a competitive advantage enabling the improvement of its performance in foreign markets (Dai et al., 2019; Ribau et al., 2019)
- Learning-by-Exporting Knowledge and experiences acquired in international markets contribute to the innovation capacity of companies (Di Cintio et al., 2019; Fassio, 2018).

These two theories coexist in the literature and highlight a causal approach to the relationship between innovation and export. They are opposed by the direction of the causality they support: is it innovation that leads to export? or is it export that promotes innovation? The lack of consensus on this direction of causality suggests that the relationship between innovation and export is complex and puts forward the possible existence of a virtuous circle with two possible entry points (Halilem et al., 2014; Zehir et al., 2015).

Based on these theoretical assumptions, we choose to consider jointly the innovation and export practices within companies, in order to provide joint innovation/export behavioral profiles. We consider that if the innovation capability of a company is high, its export capability is also supposed to be high, innovation and export being two activities having a mutual positive impact on each other (Golovko and Valentini, 2011).

Moreover, as explained in the introduction, we consider innovation and export as disruptive activities, pushing companies to adapt their behavior in order to overcome the challenges associated with the implementation of innovation and export processes in their daily routines. Mobilizing the Schumpeterian capability approach (Zawislak et al., 2014; Schumpeter and Backhaus, 2003) as a conceptual base, we consider that if a company is able to manage innovation and export in a more structured and formalized way, by implementing good practices, its innovation and export capability will increase.

We formulate then our first hypothesis.

H1: Innovation and export capabilities of companies are correlated and can be reflected by the way companies implement both innovation and export practices in their internal routines.

1.2. Contextual contingency factors:

Based on Mintzberg's contingency theory, we consider that the structure/behavior of an organization depends both on its own characteristics, but also on the nature of its environment. There are differentiating factors that reveal possible specificities in the daily practices of companies in terms of innovation and export.

One of these specificities is the characteristics of its ecosystem referring to public policies of its domestic market, regulatory context, or economic and political stability (Choi and Lim, 2017; van den Heiligenberg et al., 2017; Urbinati et al., 2018). Then, the domestic geographical area of the company seems to have an impact on the way it implements its innovation and export activities.

Then, our second hypothesis is:

H2: The domestic geographical area of a firm has an impact on its innovation/export practices.

From a market-oriented perspective the business sector might also appear as a relevant differentiating factor for innovation and export capabilities, as business practices may vary from sector to sector (Lorenzo et al., 2018; Tidd and Thuriaux-Alemán, 2016). Regarding to the competitiveness of a specific business sector (Crowley and Jordan, 2017), its technological orientation (Thornhill, 2006) or its dynamic (Korab and Koudelkova, 2016), companies may implement innovation and export differently.

Then, we formulate our third hypothesis:

H3: The business sector of a company influences its behavior regarding innovation and export.

1.3. Structural contingency factors

Finally, some researchers identified that structural characteristics of a company can also be considered as contingency factors. For example, some studies (Belas et al., 2018; Forés and Camisón, 2016) indicate that the size of companies has an impact on a company's behavior in terms of innovation practices. It indeed potentially reflects a level of internal structuring that directly affects the way a company implements innovation practices on a daily basis. The size is also usually considered as a potential differentiating factor regarding export studies (Golovko and Valentini, 2014; Majocchi et al., 2005).

Then, we formulate our fourth hypothesis:

H4: Company's size has an impact on its innovation and export practices

1.4. Conceptual approach

Based on the several hypotheses provided by the academic literature, we proposed a conceptual framework including companies' innovation and export practices, innovation and export capabilities and finally contextual and structural elements considered as potential contingency factors.

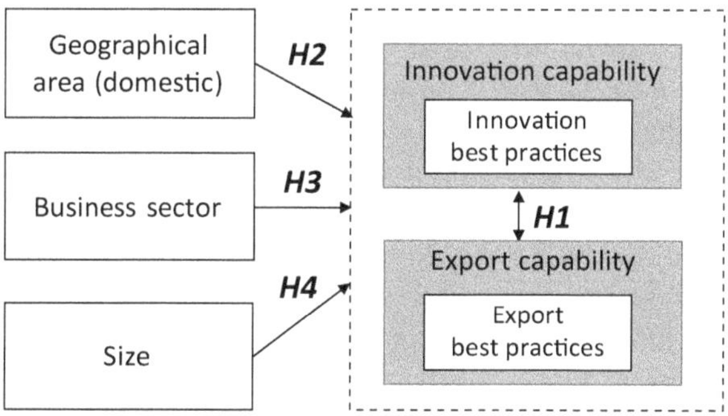

Fig. 1: Conceptual framework

2. Methodology

The ambition of this research work is to explore the hypothesis that specific behaviors of innovative and exporting companies exist and that they can be translated into typical profiles described via internal, structural and contextual factors, in the manner of a taxonomy. To achieve this objective, several steps were implemented (Fig. 2).

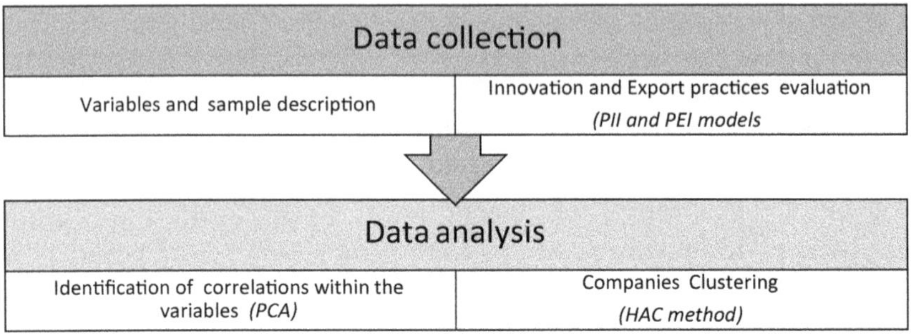

Fig. 2: Methodological steps

2.1. Data collection method: The PII and PEI models

The indicators for assessing innovation capability mark a trend towards considering internal practices and processes (ISO 56002 2019). Within these models there is consensus that the innovation capability of a company depends on several practices at the same time, so it is necessary to model it as a problem of multi-criteria analysis. Another consensus factor is that these internal practices must be measured according to the degree of maturity or performance, so one of the most used methods of evaluation of internal practices is the maturity grid (Maier et al., 2012). Therefore, we base the data collection stage of our approach on the Potential Innovation Index (PII) model. This diagnostic tool makes it possible to measure the maturity of a company concerning its innovation practices, mobilizing methodological tools such as multi-criteria analysis (in particular through AHP – Analytic Hierarchy Process (Saaty, 1980) and FlowSort (Nemery and Lamboray, 2007)) as well as maturity grids. It relies on a multi-level aggregative evaluation principle which makes it possible to construct the maturity profile of an innovative company from a reference framework of 6 innovation practices, divided into 20 activities representing the routine tasks carried out within the company. At the end of this evaluation, it is possible to classify the evaluated company in an innovation category corresponding to the maturity of its practices and reflecting its behavior in terms of innovation management: passive, reactive, preactive or proactive (Fig. 3).

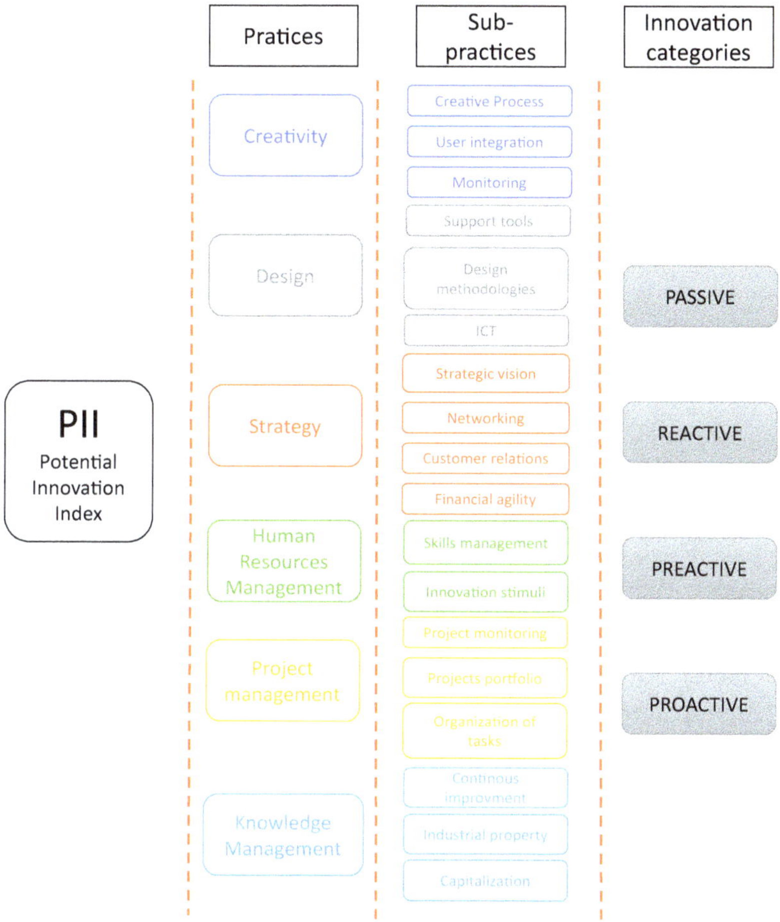

Fig. 3: Potential Innovation Index (PII) architecture

The Potential Innovation Index (PII), and its theoretically and empirically validated methodological principle (Boly et al., 2000, 2013) have also been used as the basis for the development of a tool for the assessment of export capability: the Potential Export Index (PEI). It works on the same principle. It assesses 22 export activities, aggregated into 6 best practices, and results in the identification of a category of exporting firm: homebody, traveler, explorer or adventurer (Fig. 4). The PEI will therefore constitute the model on which our evaluation of the export capability of the companies in the panel is based. Both models have been implemented in the form of a web application[1], allowing self-diagnosis. This application facilitates data collection and centralization through a single online access point.

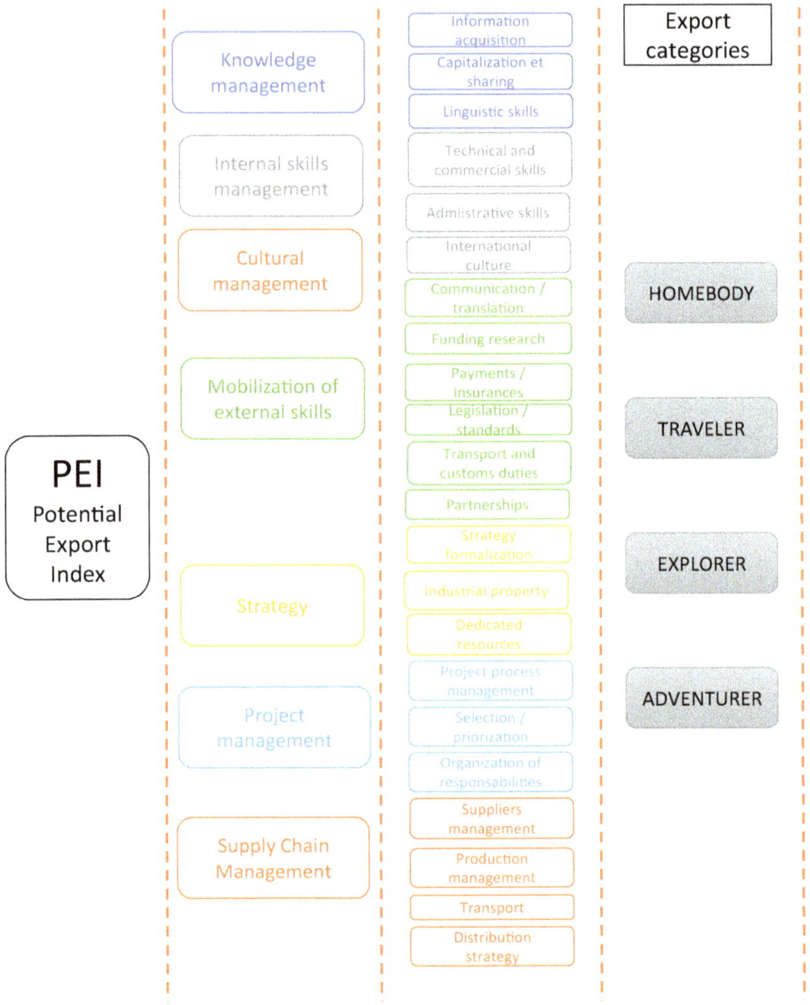

Fig. 4: Potential Export Index (PEI) architecture

1 https://diagnostic.innovation-way.com/

2.2. Data collection method: Sample and variables description

The second step of our methodology concerns the evaluation of the innovation and export capabilities of the companies included in our sample. The PII and PEI diagnoses have been realized into 25 innovative and exporting companies described in Tab. 1.

Tab. 1: Sample description

Company code	Geographical area	Nb of employees	Turnover	Business sector	Export Category	Innovation category
C1	EUROPE	3	3	Industry	HOMEBODY	REACTIVE
C2	EUROPE	10	7	Services	EXPLORER	PREACTIVE
C3	EUROPE	2	2	Services	HOMEBODY	PASSIVE
C4	EUROPE	8	7	Services	TRAVELER	REACTIVE
C5	EUROPE	3	3	Trade	TRAVELER	PREACTIVE
C6	EUROPE	6	6	Services	EXPLORER	REACTIVE
C7	EUROPE	5	6	Trade	EXPLORER	REACTIVE
C8	EUROPE	2	1	Industry	TRAVELER	REACTIVE
C9	SOUTH AMERICA	5	3	Industry	TRAVELER	REACTIVE
C10	SOUTH AMERICA	1	1	Industry	EXPLORER	REACTIVE
C11	SOUTH AMERICA	4	4	Industry	HOMEBODY	PASSIVE
C12	EUROPE	10	7	Industry	EXPLORER	PROACTIVE
C13	EUROPE	3	4	Services	HOMEBODY	REACTIVE
C14	SOUTH AMERICA	2	1	Industry	HOMEBODY	PASSIVE
C15	SOUTH AMERICA	4	1	Industry	TRAVELER	REACTIVE
C16	EUROPE	6	5	Trade	TRAVELER	REACTIVE
C17	SOUTH AMERICA	2	5	Industry	TRAVELER	PASSIVE
C18	EUROPE	8	7	Services	EXPLORER	PREACTIVE
C19	EUROPE	1	1	Trade	TRAVELER	REACTIVE
C20	EUROPE	3	4	Services	HOMEBODY	REACTIVE
C21	EUROPE	7	3	Industry	ADVENTURER	PROACTIVE
C22	EUROPE	4	4	Industry	TRAVELER	REACTIVE
C23	EUROPE	9	7	Services	EXPLORER	REACTIVE
C24	EUROPE	4	5	Services	ADVENTURER	PREACTIVE
C25	EUROPE	8	7	Services	TRAVELER	REACTIVE

These 25 companies are mainly European, but some of them are located in South America. The panel is rather balanced between companies from the industrial and services business sectors. To a lesser extent, some of them are focused on trade activities.

Regarding the size, the number of employees of the companies from our panel varies greatly, ranging from micro enterprises to large multinationals. This characteristic linked to the size of the company allows us to identify the companies that can be qualified as SMEs and those of larger size. However, the definition of an SME being very dependent on the geographical area concerned, we have chosen to rely on the definition proposed by the European Commission (2003) according to which a company is considered as an SME when its workforce does not exceed 250 employees, its annual turnover is less than EUR 50 million and, finally, its annual balance sheet does not exceed EUR 43 million. The turnover being a critical factor of this definition, it has been added as an additional variable to our sample to deepen the characterization of these companies. The variables structural variables of our panel were then defined as presented in Tab. 2.

Tab. 2: Structural variables definition

Structural variables			
Size (nb of employees)		**Turnover (€)**	
Scale	**Associated value**	**Scale**	**Associated value**
1	1–4	1	Less than 100k€
2	5–9	2	100–500k€
3	10–24	3	500k€–2m€
4	25–49	4	2–5 m€
5	50–149	5	5–25 m€
6	150–249	6	25–50 m€
7	250–499	7	More than 50 m€
8	500–999		
9	1,000–4,999		
10	More than 5,000		

Applying the PII and the PEI on the sample, the innovation and export categories of each company has been identified, as well as the maturity level of each innovation and export practices of the considered evaluation framework. For the purpose of readability, the maturity levels of each company have not been presented in Tab. 1. However, this table includes the innovation and export categories reached by each company according to the PII and PEI diagnoses. These categories (passive, reactive, preactive, proactive for innovation; home-based, traveler, explorer, adventurer for export) represents respectively the company's innovation and export capabilities and are expressed in the form of two 4-level variables that have been integrated into the analysis. They can be considered as performance variables (Tab. 3).

Tab. 3: Performance variables

Performance variables			
Innovation category		**Export category**	
Scale	**Associated value**	**Scale**	**Associated value**
1	Passive	1	Homebody
2	Reactive	2	Traveller
3	Preactive	3	Explorer
4	Proactive	4	Adventurer

2.3. Data analysis technic: A combined PCA and HAC approach

Finally, the last phase of our methodology consists in analyzing the data collected within the panel in order to propose a taxonomic characterization of these innovative and exporting companies. Through the use of a mixed multivariate data analysis method applied to our panel of 25 companies, we were able to draft 5 profiles with specific characteristics in terms of internal innovation and export practices.

First, we used the multivariate data analysis method PCA (Principal Components Analysis), with the objective of identifying the potential correlations between the variables of our conceptual framework. PCA delivers graphical representations of a sample according to two principal axes defined for the different variables (Syms, 2008). Each variable is represented by a vector brought back into a two-dimensional (2D) plane constructed by two main axes: the principal components. These two axes do not have a specific meaning in themselves but are considered as the most representative dimensions to exploit the data. If two variables are represented in the same direction, they are positively correlated. If they are represented in opposite directions, they are negatively correlated.

Finally, if the vectors of two variables are orthogonal, there is no correlation between them (Lever et al., 2017).

This first phase enabled us to question some of the hypotheses provided in the building of our conceptual framework, by analyzing the correlations between structural and contextual variables and the innovation and export capabilities of the companies within the sample.

Then, a clustering approach was carried on, through the use of a HAC (hierarchical ascending classification). This tool is based on the Ward criteria aggregation method (Ward, 1963). The principle is to create a partition obtained by aggregating 2–2 the closest individuals (or group of individuals) in an iterative manner. The functioning of this technique is based on regrouping companies by minimal distance on a plan considering as input variables the companies' maturity level according to the innovation and export practices of the PII and PEI framework. This HAC technique enables the identification of clusters grouping companies within similar behaviors in terms of innovation and export management. These profiles were then combined with contextual factors (geographical area and sector of activity) and structural factors (size and turnover) to propose an interpretation.

3. Results

Firstly, a Principal Component Analysis (PCA) was conducted within the panel of companies in order to identify potential correlations between the descriptive variables of the companies considered. Firstly, we explored the impact of structural data, such as size or turnover, on the innovation and export capabilities of companies. We therefore analyzed the correlations between these structural variables and the results of the IIP and IEP diagnoses carried out within the companies in the panel (Tab. 4).

Tab. 4: Variables integrated into the PCA analysis

Structural variables		Performance variables	
Size (n° of employees)	Turnover (k€)	Innovation category	Export category

The loading plot obtained (Fig. 5) illustrates 89 % of the data considered and the variables represented on the axes of this plot are close to the border of the circle. Thus, this loading plot can be interpreted with a certain degree of confidence. It highlights several observations. Firstly, the variables relating to the innovation and export categories are extremely close to each other. They are indeed highly correlated within our panel, which seems to support hypothesis H1 of this research work according to which companies having a good innovation capability also have a strong export capability and vice versa. Indeed, according to this plot, if a company achieves a high category in terms of innovation, it also achieves a high category in terms of exports.

On the other hand, the variables relating to company size and turnover are also relatively close, but to a lesser extent. We must therefore interpret this proximity with a little more caution.

Finally, it is interesting to note that two groups of variables are formed, the one related to performance and the other related to structural characteristics. Thus, by analyzing the position of these two groups of variables in relation to each other, it is possible to consider that these two groups of variables are rather independent. Indeed, the variables linked to turnover and size are almost orthogonal to the two performance variables (innovation and export categories). Thus, according to this PCA analysis, it would seem that the size of the firms and their turnover are not correlated with their innovation and export capabilities, questioning hypothesis H4 of our conceptual framework.

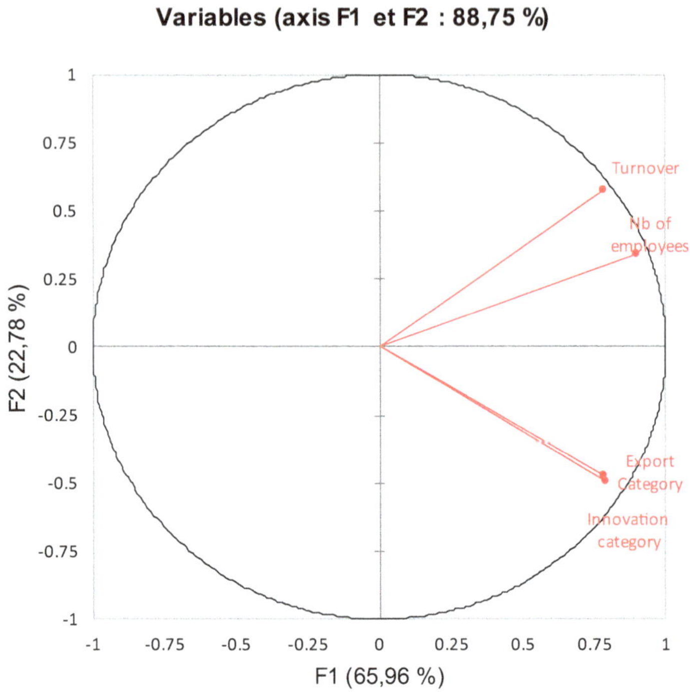

Fig. 5: Loading plot (PCA)

Finally, the biplot presented in Fig. 6 shows the distribution of the panel on the plane formed by the two main components selected. It can be seen that they are rather dispersed. Two of them stand out mainly in terms of performance: C24 and C21. It is also possible to identify the smallest companies in the panel, which are concentrated in the lower left-hand corner of the plot.

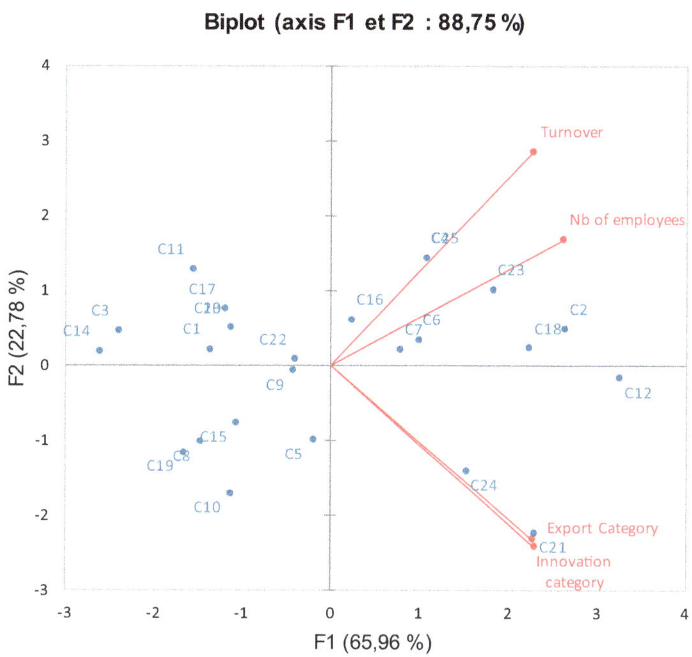

Fig. 6: Biplot (PCA)

The second step of this Principal Component Analysis consisted in integrating qualitative variables to the set of variables considered. Thus, variables related to the market characteristics of the companies were added: the business sector and the domestic geographical area (Tab. 5).

Tab. 5: Market-oriented qualitative variables

Geographical area	Business sector
EUROPE	TRADE
SOUTH AMERICA	SERVICE
	INDUSTRY

By calculating the coordinates of the barycenters representing each of these variables, it was possible to visualize their relationship with the quantitative variables previously analyzed according to their position in relation to them (Fig. 7). Concerning the geographical area, it can be seen that the two barycenters are positioned at the center of the biplot, and therefore close to the origin of the performance and structural variables. Thus, the domestic geographical area of the company does not seem to be a differentiating element within our panel, neither for the innovation and export capabilities, nor for the size and the turnover of the companies. It could be considered that South American companies are slightly smaller than European companies and that they potentially have a lower turnover, but these observations should be taken with caution, as our panel is not totally balanced in terms of geographical distribution. On the other hand, the turnover variable should also be qualified as it is also dependent on the standard of living and the monetary value of the currency used in the domestic country. These observations do not enable us to conclude about the veracity of hypothesis H2 of our conceptual framework, according to which the geographical area of the company has an impact on its innovation and export capability.

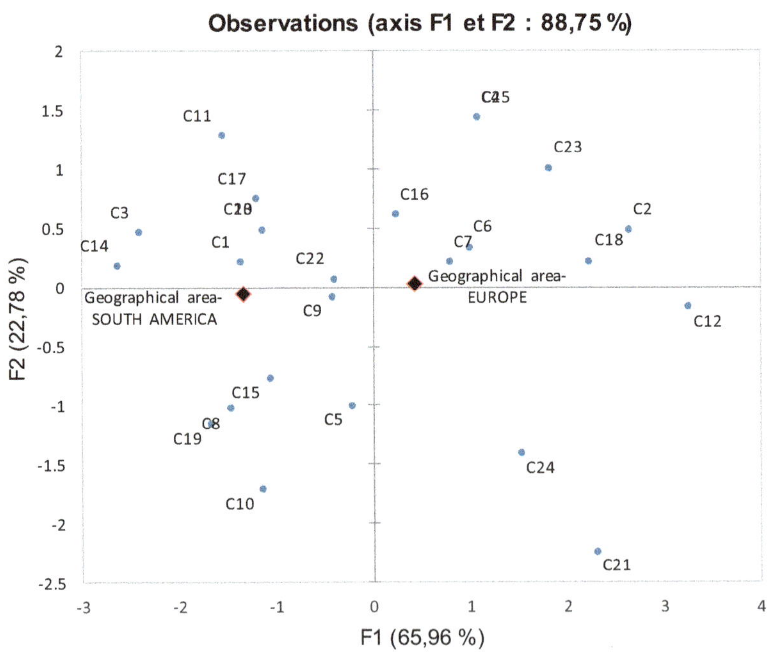

Fig. 7: Biplot – geographical area barycenters

On the other hand, according to Fig. 8, the business sector seems to be a little more differentiating, particularly in the case of service firms. While the barycenter of the industrial and trade firms are very close to each other and located in the center of the plot, the barycenter of the service firms seems to be oriented towards the upper right-hand quadrant, representative of larger firms with a higher turnover. We could then consider that hypothesis H3 may be relevant in the specific case of service companies, showing a stronger innovation and export capability.

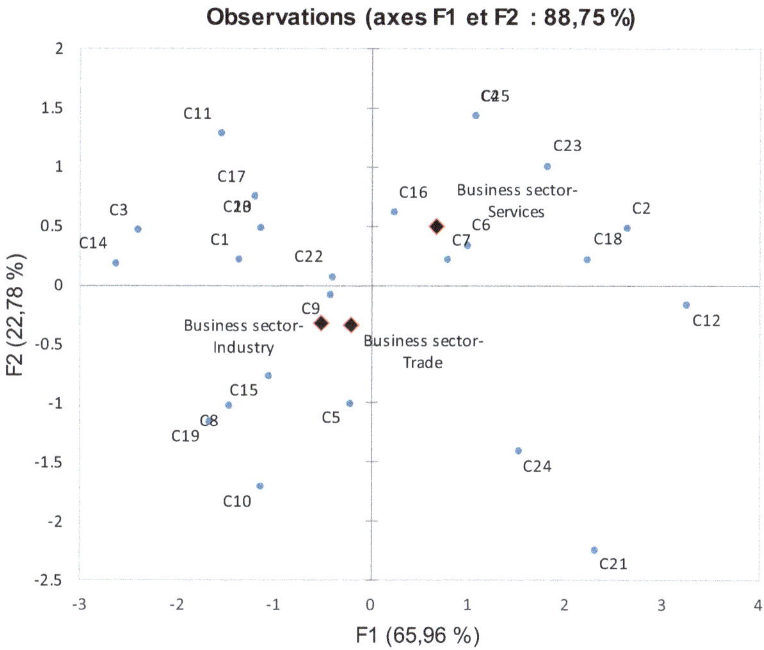

Fig. 8: Biplot – business sector barycenters

After looking at the potentially differentiating factors that can impact the innovation and export capabilities of the companies in the panel, we carried out an analysis of the practices implemented within the companies on a daily basis. From the evaluations obtained during the IIP and IEP diagnostics, we were able to collect the respective maturity levels of the companies for each of the innovation and export practices considered by these evaluation models. This maturity level is expressed through a maturity grid allowing to assign a value between 1 and 5 representing the level of mastery of the company for each practice of the PII and the PEI. Thus, each company was evaluated through 20 scores between 1 and 5 for its innovation practices and 22 scores between 1 and 5 for its export practices. From this database, a hierarchical ascending classification (HAC) was then carried out in order to identify clusters grouping together companies with similar maturity profiles in terms of both innovation and export. These clusters form 5 different classes (see Fig. 9a and 9b) reflecting the average level of maturity of the companies making up the class with regard to the 22 export practices of the IEP, and the 20 innovation practices of the IIP. In addition, these classes were analyzed according to the structural (size, turnover) and market (business sector and geographical area) characteristics of the companies that make them up, in order to compare the results of the PCA analysis carried out previously. Thus, each of these classes could be studied and described according to its average practices profile and intrinsic characteristics.

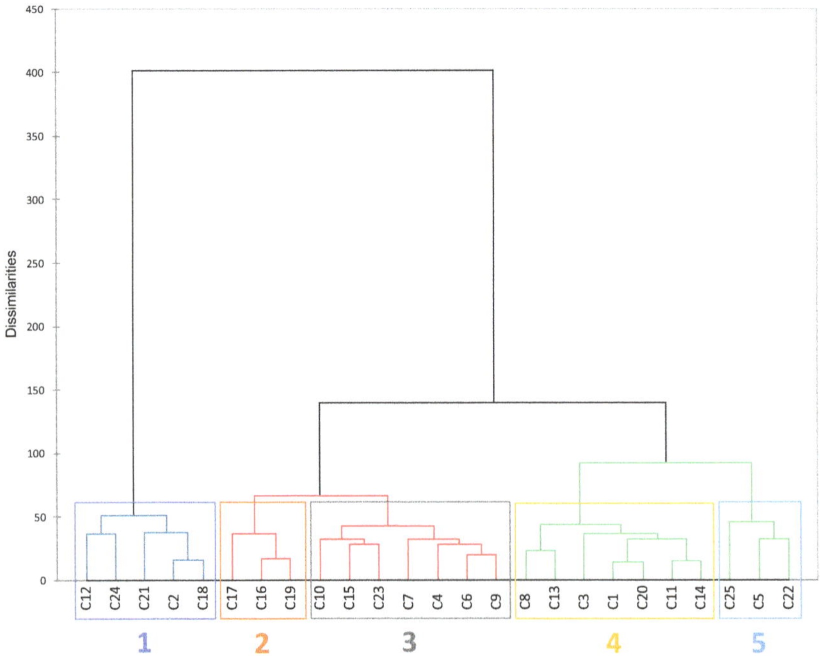

Fig. 9a: HAC dendogram

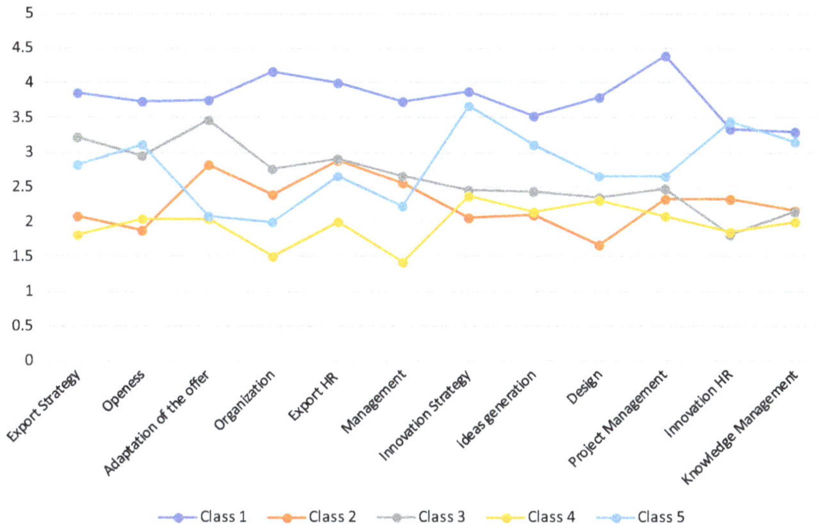

Fig. 9b: Average maturity profiles

3.1. Class 1: Structured companies

It includes five companies from the panel. These are the "best in class", as their profile is the most mature. None of their practices was evaluated below three. They are particularly distinguished by their strength in terms of organization and project management, both for innovation and for export. These practices are indeed much better mastered than in the other classes. In terms of structural characteristics, the majority of companies in this class are the largest in the panel. Only one company in this class has fewer than 250 employees. This large size, although not considered a differentiating factor in the PCA analysis, certainly has an impact on the profile of these companies, which are more structured. This explains the existence of more formalized organizational processes, both for international activities and for innovation. In terms of the market, these companies come from the industrial and service sectors in equal measure. However, they are all European.

3.2. Class 2: Adaptation as the watchword

This class includes companies with an average profile in terms of maturity. Their strengths lie in their adaptation capacity and in their human resources, both in relation to innovation and export activities. These are fundamental pillars for them. This class of companies is therefore reactive, adapting to the disruptions in their environment by relying on the skills of their workforce. On the other hand, they seem to lack a long-term vision and strategy and their capacity for design/experimentation seems limited. This last observation can be explained by the fact that two out of three companies in this class are from the trade sector. Thus, product/service design is not part of their daily activities, as it might be for industrial or service companies. In terms of size and turnover, these factors vary within this class, although the largest number of employees recorded does not exceed 250. These are both European and South American SMEs.

3.3. Class 3: International-oriented companies

This class includes seven enterprises with different structural and market characteristics. It includes both micro-enterprises and companies with more than 1,000 employees. They are equally distributed between Europe and South America. Their turnover, on the other hand, does not exceed €5m and they are exclusively from the industrial and service sectors. Their profile is characterized by a high level of maturity in export-related practices, particularly with regard to international strategy and the adaptation of their offer. Their maturity concerning innovation practices is significantly weaker, with an important point of vigilance on the management of human resources assigned to innovation projects. These companies are therefore internationally-oriented, they are able to adapt their existing offer to foreign markets but have difficulties in building a structured innovation process on a daily basis. They are in a logic of optimization.

3.4. Class 4: Small innovative companies

This class includes the smallest companies in the panel. They all have the fewer than 50 employees and a turnover of less than €5m. In terms of the business sector, they are equally divided between industry and services and are mostly European. In contrast to class 3, these companies have an innovation-oriented profile, although it is relatively low in terms of maturity (average ratings below 2.5). These companies have limited resources due to their small size, but show a rather good strategic vision with regard to innovation, as well as a high capacity for experimentation and design. Their lack of internal resources indeed seems to be compensated by a propensity for openness and partnerships, and they also seem to have a strong adaptation capacity. This last characteristic is certainly reinforced by the fact that their small size and their innovation dynamics give them certain flexibility. On the other hand, their weak points are linked to the organization and management of the administrative aspects of exporting, and to their international strategy, which seems to be little formalized. These companies show a profile of primary exporting SMEs.

3.5. Class 5: Open companies

This last class includes three European companies of various sizes (from 10 to 1,000 employees) and from a wide range of sectors (industrial, service and trade). Their maturity profile is very heterogeneous. However, their main driver is clear: these companies have a strong openness. They are able to work in partnerships, both for their export and innovation activities, and they also rely heavily on the skills of their human resources. They are also very creative and have a long-term strategic vision. On the other hand, they are poorly structured in terms of organization and the formalization of their administrative and project management processes clearly appears to be an obstacle. These companies therefore rely on their network and the skills of their human resources to overcome these difficulties.

Discussions et conclusions

The objective of this research work was to explore the possibility of identifying different profiles regarding the innovation and export practices management of companies.

Relying on an evaluation of 25 companies' maturity regarding 6 innovation practices and 6 export practices, and putting them in relation to structural (size and turnover) and market-oriented (geographical area and business sector) characteristics, 5 profiles have been identified. These five profiles reflect different behaviors in terms of innovation and export practices and specific orientation in the way companies manage their internal processes.

Although this research work is primarily exploratory and not statistically representative, it may pave the way for different implications concerning both scientific research and practitioners. Combining a Principal Component Analysis (PCA) with a clustering approach (HAC), the results highlight that the structural factors of the companies (size and turnover) do not seem to be correlated to their innovation and export capability. While the bigger companies seem to adopt more structured and formalized practices in terms of organization, smaller companies may nevertheless achieve strong levels of maturity on internal practices more adapted to their agile and flexible functioning (for example, adaptation of the offer, human resources management, design and openness). So, the structural factors seem to impact the way companies manage their internal practices (their behaviors) both in terms of export and innovation, but they are not associated with a specific level of innovation or export capability.

Regarding the market-oriented characteristics, the results of the analysis have to be considered in a more careful way. Our panel is indeed not well balanced in terms of business sector and geographical area. Most of the companies are Europeans and they also are generally the biggest ones. It also seems that the service companies in the panel show a higher size than the companies from the industrial and trade sector. So, taking these limitations into account, it seems that the business sector and the domestic market of the companies do not seem to be correlated with their innovation and export capability either. However, a deeper analysis has to be taken into consideration, within a larger and more balanced sample in order to be able to propose robust conclusions. This raises interesting research perspectives, which are oriented towards a finer decomposition of structural and market-oriented variables, as well as the integration of additional factors such as the companies' level of technological intensity or their targeted foreign markets.

So, further analysis and the proposal of a more refined and extended taxonomy could then make a strong contribution to the innovation and export support for companies. It is a way to promote the interest of considering innovation and export activities as a joint challenge that requires specific profiles in terms of internal processes management. Moreover, this taxonomy could be a way to highlight the benefit of providing a contextualized support according to criteria that are both market- and structure-oriented, and adapted to the companies' behavior regarding simultaneously innovation and export.

References

Belas, J., Ivanova, E., Rozsa, Z., Schonfeld, J. 2018. "Innovations in sme segment: Important factors and differences in the approach by size and age of the company." Transformations in Business & Economics 17 (3): 55–71.

Boly, V., Morel, L., Assielou G., and Camargo M. 2013. "Evaluating Innovative Processes in French Firms: Methodological Proposition for Firm Innovation Capacity Evaluation." Research Policy 43(3): 608–622. https://doi.org/10.1016/j.respol.2013.09.005

Boly, V., Morel, L., Renaud, J., and Guidat, C. 2000. "Innovation in Low Tech SMBs: Evidence of a Necessary Constructivist Approach." Technovation 20 (3): 161–68. https://doi.org/10.1016/S0166-4972(99)00099-1

Choi, Y. S., and Lim, U. 2017. "Contextual Factors Affecting the Innovation Performance of Manufacturing SMEs in Korea: A Structural Equation Modeling Approach." Sustainability (Switzerland) 9 (7): 1193. https://doi.org/10.3390/su9071193

European Commission. 2003. "Les PME En Europe." European Network for SME Research (ENSR), report n°7.

European Commission. 2007. "Supporting the Internationalisation of SMEs." Final Report of the Expert Group. Entrepreneurship Unit, Directorate-General for Enterprise and Industry.

Crowley, F., and Jordan, D. 2017. "Does More Competition Increase Business-Level Innovation? Evidence from Domestically Focused Firms in Emerging Economies." Economics of Innovation and New Technology 26 (5): 477–88. https://doi.org/10.1080/10438599.2016.1233627.

Dai, M., Liu, H., and Lin, L. 2019. "How Innovation Impacts Firms' Export Survival: Does Export Mode Matter?" World Economy. https://doi.org/10.1111/twec.12847.

Di Cintio, M., Ghosh, S., and Grassi, E. 2019. "Direct or Indirect Exports: What Matters for Firms' Innovation Activities?" Applied Economics Letters 27 (2): 93–103. https://doi.org/10.1080/13504851.2019.1610693.

Fassio, C. 2018. "Export-Led Innovation: The Role of Export Destinations." Industrial and Corporate Change 27 (1): 149–71. https://doi.org/10.1093/icc/dtx028

Forés, B., and Camisón, C. 2016. "Does Incremental and Radical Innovation Performance Depend on Different Types of Knowledge Accumulation

Capabilities and Organizational Size?" Journal of Business Research 69 (2): 831–48. https://doi.org/10.1016/j.jbusres.2015.07.006

Golovko, E., and Valentini, G. 2011. "Exploring the Complementarity between Innovation and Export for SMEs Growth." Journal of International Business Studies 42 (3): 362–80.

Golovko, E., and Valentini, G. 2014. "Selective Learning-by-Exporting: Firm Size and Product Versus Process Innovation." Global Strategy Journal 4 (3): 161–80. https://doi.org/10.1002/gsj.1080

Halilem, N., Amara, N., and Landry, R. 2014. "Exploring the Relationships between Innovation and Internationalization of Small and Medium-Sized Enterprises: A Nonrecursive Structural Equation Model." Canadian Journal of Administrative Sciences / Revue Canadienne Des Sciences de l'Administration 31 (1): 18–34. https://doi.org/10.1002/cjas.1272

Heiligenberg, H. A. R. M. van den, Heimeriks, G. J., Hekkert, M. P., and Van Oort, F. G. 2017. "A Habitat for Sustainability Experiments: Success Factors for Innovations in Their Local and Regional Contexts." Journal of Cleaner Production 169: 204–15. https://doi.org/10.1016/j.jclepro.2017.06.177

ISO 56002. 2019. "ISO 56002:2019 – Innovation Management System."

Jong, J. P. J. de, and Marsili, M. 2006. "The Fruit Flies of Innovations: A Taxonomy of Innovative Small Firms." Research Policy 35 (2): 213–29. https://doi.org/10.1016/j.respol.2005.09.007

Korab, V., and Koudelkova, P. 2016. "What Determines Innovation in Small and Medium Enteprises? A Case Study from the Czech Republic." Transformations in Business & Economics 15 (2): 78–88.

Lever, J., Krzywinski, M., and Altman, N. 2017. "Principal Component Analysis." News. Nature Methods 14 (7): 641–42. https://doi.org/10.1038/nmeth.4346

Lorenzo, J. R. F, Maza Rubio, M. T., and Garcés, S. A. 2018. "The Competitive Advantage in Business, Capabilities and Strategy. {What} General Performance Factors are Found in the Spanish Wine Industry?" Wine Economics and Policy 7 (2): 94–108. https://doi.org/10.1016/j.wep.2018.04.001

Love, J. H., and Roper, S. 2015. "SME Innovation, Exporting and Growth: A Review of Existing Evidence." International Small Business Journal 33 (1): 28–48. https://doi.org/10.1177/0266242614550190

Maier, A. M., Moultrie, J., and Clarkson, P. J. 2012. "Assessing Organizational Capabilities: Reviewing and Guiding the Development of Maturity Grids."

IEEE Transactions on Engineering Management 59 (1): 138–59. https://doi.org/10.1109/TEM.2010.2077289

Majocchi, A., Bacchiocchi, E., and Mayrhofer, U. 2005. "Firm Size, Business Experience and Export Intensity in SMEs: A Longitudinal Approach to Complex Relationships." *International Business Review* 14 (6): 719–38. https://doi.org/10.1016/j.ibusrev.2005.07.004

Mintzberg, H. 1979. *The Structuring of Organizations*. Englewood Cliffs, N.J: Pearson.

Nemery, P., and Lamboray, C. 2007. "FlowSort: A Flow-Based Sorting Method with Limiting or Central Profiles." *TOP* 16 (1): 90–113. https://doi.org/10.1007/s11750-007-0036-x

Ribau, C. P., Moreira, A. C., and Raposo, M. 2019. "The Role of Exploitative and Exploratory Innovation in Export Performance: An Analysis of Plastics Industry SMEs." *European Journal of International Management* 13 (2): 224–46. https://doi.org/10.1504/EJIM.2019.098149

Saaty, T. L. 1980. *The Analytic Hierarchy Process: Planning, Priority Setting, Resource Allocation*. McGraw-Hill, New York, USA.

Schumpeter, J., and Backhaus, U. 2003. "The Theory of Economic Development." In *Joseph Alois Schumpeter: Entrepreneurship, Style and Vision*, edited by Jürgen Backhaus, 61–116. The European Heritage in Economics and the Social Sciences. Boston, MA: Springer US. https://doi.org/10.1007/0-306-48082-4_3

Syms, C. 2008. "Principal Components Analysis." In *Encyclopedia of Ecology*, edited by Sven Erik Jørgensen and Brian D. Fath, 2940–49. Oxford: Academic Press. https://doi.org/10.1016/B978-008045405-4.00538-3

Thornhill, S. 2006. "Knowledge, Innovation and Firm Performance in High- and Low-Technology Regimes." *Journal of Business Venturing* 21 (5): 687–703.

Tidd, J., and Thuriaux-Alemán, B. 2016. "Innovation Management Practices: Cross-Sectorial Adoption, Variation, and Effectiveness." *R&D Management* 46 (S3): 1024–43. https://doi.org/10.1111/radm.12199

Torrès, O., and Julien, P. A. 2005. "Specificity and Denaturing of Small Business." *International Small Business Journal* 23 (4): 355–77. https://doi.org/10.1177/0266242605054049

Urbinati, A., Chiaroni, D., Chiesa, V., Franzò, S., and Frattini, F. 2018. "An Exploratory Analysis on the Contextual Factors That Influence Disruptive Innovation: The Case of Uber." *International Journal of*

Innovation and Technology Management 15 (3). https://doi.org/10.1142/S0219877018500244

Ward, J. H. 1963. "Hierarchical Grouping to Optimize an Objective Function." *Journal of the American Statistical Association* 58 (301): 236–44. https://doi.org/10.1080/01621459.1963.10500845

Zawislak, P. A., Gamarra, J. T., Alves A. C., Barbieux D., and Reichert F. M. 2014. "The Different Innovation Capabilities of the Firm: Further Remarks upon the Brazilian Experience." *Journal of Innovation Economics Management* 13 (1): 129–50.

Zehir, C., Köle M., and Yıldız H. 2015. "The Mediating Role of Innovation Capability on Market Orientation and Export Performance: An Implementation on SMEs in Turkey." *Procedia – Social and Behavioral Sciences*, 11th International Strategic Management Conference, 207 (October): 700–708. https://doi.org/10.1016/j.sbspro.2015.10.141

Chapter 7

Collaboration between SMEs: A lever to innovate and expand internationally

Jean-Christophe Gessler

Introduction

A major challenge for firms expanding internationally is being able to offer goods and services that meet the expectations of the international target markets: They may lack the products demanded by external markets (Haase and Franco, 2015; Paul et al., 2017). For SMEs, designing new products that meet the specific needs of their target markets is a more difficult goal than it is for major corporations (Leonidou, 2004). Calantone et al., (2006; p. 178) define product adaptation strategy as "a firm's consistent and planned activities to meet local consumers' preferences and values (Cavusgil and Zou, 1994)". Given the high market openness of the last several decades, most markets already have products that meet the various needs consumers have expressed. This observation is even more valid in a context of heightened competition, with companies from emerging economies joining the list of competitors. Consumers who wish to acquire a capital good such as a refrigerator, smartphone, or car have a much wider selection than they did at the beginning of the 2000s, now that there are attractive products from Turkey, China, and other emerging economies.

Therefore, to create value, companies need to differentiate their products; if production is located in countries with high labour costs like France, differentiation happens through innovation. In the literature, there is no universal definition of innovation. The approach proposed by the OECD in the Oslo Manual (2005) distinguishes between four types of innovation (product, process, marketing, and organizational); in this chapter we focus on product innovation, defined as the introduction of a new product or service on the market. From our perspective, this innovation is driven by the demand identified in international markets.

SMEs, unlike large corporations, experience a double bind in terms of innovation. On the one hand, they have access to fewer resources than do large corporations for innovation (budgets, technical means, employees) and are constrained to implement less structured innovation processes (Lichtenthaler, 2008). They have lower budgets available as well as less ability to recruit experts; in addition, their innovation portfolio is thinner, which hinders SMEs from spreading the risk of failure (Van de Vrande et al., 2009). On the other hand, SMEs have fewer skills and knowledge available to implement collaborative innovation than do large corporations (Jeon and Degravel, 2019).

A collaborative innovation approach makes it possible for SMEs to pool resources in order to adopt shared forms of innovation. Entrepreneurs can build an "innovation ecosystem" (Grandstrand and Holgersson, 2020) involving collaborative relationships with their peers and even with their competitors. Deltour, Le Gall and Lethiais (2017) find, for example, that among 117 Breton SMEs that have innovated with new products and/or processes, 37.8 % did so in collaboration with external actors (companies, research centres, consultants) rather than internally. These partnerships, which especially aim to access knowledge as well as material and technical resources, involve domestic actors over 75 % of the time. However, research shows that SMEs are reluctant to collaborate with other companies, especially when they are not clients or suppliers. Relationships with research centres, government agencies, or universities seem less risky to them (D'Angelo and Baroncelli, 2020); Santoro et al. (2016), thus find that among a sample of SMEs, only 31 % of partnerships are built with other companies.

In our approach, collaboration can be formal or informal; it does not necessarily reach the level of formality commonly connoted in the term alliance. SME executives often display a "fortress mentality" (Huggins, 2010) that prioritizes independence, informal agreements, and flexible governance arrangements. We take a very flexible approach to how SMEs may collaborate with each other. Shared innovation can in fact vary widely in its duration, focus, and the formality of agreements. In this paper, we look at forms of inter-firm collaboration through which SMEs seek to innovate for the purpose of international expansion.

We are, however, more restrictive in the scope of collaboration. We will focus only on collaborative relationships between SMEs and not on major corporations or other actors such as government organizations or research centres, for example. There are several reasons for this. First, collaborations between SMEs and large corporations generally involve asymmetric power relationships. However, we believe that SMEs should be encouraged to deliberately work together as equals. Since they have assets like agility, flexibility, and responsiveness, they can quickly integrate external innovation and benefit from it more than can large corporations (Torchia and Calabro, 2019). The challenge is enabling SMEs to find the levers to innovate and export more by drawing upon their available resources. Finally, relationships with other types of partners (research centers, universities, etc.) raise other issues and will thus not be discussed here.

Different types of SMEs can innovate together (Jeon and Degravel, 2019): clients, suppliers, competitors, complementary companies not in direct competition, etc. Above all, it is important to understand the market and decide to co-create a response to its needs. We thus distinguish between business-to-business relationships like purchasing a service or consulting from another firm. In our study, SMEs themselves serve as the crucible of innovation through a joint, non-market approach.

Based on the resource approach, network theory, and the literature on open innovation, we show how SMEs can benefit from shared innovation in order to expand internationally. We use research elements from the academic literature along with our own study of a sample of French SMEs. This chapter is divided into four parts: (1) collaborating to innovate, (2) collaborating to innovate and expand internationally, (3) success factors, and (4) future perspectives and avenues of research.

1. Collaborating to innovate

The key question of innovation has been examined in the literature from many angles. It is regularly put forward as a pillar of a company's competitive advantage, development, and survival. When it is implemented, the same questions arise as with any business activity: whether to do it oneself, have it done, or join forces with others – the "make, buy, or ally" decision. The heterogeneity of resources available to different firms (Lockett, Thompson and Morgenstern, 2009) is more difficult to overcome because resources are assets that cannot be easily acquired on the market (Teece, 2007). SMEs often do not have the human, technical, or financial resources to innovate enough (Huggins and Thompson, 2015), so collaborating with other SMEs becomes an option (Blomqvist and Levy, 2006). Similarly, for Rinjsoever et al. (2017), the choice to join forces involves developing shared knowledge with one or more partners rather than acquiring it on the market. Ahuja (2000) finds that collaboration on innovation enables the sharing of knowledge and complementary skills and the attainment of economies of scale.

Generally speaking, the collaborative approach has grown considerably since the pioneering work of Granovetter in the 1970s (1973, 1985). Originating in sociology, this research sets individuals within a network of interconnected actors. This approach then spread to the management and business literature. Entrepreneurs are thus embedded in a web of relationships, and networks are seen as an asset, or social capital. Business networks, which have gradually become independent from personal networks, are seen as all the entities a firm has relationships with. Beyond a simple static or passive approach, these networks can be extended and guided strategically in order to attain specific economic objectives. The nature and number of partners thus become key issues. These partners may be proactively approached by SME leaders (Sullivan et al., 2006; Lockett et al., 2009; Tang, 2011) to establish collaborations. In this case, these are not relationships based on purely business transactions between the parties but more a "calculative commitment" (Blomqvist and Levy, 2006; p. 40) that is also rational, driven by the hope of economic benefits, particularly through knowledge transfer (Huggins, 2010).

Beyond the network theory approach, inter-firm collaboration can also be seen in the resource approach (Wernerfelt, 1984; Barney, 1991). Resources, which are assets available to firms that allow them to build competitive advantage, can be material or immaterial. This approach is rather smoothly linked to the network theory: resources are assets that can circulate throughout networks. For a company, the important thing is not to own resources but to have access to and be able to use them. Networks thus become assets and resources in themselves; they enable the exchange of resources. This perspective leads Popli et al. (2017) to evoke an "extended relational-based view" assuming that access to "resources, assets and skills" (p. 22) takes precedence over their ownership and gives relationships with other companies a central role (Arya and Lin, 2007; Dyer and Singh, 1998).

The open innovation literature (Chesbrough, 2003) has gradually embedded innovation within networks and business environments. Chesbrough (2003) defines open innovation as "a paradigm that assumes that companies can and should use external ideas as well as internal ideas." It is "a multi-actor exchange process in which various actors exchange resources (e.g. ideas, knowledge, materials) that have potential value-in-use for other actors" (Chesbrough et al., 2018; p. 932).

This approach suggests that companies have an interest in innovating with external actors rather than exclusively internally: new knowledge should not be created only by internal R&D. Large companies use these practices commonly, especially in the industrial and automotive sectors. Competing automobile companies can thus develop a shared platform that can be used for light or electric vehicles (Ford and Volkswagen)[1] or commercial vehicles (Renault and Daimler)[2] of both partner brands. Open innovation research has focused on major corporations (Gassman and Enkel, 2010; Hinteregger et al., 2018). However, this seems counter-intuitive because the network approach has broadly included SMEs over the last several decades, which seems logical since SMEs make up over 95 % of companies in developed economies.

The open innovation literature thus considers that companies should draw inspiration from their environments in order to obtain various resources, especially knowledge and new ideas, to innovate. This is the inbound open innovation view. Gradually, the barrier between internal and external should be lowered for the resources available to SMEs that other companies might value. Researchers in the open innovation literature thus encourage entrepreneurs to release these resources so other companies can use them to create value, also known as outbound open innovation. This occurs, for example, when a company has developed a technology or skill but does not want to market it on a large scale. Open innovation researchers encourage this kind of company to make its resources available to external actors in the form of out-licensing, for example. Its partners could create value on a large scale by developing a range of products and services, especially for international markets. In this case, innovation is not necessarily co-developed from the project onset: the inventor passes the baton to the developer, who will market the product. This is obviously collaborative innovation since the progress of

---

1 https://www.usinenouvelle.com/article/ford-et-volkswagen-scellent-une-alliance-strategique-mais-gardent-leur-independance.N793194

2 https://www.latribune.fr/depeches/reuters/KBN2A21SK/renault-et-daimler-pourraient-collaborer-dans-les-grands-fourgons-selon-des-sources.html

some also benefits others. For example, the Metalskin[3] company, which invented a solution for disinfecting contact surfaces in public places based on a patented copper-based coating, made its invention available to partners who then adapted it into solutions for various markets: hospitals, local governments, retail outlets, and public transportation. This approach considerably reduced the time to market of these products and sped up the inventor's return on investment through royalties.

To describe open innovation, Chesbrough (2006; p. 20) offers an enriched and expanded definition: "the use of purposive inflows and outflows of knowledge to accelerate internal innovation and expand the markets for external use of innovation" To clarify our use of this definition in our work, several comments are in order. First, these flows are deliberate and part of a voluntary and guided process. For the inbound aspect, the company will identify the resources in its environment and integrate that knowledge so that it can innovate more quickly. For outbound innovation, knowledge transfer is voluntary, not a leak or an externality. A given company will grant external actors access to elements it has developed so that they can innovate more quickly. This concept has been built on through other definitions like that of Chesbrough and Bogers (2014): "a distributed innovation process, based on purposively managed knowledge flows across organizational boundaries, using pecuniary and non-pecuniary mechanisms, in line with the organization's business model." In their review of the literature, Torchia and Calabro (2019) show that the open innovation approach is now organized into three components: inbound innovation, in which companies internally transfer knowledge available from their partners; outbound innovation, in which companies transfer their own ideas, concepts, or technologies to others to leverage their skills; and coupled open innovation, which combines internal use of external resources and the external enhancement of internal resources.

There are many benefits to joint innovation. It makes it possible to pool financial and material resources as well as intellectual resources in the ideas, creativity, analytical skills, and discernment of the partners. Collaboration makes it possible to build on external expertise. On the other hand, the pooling of resources makes it possible to reach thresholds

---

3 https://www.lesechos.fr/industrie-services/industrie-lourde/stephane-penari-fait-surface-contre-le-coronavirus-1294511

that would be too high for individual actors. Innovation requires significant budgets to finance design expenses and prototypes, establish copyright protection, etc. These expenses can be spread among several partners. Moreover, the risk of failure is also borne by several actors rather than making one company shoulder the cash flow and balance sheet costs (Torchia and Calabro, 2019). Finally, joint innovation can help disseminate a stronger innovation culture among all the partners with not only a ripple effect but also the ability to set goals, meet deadlines, and reduce time to market for new products. The routines established with the partners break up the inertia that can hinder attempts to innovate alone, especially when the teams are shared across several projects. Douglas et al. (2018) use a sample of European SMEs to show that collaborating for innovation increases companies' level of innovation and their business outcomes. The authors observe this effect for two dimensions of innovation: technological (product and process) and non-technological (organizational and marketing). They show that the companies bring together complementary resources and that it is thus possible to speak of "symbiotic collaborations" in the case of vertical relationships with suppliers and clients. Furthermore, D'Angelo and Baroncelli (2020) show that open innovation in SMEs in the form of inter-firm innovation has an effect not only on the level of innovation but also on economic spillovers, unlike collaborations with universities, which only affect innovation level.

Now that we have presented the theoretical framework of joint innovation, we will look at the specific challenges of innovation for international expansion.

2. Collaborating to innovate and expand internationally

Through a joint innovation process, SMEs can aim to develop specifically for international markets. If the target market is a mature economy, the technological and innovative nature of their product is essential. If it is an emerging or developing economy, the approach might take the form of a "bottom of the pyramid" strategy (Prahalad, 2004) to serve a large number of customers with very small discretionary incomes.

The link between innovation and international expansion in firms has been confirmed in the literature (Paul et al., 2017; De Massis et al.,

2018). On the other hand, the study of SME international expansion through a collective rather than individual approach is an area that has received a great deal of attention over the last two decades (Hoang and Antoncic, 2003; Kazlauskaite et al., 2015; Agostini and Nosella, 2018).

In this article, we are taking a very broad approach to innovation, which may begin very early in the product design process (Jeon and Degravel, 2019). For example, the French companies Sleever and Tecma Aries jointly designed and developed a packaging system called Dreamoncup[4]. This concept, which won the Packaging Award in 2017, is considered a disruptive innovation that was destined for the global market from the outset[5].

3. What are the results?

Having presented our approach, we will now highlight the main results related to collaborations between SMEs for the purpose of innovating for international expansion. Mesquita and Lazzarini (2008) find that horizontal collaborations between SMEs (companies in the same business sector or offering complementary products) have a positive effect on their level of product innovation, which favorably influences the access to international markets in the companies studied. This effect has been found in American, South Korean, and Japanese companies (Calantone et al., 2006). The partners can share the costs and risks inherent in the product development process (Rinjsoever et al., 2017), reduce the time to market for their new products (Enkel et al., 2009), and increase their market power (Torchia and Calabro, 2019). The ability to offer new products makes it possible to enter a larger number of markets more quickly than if the innovative process were not collaborative. Thus, Paul et al. (2017) emphasize the link between innovation and international success, especially for born-global companies (Cavusgil and Knight, 2015). They state, building on Golovko and Valentini (2011), that innovation and international expansion support each other. They find that some SMEs have a higher share of revenue from international

4 www.dreamoncup.com

5 https://www.emballagesmagazine.com/tous-secteurs/dreamoncup-demarre-plein-pot.44587

markets because they innovate more, including collaboratively. More generally, innovative products have a greater differentiation potential that makes them more competitive and increases their international sales (Nunes et al., 2017).

In a doctoral dissertation (Gessler, 2019), we studied the effects of several types of collaborative practices (innovation, prospecting, distribution, logistics, and related services carried out jointly) on the amount of international expansion in a sample of 181 French exporting SMEs. Using a 7-point Likert scale, we asked respondents if they had used each of the four practices over the previous three years. In terms of innovation, this occurred in collaborations with other SMEs to develop new products for international markets. We looked at the effect on three components of the level of international expansion: the share of revenue from international markets (export intensity), the number of markets served (countries and regions), and the speed of international expansion. The latter can be seen as the time elapsed between two successive entries on different new markets. We used six control variables: firm age, firm size, whether the firm was a family firm, the earliness of internationalization, the business sector, and the manager's education level.

The survey was carried out in 2018 in the form of an online questionnaire. The sample was made up of SMEs in the capital goods (40.9 %), consumer goods (40.9 %), new technologies (7.2 %), services, and trade sectors (11 %).

With an average staff of 53.61 (mean of 27) and an average revenue of 11,877,216 euros (mean of 4 million euros), the respondents clearly belong in the category of small and medium-sized enterprises. Moreover, more than half of the companies has existed for about three decades (mean of 37.82 years). Two-thirds of the companies (67.4 %) are family-owned (dual ownership and management), which would seem to represent the fabric of the French economy. A considerable proportion of the companies entered international markets as soon as they were created (24.3 %) or in the three succeeding years (16 %). In contrast, many of them did not make this move until they were 3–6 years old (17.1 %), and this was most common after the age of 6 (42.5 %). The range of the results on the percentage of revenue from international markets is very broad (between 1 and 100 % of revenue from international markets); the mean is at 31.9 % and the median is 24 %, which reflects a share that is considerably higher than the mean of French goods exporters, estimated to be 19 % (excluding micro-enterprises)[6]. It is, however, a similar order of magnitude to other studies on French and European SMEs (D'Angelo and Buck, 2019). In terms of the number of markets served, the most frequently reported results are one to five countries and two world regions.

Below is our research model illustrating open innovation and our three hypotheses (Fig. 1); they posit a positive effect of collaborative innovation on the share of revenue from international markets, the number of markets served, and the speed of international expansion.

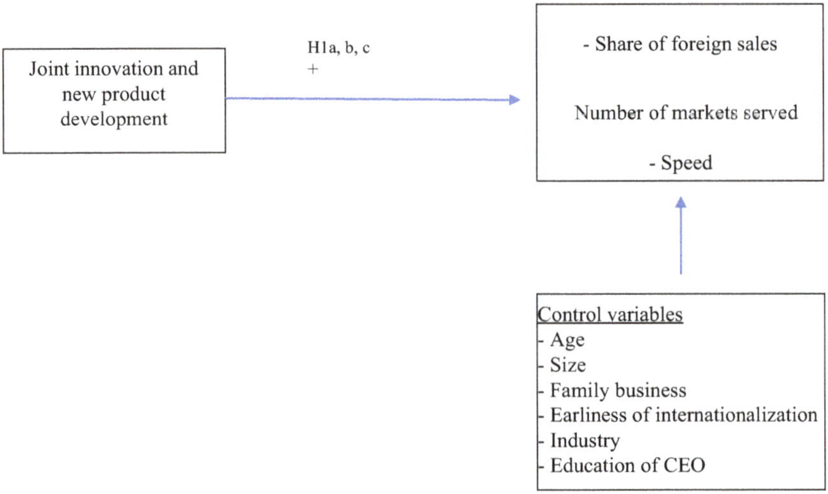

Fig. 1: Research model

We use a stepwise backwards regression in our statistical tests: by first integrating all the variables into the model, it is then possible to remove the independent variable being studied (joint innovation) to identify its explanatory power on the observed dependent variable. The results are presented below (Tab. 1). If the model is statistically significant in both cases, we look at the share of variance (ΔR^2) explained by the independent variable.

6 L'internationalisation des PME et ETI françaises (2014). Direction Générale du Trésor. Paris.

Tab. 1: Regression results

	Share of foreign sales	**Number of markets served**	**Speed**
	Model 1	**Model 2**	**Model 3**
Constant	46,307	8,331	3,189
Age	4,355**	1,383***	-0,024
Size (employees)	-0,010	0,739***	0,021
Earliness	-7,132***	-0,682**	-0,030
Family business	-11,390***	-1,092*	-0,364**
Activity : new technologies [a]	-14,275**	-0,671	-0,124
Activity : consumer goods [a]	-11,844***	-0,897	0,175
Activity : services and commerce [a]	-10,910**	-0,540	0,01
CEO education	1,958	0,000	0,101
Joint innovation	**4,100**** **(0,019)**	0,433*	0,090
Significance	0,000	0,000	0,203
R^2	0,232	0,234	0,068
Adjusted R^2	0,191	0,193	0,019
ΔR^2	0,025	0,013	0,009
Durbin Watson	1,941	2,100	2,177
F	5,698	5,790	1,375
VIF	1,031	1,031	1,031
N	180	181	180

Unstandardized coefficients
a Reference group: capital goods

First, our dissertation, which looked at eight collaborative practices, had an important finding: the development of new products is the least used form of collaboration among the companies that responded, with an average score of 2.35/7 for new products; by comparison, the score for knowledge transfer on new markets was 3.27/7, 3.09/7 for prospecting, and 2.72/20 for joint distribution. This finding raises questions about the possible obstacles to collaboration. Do companies want to innovate together but not know how to go about it? Are they reluctant to engage in this practice? Have they tried but not succeeded? Do they collaborate with other actors? This aspect remains to be resolved.

Moreover, statistical tests show a positive and significant effect of joint innovation on the share of revenue from international markets. For information purposes and to emphasize the importance of this result, we note that among the eight practices we studied, innovation is the only collaborative practice that has a positive influence on revenue from international markets. In contrast, the number of markets served and the speed of international expansion are not influenced by collaboration.

We then carried out more sophisticated tests in order to isolate certain business sectors to see if they would react differently to the implementation of collaboration. This result is a surprising aspect of our work. We find that for capital goods companies, the design of new products has a positive and significant effect on the share of revenue from international markets, as it did for the entire sample. The coefficient is slightly higher in this case (4.668 as opposed to 4.1) as is the share of explained variance (ΔR^2 = 3.8 % as opposed to 2.5 %). For capital goods companies, joint innovation has a positive (coefficient of 2.446) but not significant effect. This thus shows a divide between capital goods companies and others: capital goods companies do not derive a significant benefit from collaborating for innovation.

Tab. 2: Regression results for non-capital goods/capital goods companies

	Share of foreign sales – other than capital goods	**Share of foreign sales – capital goods**
Constant	33,3	46,083
Age	3,664*	5,611
Size	-2,460	3,508
Earliness	-9,568*	-9,83***
Family business	0,137	-11,936*
CEO education	-6,126**	5.316*
Joint innovation	**4,668****	2.446
Significance	*0,01*	*0,001*
R^2	*0,168*	*0,286*
Adjusted R^2	*0,118*	*0,222*
ΔR^2	*0,038*	*0,007*
Durbin Watson	*1,737*	*1,818*
F	*3,360*	*4,465*
VIF	*1,015*	*1,054*

Unstandardized coefficients

We base our study on literature that takes a generally favourable position on collaborative innovation. However, our results show more mixed effects. First, our study shows that only one indicator of international expansion is positively affected. We first observe that joint innovation does not increase the number of markets served. This thus depends on other factors: opportunities identified on the market, resources available for prospecting, etc. The same is true for the speed of international expansion. Thus, joint innovation does not seem to affect the scope of international expansion or the speed of international growth.

At the same time, it seems that SMEs that innovate together have a greater proportion of international business in their revenues. This result thus suggests that when they pool their resources, companies can generate synergies that enable them to further advance the innovation process. Together they can develop a more differentiated product with a higher value added and thus obtain an increase in their revenue from international markets.

Furthermore, the positive effect is limited to companies that do not deal in capital goods. This raises the question of what might be happening in the capital goods sector since synergies have not been identified. These results are in line with those of Jeon and Degravel (2019), who note that 60–70 % of projects do not reach their objectives. Delays can multiply and be costly, goals may diverge, and a short-term approach may prevail. The costs of coordinating and protecting non-transferable knowledge also need to be considered. After all, collaborative innovation involves the "openness paradox" (Laursen and Salter, 2014) highlighted by Chesbrough et al. (2018): companies must demonstrate openness while remaining able to capture created value.

On the other hand, these results are also in line with Torchia and Calabro, who in their literature review point to studies that dispute the advantages of open innovation. For example, Saetta et al. (2013) find that product development may be more difficult as a group than alone if none of the companies provides dynamic leadership on the project. We also suggest that for capital goods SMEs, innovation involves greater commitments than for consumer goods, with high technological requirements, longer development cycles, and relatively expensive experimental conditions. It could be that SMEs that collaborate have not known how to guide the process effectively over time, making the attainment of results take longer (Kessler et al., 2007), which can discourage the parties and even lead to termination of the project. This motivates us to consider possible success factors. Finally, we can also posit that innovation cycles are longer in these industries and that any collaborations established in the period observed (the three years previous to the survey) had not yet had time to bear fruit.

4. Success factors

In their description of the relational rents that companies obtain by collaboration through what they call a "heterarchical" relationship because it involves neither the market nor integration, Dyer and Singh (1998) identify four factors: relation-specific assets, knowledge-sharing routines, complementary resources and skills, and effective governance. Other researchers stress the nature of the relationship or the necessary synergies. We will look at several elements in turn: the initiation of partnerships, the evaluation and choice of potential partners, the governance framework and routines, the development of specific skills, and the allocation of rents.

4.1. Initiation of partnerships

Some companies have attractive and desirable resources (Lavie, 2006; Gulati et al., 2011): for example, complementary product suppliers involving new technology (Lindstrand and Hånell, 2017). SMEs that wish to jointly innovate need to identify desirable resources that can create synergies at an early stage so that the target companies and their managers can be approached clearly and deliberately. In this case, the entrepreneurs take a clear strategic and/or calculative network approach with an economic goal.

The scope of identification varies. Interpersonal social networks can provide opportunities in international markets or techniques for international expansion; exporters are strongly inclined to exchange information on these subjects. In the case of innovation collaborations, however, SME managers have more targeted expectations and needs for specific skills or technologies. Synergies will mostly arise through inter-firm networks and are likely to be found beyond the existing network or even in other business sectors. In this case, entrepreneurs should use their economic intelligence to identify relevant technologies, the SMEs that market them or that work in that area, complementary businesses, etc. Their managers need to be open and curious; for example, they could attend trade fairs that are not directly connected to their business. Once they have identified potential partners, they then need to make contact.

4.2. Assessment and selection of potential partners

This stage is sensitive by definition and involves choosing partners that make it possible to maximize potential profit while minimizing risks. However, since it takes place very early on, the process is based on asymmetric information between the partners. The literature emphasizes the role of trust between partners, but when there has been no previous relationship, there is neither trust nor relational capital to rely on. It is difficult to advise exporters to implement a gradual approach, as can be the case for information exchanges or joint prospecting. In fact, the entry for these types of collaborations is more affordable; the companies can engage in more modest joint actions like, for example, participating in a trade fair abroad. These actions make it possible for the actors to observe each other in the field and develop social capital that can be gradually built upon. This gradual approach seems more difficult to implement in an innovation process, which requires more commitment from the outset. We thus recommend that entrepreneurs use different sources of information to study trust signals (Barney and Clark, 2007) and the other companies' reputations. Torchia and Calabro (2019) suggest carrying out a strategic value assessment (SVA) to choose partners. This method assesses how potential collaborations could contribute to the company's long-term objectives. When applied at the very early stages of the collaborative process (Braun et al., 2012), this makes it possible to choose partners that are especially advanced in certain technological domains and to take a rational approach.

It also seems important to clarify needs and expectations from the outset and present the resources that can be contributed to the relationship. Dyer and Singh (1998) explain that partners "must find each other and recognize the potential value of combining resources" (p. 667). Identifying common goals improves the chances of successful technological development (Lichtenthaler, 2005; Lee et al., 2010).

It is also advisable to plan social gatherings to build this relationship; for example, the partners could make joint visits to different production sites. This could be an opportunity for both parties to assess one another during informal conversations.

4.3. Establishing a framework and governance routines

Once a relationship is established, it seems essential to set up formal protection mechanisms based on deterrence through structural trust (Madhok, 1995). Intellectual property is the main issue here. Dyer and Singh (1998) recommend self-regulation mechanisms like trust or a mutual hostage situation rather than relying on a third party.

This also involves establishing inter-organizational trust mechanisms (Gulati et al., 2011) until interpersonal trust emerges.

4.4. Developing specific skills

The success of partnerships that have been initiated for the purpose of innovation must rely on specific skills.

The development of absorptive capacity to maximize advantages in alliances and collaborations is a recurring theme in the research on the subject. For Cohen and Levinthal (1990; p. 128), absorptive capacity is "the ability of a firm to recognize the value of new, external information, assimilate it, and apply it to commercial ends".

Moreover, Dyer and Singh (1998) emphasize the importance of relational skills, defined as the firm's desire and ability to collaborate. Blomqvist and Levy (2006) and Gincing (2014) emphasize the role of collaborative skills as an essential element in the process of continued and sustainable innovation. Nahapiet and Ghoshal (1998) recommend that partners increase their social interactions and build trust so that the knowledge each party contributes can combine and create new intellectual capital. Joint activities should be clustered around a clearly identified shared identity. This identity can serve as a foundation of projects, routines, and activities; it thus seems essential for the joint project to have a name. This will increase awareness of the project and create a sense of belonging.

According to Powell et al. (1996), innovation is based on a social process that enables the circulation and recombination of knowledge. The authors state that collaboration related to innovation needs to be a mutually beneficial process that makes it possible for participants to learn to exchange with others and become organized accordingly. The firm thus develops the skills and know-how needed for absorption, which will then be useful in future collaborations. Not connecting thus handicaps companies that do not take this approach. It should be noted that other factors are also at play: Jeon and Degravel (2019) point to the technical skills of the SMEs, the quality of the technological transfer, and the ability to allocate enough time and attention to the process. These last two aspects are attributed to managers and their ability to allocate the necessary availability and resources to their partners and collaborative activities.

4.5. Rent allocation conditions

Relational rent (Dyer and Singh, 1998) is the additional profits jointly generated through collaborations. It belongs to the companies that have created it together, which raises the essential question of it being shared beyond its creation (Chesbrough et al., 2018). Lavie (2006) states that the ability to capture a large portion of relational rent stems from several factors: the company's bargaining power with its partners, the proportion of resources compared to those contributed by partners, the relative absorption capacity, existing contractual agreements, and the partner's potential lack of loyalty. Lavie (2006) argues that the outcome of a collaboration can only be evaluated by calculating the difference between the rent that the company captures and the internal resources that may be captured by partners. This balance is based on both gains and potential losses or spillovers; it could be more or less than what drawing exclusively upon internal resources would have generated.

The diagram below (Fig. 2) represents the three main phases of the collaborative innovation process.

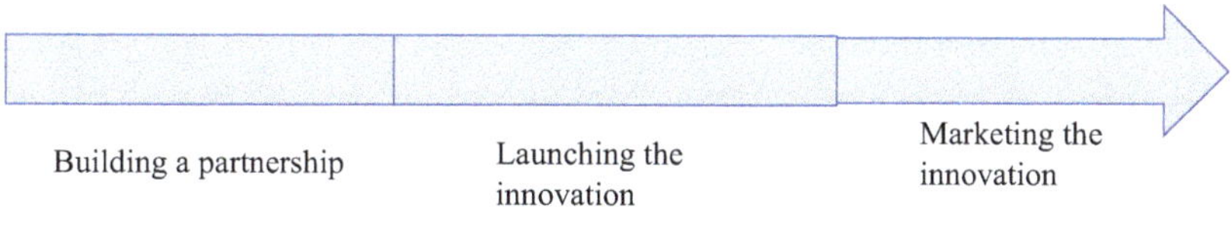

Fig. 2: Collaborative innovation process – based on Torchia and Calabro (2019)

Each phase presents specific challenges for the project's success. The first phase relies on the choice of partner and the definition of shared objectives. The second phase depends on the ability to exchange resources – especially knowledge – and recombine them to create value. The third phase is related to marketing the innovation and sharing the jointly generated relational rent.

5. Future research and perspectives

The accelerating pace of innovation in general, technological change in many sectors, new needs for sustainable development, and the increase in international competition are some of the factors that might lead SMEs to innovate more in the future so that they can sell their products in international markets. It is thus important to continue studying collaboration in these areas, optimize the results, and share the best practices. Chesbrough et al. (2018) thus encourage future research on "open innovation capability", defined as "the processes that enable a firm to optimize value from open innovation" (p. 934). The authors encourage research on equity, trust, and companies' ability to disclose knowledge to each other. They also call for studies that will shed light on the crucial decision of whether to join a collaborative venture.

On the other hand, little research has been done on the optimal number of partners and size of collaborative partnerships as well as their geographic scope, which can go beyond the domestic sphere, as Jeon and Degravel (2019) have shown. They observe three configurations in a sample of Korean firms: closed innovation, local open innovation, and global open innovation. The characteristics of these two last formats deserve to be better known and compared.

Certain features of specific business sectors, like those found in our own studies, deserve to be better understood and should thus be the subject of future research.

Finally, on a more operational level, it appears that every new collaborative project in France raises the question of the framework to be used. If it is not an informal collaboration, it needs to be based on a structure in the French ecosystem, which is unfortunately not yet standardized. There are no identified and generalizable best practices. We thus urge the actors in that ecosystem to adopt a specific program that is both structured and flexible, whose clear aim will be to enable SMEs to collaborate by gaining a shared outlook. The network contract (Contratto di rete) adopted in Italy in 2009 can be an example to follow here.

Conclusion

Throughout this study, we have synthesized several foundational approaches that connect inter-firm collaboration, innovation, and international expansion of SMEs. Drawing on several strands of the literature as well as our own research, we have shown that SMEs have an interest in engaging in a collaborative approach to innovation and international expansion. SMEs often possess niche technologies and know-how that give them a high degree of expertise; by working with their peers, they can offer new solutions with high added value. However, these benefits are not automatic but depend on a combination of careful choices and fine-tuning of the process, from the earliest stages until the sharing of joint created value.

We believe there is still much to do to show SME managers and the broader export ecosystem the potential benefits that collaborative innovation can bring to international expansion. SME leaders should also increase their collaborative skills to that end.

On the other hand, we encourage researchers to delve deeper into the success factors for collaborative innovation; it seems important to shed more light on the different effects according to business sector, partner type, or implementation method. Ideally, these studies would identify and disseminate best practices while highlighting inspiring success stories.

References

Agostini, L., and Nosella, A. (2018), « Inter-Organizational Relationships Involving SMEs: A Bibliographic Investigation into the State of the Art », Long Range Planning, vol. 52, n° 2, pp. 1–31.

Ahuja, G. (2000), « Collaboration Networks, Structural Holes, and Innovation: A Longitudinal Study », Administrative Science Quarterly, vol. 45, no 3, pp. 425.

Arya, B., and Lin, Z.(2007), « Understanding Collaboration Outcome From an Extended Resource-based View Perspective: the Roles of Organizational Characteristics, Partner Attributes, and Network Structures », Journal of Management, vol. 33, n° 5, pp. 697–723.

Barney, J. (1991), « Firm Resources and Sustained Companditive Advantage », Journal of Management, vol. 17, no 1, pp. 99–120.

Barney, J., and Clark, D. (2007), Resource-Based Theory, Oxford University Press, Oxford, 316 p.

Blomqvist, K., and Levy, J. (2006), « Collaboration Capability – a Focal Concept in Knowledge Creation and Collaborative Innovation in Networks », International Journal of Management Concepts and Philosophy, vol. 2, n° 1, pp. 31–47.

Braun, A., Mueller, E., Adelhelm, S., and Vladova, G. (2012) « Knowledge Flow at the Fuzzy Front-end of Inter-firm R&D collaborations? Insights into SMEs in the Pharmaceutical Industry », International Journal of Entrepreneurship & Innovation Management, vol. 15, n° 1, pp. 29–46.

Calantone, R., Kim, D., Schmidt, J., and Cavusgil, S. (2006), « The Influence of Internal and External Firm Factors on International Product Adaptation Strategy and Export Performance: A Three-Country Comparison », Journal of Business Research, vol. 59, no 2, pp. 176–85.

Cavusgil, S., and Knight, G. (2015), « The Born Global Firm : An Entrepreneurial and Capabilities Perspective on Early and Rapid Internationalization », Journal of International Business Studies, vol. 46, no 1, pp. 3–16.

Chesbrough, H. (2003), Open Innovation: The New Imperative for Creating and Profiting from Technology, Harvard Business School Press, Boston, MA, 227 p.

Chesbrough, H. (2006), Open Business Models: How to Thrive in the New Innovation Landscape, Harvard Business School Press, Boston.

Chesbrough, H., and Bogers, M. (2014), « Clarifying an Emerging Paradigm for Understanding Innovation ». In New frontiers in Open Innovation, ed. H. Chesbrough, W. Vanhaverbeke, and J. West, pp. 3–28, Oxford University Press, Oxford.

Chesbrough, H., Landtl, C., and Ritter, T. (2018), "Value Creation and value Capture in Open Innovation", Journal of Product Innovation Management, vol. 35, n°6, pp. 930–938.

Cohen, W., and Levinthal, D. (1990), « Absorptive capacity: A new perspective on learning and innovation », Administrative Science Quarterly, pp. 128–152.

D'Angelo, A., and Baroncelli, A. (2020), « An Investigation over Inbound Open Innovation in SMEs: Insights from an Italian Manufacturing Sample », Technology Analysis & Strategic Management, vol. 32, n°5, pp. 542–560.

D'Angelo, A., and Buck, T.(2019), « The Earliness of Exporting and Creeping Sclerosis? The Moderating Effects of Firm Age, Size and Centralization », International Business Review, vol. 28, n° 3, pp. 428–437.

De Massis, A., Audrandsch, D., Uhlaner, L., and Kammerlander, N. (2018), « Innovation with Limited Resources: Management Lessons from the German Mittelstand », Journal of Product Innovation Management, vol. 35, no 1, pp. 125–146.

Deltour, F., Le Gall, S., and Landhiais, V. (2017), « La spatialité des coopérations pour l'innovation à l'ère du numérique: une investigation multi-méthodes auprès de PME », 26ème Conférence AIMS, Lyon.

Dyer, J., and Singh, H. (1998), « The Relational View: Cooperative Strategy and Sources of Interorganizational Companditive Advantage », Academy of Management Review, vol. 23, n°4, pp. 660–679.

Enkel, E., Gassmann, O., and Chesbrough, H. (2009), « Open R&D and Open Innovation: Exploring the Phenomenon », R&D Management, vol. 39, n° 4, pp. 311–316.

Gessler, J.-C. (2019), Les pratiques collaboratives des PME françaises pour se développer à l'international (thèse de doctorat non publiée). Université Lyon II, France.

Gassmann, O., Enkel, E., and Chesbrough, H. (2010), « The Future of Open Innovation », R&D Management, vol. 40, n° 3, pp. 213–21.

Ginting, G. (2014), « How Network Capital Influences Degree of Internationalization? Case: Small Medium Industries in Indonesia », Review of Integrative Business and Economics Research, vol. 3, n°2, pp. 210–218.

Golovko, E., and Valentini, G. (2011), « Exploring the Complementarity Bandween Innovation and Export for SMEs' Growth », Journal of International Business Studies, vol. 42, no 3, pp. 362–380.

""Granovetter, M. (1973), « The Strength of Weak Ties », American Journal of Sociology, vol. 78, no 6, pp. 1360–1380.

Granovetter, M. (1985), « Economic Action and Social Structure : The Problem of Embeddedness », American Journal of Sociology, vol. 91, no 3, pp. 481–510.

Granstrand, O., and Holgersson, M. (2020), « Innovation Ecosystems: A Conceptual Review and a New Definition », Technovation, vol. 90, pp. 1–12.

Gulati, R., Lavie, D., and Madhavan, R. (2011), « How Do Networks Matter? The Performance Effects of Interorganizational Networks », Research in Organizational Behavior, vol. 31, pp. 207–224

Haase, F., and Franco, M. (2015), « When Small Businesses Go International: Alliances as a Key to Entry », Journal of Business Strategy, vol. 36, n° 3, pp. 37–45.

Hinteregger, C., Durst, C., Temel, S., and Yesilay, R. (2018), « The Impact of Openness on Innovation in SMEs », International Journal of Innovation Management, vol. 23, n° 01 1950003.

Hoang, H., and Antoncic, B. (2003), « Network-Based Research in Entrepreneurship », Journal of Business Venturing, vol. 18, no 2, pp. 165–187.

Huggins, R. (2010), « Forms of Network Resource: Knowledge Access and the Role of Inter-firm Networks », International Journal of Management Reviews, vol. 12, n° 3, pp. 335–352.

Huggins, R., and Thompson, P. (2015), « Entrepreneurship, Innovation and Regional Growth: A Network Theory », Small Business Economics, vol. 45, no 1, pp. 103–128.

Jeon, R., and Degravel, D. (2019), « Open Innovation, a Tool for Globalization: The Case of South Korean SMEs », Journal of Management Policy and Practice, vol. 20, n° 2, pp. 51–74.

Kazlauskaite, R., Abramavicius, R., Sarapovas, T., Gelbuda, M., and Venciūtė, D. (2015), « Network Research on Internationalization of Firms from the Emerging Economies: Literature Review and Propositions », European Journal of Business and Economics, vol. 10, no 1, pp. 26–30.

Kessler, E., Allocca, M., and Rahman, N. (2007), « External Knowledge Accession and Innovation Speed in the Small and Medium Sized Enterprise (SME) », Small Enterprise Research, vol. 15, n° 1, pp. 1–21.

Laursen, K., and Salter, A. (2014), « The Paradox of Openness: Appropriability, External Search and Collaboration », Research Policy, vol. 43, n° 5, pp. 867–78.

Lavie, D. (2006), « Interconnected Firms and the Value of Network Resources », Advances in Mergers & Acquisitions, vol. 5, Emerald, Bingley, pp. 127–141.

Lawson, B., and Samson, D. (2001), « Developing Innovation Capability in Organisations: A Dynamic Capabilities Approach », International Journal of Innovation Management, vol. 5, n° 3, pp. 377–400.

Lee, S., Park, G., Yoon, B., and Park, J. (2010). « Open Innovation in SMEs: An Intermediated Network Model », Research Policy, vol. 39, pp. 290–300.

Leonidou, L. (2004), « An Analysis of the Barriers Hindering Small Business Export Development », Journal of Small Business Management, vol. 42, no 3, pp. 279–302.

Lichtenthaler, U. (2005), « External Commercialization of Knowledge: Review and Research Agenda », International Journal of Management Reviews, vol. 7, pp. 231–255.

Lichtenthaler, U. (2008). « Open Innovation in Practice: An Analysis of Strategic Approaches to Technology Transactions », IEEE Transactions on Engineering Management, vol. 55, pp. 148–157.

Lindstrand, A., and Hånell, S. (2017), « International and Market-Specific Social Capital Effects on International Opportunity Exploitation in the Internationalization Process », Journal of World Business, vol. 52, n°5, pp. 653–663.

Lockett, A., Thompson, S., and Morgenstern, U. (2009), « The Development of the Resource-Based View of the Firm: A Critical Appraisal », International Journal of Management Reviews, vol. 11, no 1, pp. 9–28.

Madhok, A. (1995), « Opportunism and Trust in Joint Venture Relationships: An Exploratory Study and a Model », Scandinavian Journal of Management, vol. 11, n° 1, pp. 57–74.

Mesquita, L., and Lazzarini, S. (2008), « Horizontal and Vertical Relationships in Developping Economies : Implications for SME's Access to Global Markands », Academy of Management Journal, vol. 51, n° 2, pp. 359–390.

Nahapiet, J., and Ghoshal, S. (1998), « Social Capital, Intellectual Capital, and the Organizational Advantage », Academy of Management Review, vol. 23, no 2, pp. 242–266.

Nunes, S., Lopes, R., and Fuller-Love, N. (2017), « Networking, Innovation, and Firms' Performance: Portugal as Illustration », Journal of the Knowledge Economy, novembre 2017, pp. 1–22.

OECD (2005), Oslo Manual. Guidelines for Collecting and Interpreting Innovation Data, OECD, Paris.

Paul, J., Parthasarathy, S., and Gupta, P. (2017), « Exporting Challenges of SMEs: A Review and Future Research Agenda », Journal of World Business, vol. 52, no 3, pp. 327–342.

Popli, M., Ladkani, R., and Gaur, A. (2017), « Business Group Affiliation and Post-acquisition Performance: An Extended Resource-based View », Journal of Business Research, vol. 81, pp. 21–30.

Powell, W., Koput, K., and Smith-Doerr, L. (1996), « Interorganizational Collaboration and the Locus of Innovation: Networks of Learning in Biotechnology », Administrative Science Quarterly, vol. 41, no 1, pp. 116–145.

Radicic, D., Douglas, D., and Pugh, G. (2019), « Cooperation for Innovation and its Impact on Technological and Non-technological Innovations: Empirical Evidence for European SMEs in Traditional Manufacturing Industries », International Journal of Innovation Management, vol. 23, n° 05; 1950046.

Rinjsoever, F., Kempkes, S., and Chappin, M. (2017), « Seduced into Collaboration: A Resource-based Choice Experiment to Explain Make, Buy or Ally Strategies of SMEs », Technological Forecasting and Social Change, vol. 120, pp. 284–297.

Saetta, S., Tiacci, L., and Cagnazzo, L. (2013), « The Innovative Model of the Virtual Development Office for Collaborative Networked Enterprises: The GPT Network Case Study », International Journal of Computer Integrated Manufacturing, vol. 26, n° 1, pp. 41–54.

Santoro, G., Ferraris, A., Giacosa, E., and Giovando, G. (2016), « How SMEs Engage in Open Innovation: A Survey », Journal of Knowledge Economy, vol. 9, pp. 651–574.

Sullivan Mort, G., and Weerawardena, J. (2006), « Networking Capability and International Entrepreneurship: How Networks Function in Australian Born Global Firms », International Marketing Review, vol. 23, no 5, pp. 549–572.

Tang, Y. K. (2011), « Influence of Networking on the Internationalisation of SMEs: Evidence from Internationalised Chinese firms », International Small Business Journal, vol. 29, n° 4, pp. 374–398.

Teece, D. (2007), « Explicating Dynamic Capabilities: The Nature and Microfoundations of (Sustainable) Enterprise Performance », Strategic Management Journal, vol. 28, no 13, pp. 1319–1350.

Torchia, M., and Calabrò, A. (2019), « Open innovation in SMEs: A Systematic Literature Review », Journal of Enterprising Culture, vol. 27 n° 2, pp. 201–228.

Van de Vrande, V., De Jong, J. P., Vanhaverbeke, W., and De Rochemont, M. (2009), « Open innovation in SMEs: Trends, Motives and Management Challenges », Technovation, vol. 29, n° 6, pp. 423–437.

Wernerfelt, B.(1984), « A Resource-based View of the Firm », Strategic Management Journal, vol. 5, no 2, pp. 171–180.

Chapter 8

Degree of digitalization and entrepreneurial orientation of internationalizing micro-, small- and medium-sized enterprises: The mediating roles of self-concept traits

Annaële Hervé, Christophe Schmitt, and Rico Baldegger

Introduction

Although the widespread adoption of digital technologies creates an enabling business environment based on wide scalability and powerful resources for processing and storing information, the digital context also accentuates the competitive landscape all around the world. As it shapes spatial and temporal boundaries of entrepreneurial processes and outcomes (Nambisan, 2017), digital technologies reduce many barriers as regards reaching the global marketplace. This context allows new players to compete and completely transforms the patterns of both domestic and international trade. In such a competitive environment, micro-, small- and medium-sized enterprises (MSMEs), and especially internationalizing ones, are required to adjust their efforts by aggressively trying to preserve a market advantage and demonstrate a strong entrepreneurial orientation (EO) (Covin and Slevin, 1989). EO refers to strategic behaviors that are entrepreneurial in nature, in other words, it consists of decision-making practices that demonstrate innovativeness, proactiveness and risk-taking (Anderson et al., 2009). In that regard, by allowing more variability in entrepreneurial activities and in value creation, integrating digital technologies into internal and external firms' operational dimensions might offer new opportunities, not only for building strong competitive advantage, but also for optimizing managerial and strategic decisions (Hull et al., 2007; Bharadwaj et al., 2013; Nambisan, 2017; Autio et al., 2018; Kraus et al., 2019). At a firm level, digital technologies are a major type of external enabler that have a paradigm-shifting role in entrepreneurship (Nambisan, 2017; von Briel et al., 2018). They have rendered entrepreneurial activities less bounded and have decentralized and distributed firm governance between groups of actors, thereby enabling innovation collectives and the sharing of value creation (Nambisan, 2017). However, even if the change in competitive and technology landscapes creates entrepreneurial opportunities to be discovered and pursued by entrepreneurs (Schumpeter, 1934; Shane, 2000), those individuals need to be aware of these new possibilities in order to reinforce the entrepreneurial behaviors of their firms and be ready for sustainable innovations (Shane, 2000; Kraus et al., 2019). As acknowledged by Schumpeter (1934), it is individual characteristics that influence the discovery and exploitation of opportunity – and thus, personal traits. Prior knowledge, as well as technology and managerial capabilities are also required (Shane, 2000; Grégoire and Shepherd, 2012; Gruber et al., 2012). In the literature, despite the burgeoning scholarly interest in the digital area, a number of ontological questions persist. Indeed, minimal research has addressed the role of digital technologies in shaping entrepreneurial opportunities, decisions, actions and outcomes (Nambisan, 2017).

Within the entrepreneurship domain, particularly in a context of rapid technological advances, many researchers have been interested in profiling the specific characteristics that define the entrepreneur and his entrepreneurial actions (Schumpeter, 1934; Shane, 2000; Rauch and Frese, 2007; Gruber et al., 2012). As self-motivated individuals, entrepreneurs rely primarily on themselves to achieve their goals and thus, are a central driver in taking advantage of technological changes and defining competitive strategies (Schumpeter, 1934). Similarly, recurrent debates in scientific literature associated the personal traits of managers with a firm's EO (Miller and Friesen, 1982; Miller, 1983; Mueller and Thomas, 2001; Poon et al., 2006; Khedhaouria et al., 2015; McGee and Peterson, 2019). As contended in the Miller and Friesen (1982) study, executive goals and traits are central to driving a firm's EO. At the individual level, there are many self-concept traits that have a theoretical relationship with a firm's strategic posture. The most popular concepts in the field of entrepreneurship are self-efficacy, which refers to individuals' perceived ability to accomplish a certain level of performance (Bandura, 1986) and locus of control, which refers to the disposition of a manager to perceive control over the environment (Rotter, 1966). In our research, we suggested that entrepreneurs have several opportunities to maintain their firms' competitive and entrepreneurial strategic posture by reinforcing EO capabilities with the use of digital technologies. Nevertheless, in the literature, only few empirical studies have explored these dimensions together in order to understand how the integration of digital technologies into firms may drive EO (Hervé et al., 2020a). In our research, we thus extended the theoretical boundary and contributed to the entrepreneurship literature by testing a comprehensive model that used both firm-level and individual-level variables to explain the EO of MSMEs. Specifically, drawing on digital and technology entrepreneurship, on EO and the theories of self-concept traits, we argued that the integration of digital technologies into internal and external dimensions of a firm is central to reinforcing the strategic posture of entrepreneurially internationalizing MSMEs and proposed that individuals are the central driver of this strategic approach. In sum, we aimed to investigate the effect of the digitalization of MSMEs on their EO as well as examine the role of individuals' behaviors as potential mediating variables to explain this relationship. Toward these ends, we developed a model linking four levels of digital transformation (i.e., process and infrastructure – people and culture – digital sales – customer involvement) to the three main EO components (i.e., innovativeness – proactiveness – risk-taking) and measured how the relationship transits through self-concept traits (i.e., self-efficacy and locus of control). Based on parallel mediation analysis, the model was empirically tested using 143 Swiss internationalizing MSMEs. Our study made two distinct contributions to theory on entrepreneurship. First, by using an integrative perspective, it provided new impetus to research on the effect on the firms' EO of integrating digital technologies into operational dimensions. Second, our research shed new light on the important role of individuals in shaping these digital opportunities to reinforce strategic posture. By providing empirical evidence of the mediating role of individual behaviors, we demonstrated that self-efficacy can be a way forward to strategically use digital technologies in order to reinforce EO and, simultaneously, to provide competitive advantage of internationalizing firms.

1. Theoretical developments

1.1. Digital entrepreneurship

Firms are evolving at the heart of digital disruption that involves changes in the competitive landscape. Resulting from the use of digital technologies by new market entrants or existing competitors, these changes directly impact current offers and market strategic approaches of established firms (Ross et al., 2016). Simultaneously, the use of emerging and readily accessible technologies presents firms with opportunities to define new value propositions based on the combination of existing competencies and the capabilities allowed by technologies. This is especially true for MSMEs, which move more quickly (Ross et al., 2016). These emerging technologies have an increasing paradigm-shifting role in entrepreneurship and engender profound effects in shaping entrepreneurial processes, outcomes and opportunities (Nambisan, 2017). Because they create more fluidity and nonlinearity across time and space, the use of digital technologies completely reshaped the very nature of entrepreneurship (Nambisan, 2017). From this perspective, the use of digital technologies can be introduced as input for entrepreneurship opportunities (Giones and Brem, 2017). In scientific research, the phenomenon of digitalization is of growing interest to more and more scientists and gave birth to DE a decade ago (Hull et al., 2007; Davidson and Vaast, 2010; Giones and Brem, 2017; Nambisan, 2017; Kraus et al., 2019). At the intersection of digitalization and entrepreneurship theories, DE is described as a subcategory of entrepreneurship "in which some or all of what would be physical in a traditional organization has been digitized" (Hull et al., 2007). In other words, it is the association of traditional entrepreneurship with the new approach of creating value and doing business in a digital context. Considering the strong emergence of digital technologies in various aspects of innovation and entrepreneurship, DE can be defined as "the pursuit of opportunities based on the use of digital media and other information and communication technologies" (Davidson and Vaast, 2010).

Although DE entrepreneurship is gaining increasing importance in scholarly community, the field still struggle in providing a consolidated definition (Kraus et al., 2019). Furthermore, even if the research field is of high topically, literature on the topic is quite scarce (Kraus et al., 2019). Limited efforts have been made in theorizing opportunities, challenges and success factors of DE and researchers have overlooked the role of digital technologies in entrepreneurial activities (Nambisan, 2017; Kraus et al., 2019). By combining insights from entrepreneurship field and DE, our paper highlighted several insights into the major role of the use of digital technologies in adopting strategic orientations, both at the corporate and at the individual levels.

1.2. At the firm level – entrepreneurial orientation in a digital context

As reported by Porter (1985), technological change represents one of the main drivers of competition and significantly affects competitive advantage of firms. Consequently, as highlighted by Covin and Slevin (1989), in such a competitive environment companies need to adapt their efforts to current conditions by aggressively trying to benefit from or preserve their market advantage. In order to access such an advantage, entrepreneurial firms would have to build and adopt an EO as their strategic posture (Covin and Slevin, 1989; Lumpkin and Dess, 1996; Anderson et al., 2009; Rauch et al., 2009). This orientation has generally been conceptualized as an organizational trend in decision-making that favors entrepreneurial activities (Lumpkin and Dess, 1996; Anderson et al., 2009). To identify this trend, Covin and Slevin (1989, 1991) defined a continuum ranging from a more conservative posture to a more entrepreneurial one. In this regard, EO is the ability to adopt new behaviors in order to manage future changes in the external environment and the propensity to engage in investments with uncertain returns (Covin and Slevin, 1989; Lumpkin and Dess, 1996). In scientific literature, researchers have suggested that EO is a capacity that provides the main abilities for consolidating competitive advantage (Covin and Slevin, 1989; Lumpkin and Dess, 1996). Since EO is based on this potential source of competitive edge, entrepreneurship researchers agreed that firms with a high level of EO perform better than other firms (Anderson et al., 2009; Rauch et al., 2009). Alongside the literature, EO has been discussed from a primarily firm-level perspective (Covin and Slevin, 1991; Lumpkin and Dess, 1996). Some authors have nonetheless contended that there is no entrepreneurship without the entrepreneur and have adopted EO as an individual-level process by using a personal traits and behavioral approach (Poon et al., 2006; Rauch et al., 2009; Khedhaouria et al., 2015). In our study, we have considered EO to be a firm-level concept and took into consideration founders and decision-makers as a lever of influence to operationalize the orientation of strategic decisions (Covin and Slevin, 1991). As Miller (1983) suggested, the firm's degree of entrepreneurship could be characterized by the proclivity of a firm to value innovative, proactive and risk-taking actions. In other words, adopting an EO as a strategic posture is demonstrative of innovative, proactive and risk-taking efforts to better recognize and exploit opportunities as well as outperform competitors (Miller, 1983). Thus, the most common conceptualization of EO is based on a unidimensional strategic orientation towards three components: innovativeness, which represents the firm's ability and willingness to encourage novel and creative processes, new insights and experimentation for launching new products and services: proactiveness, which describes the propensity of a company to identify and pursue opportunity for improving competitive situations, anticipate change and shape the business environment: risk-taking, which refers to the uncertainty that follows when an entrepreneur or a firm behaves entrepreneurially and engages in risky actions (Covin and Slevin, 1989; Lumpkin and Dess, 1996). By providing the main abilities for consolidating competitive advantage in markets, the concept of EO is often applied in the research stream of international entrepreneurship (IE) (McDougall and Oviatt, 2000). In the literature, academic researchers have even developed the multi-dimensional concept of international entrepreneurial orientation (IEO) that refers to the willingness of entrepreneurs in demonstrating innovativeness, proactiveness and take risks in international trades (Covin and Miller, 2014).

As introduced at the beginning, strategic entrepreneurship researchers exploring technological change have advocated from the outset that technological capabilities are paramount in the process of gaining competitive advantage and improving business performance (Porter, 1985). Today, with the advances in digital technologies, the basis of competitive advantage is being significantly transformed. The use of digital tools allows firms to think differently about business and to expand the possible approaches in solving problems (Weinman and Euchner, 2015). As Grégoire and Shepherd (2012) suggested, "an opportunity is neither solely about a new technology nor solely about a current market situation; rather, it is about the possibility of changing the current market situation by using the new technology". Based on wide scalability and powerful resources for processing and storing information, digital technologies favor an enabling business environment for MSMEs and allow firms to overcome several issues, such as the way to deal with uncertainty in entrepreneurial activities (Nambisan, 2017). At the firm level, the unique attributes of digital technologies have affected the fundamental character of corporate strategic orientation and is providing more variability in entrepreneurial activities, especially for internationalizing MSMEs (Hervé et al., 2020b). As outlined by Nambisan (2017), the digital context has reshaped two major assumptions of entrepreneurial processes and outcomes. First, digital technologies have rendered entrepreneurial processes and outcomes less bounded and allow more flexibility and continuous improvement in activities. Second, by involving a more diverse set of actors in activities, the digital context drives to more collective ways of undertaking entrepreneurship in order to bring together new ideas and resources. Furthermore, as the structural connections of digital technologies make them interactive, it also leads to the creation of digital affordances that improve existing functions or perform entirely new ones (von Briel et al., 2018). Thus, it provides opportunities, especially for established MSMEs, to proactively deliver and capture value in the interactions with their entire ecosystem, including customers, partners, suppliers and stakeholders (Autio et al., 2018). Whether to develop and customize offers or optimize processes, involve new actors, improve managerial decisions and rethink current business models, the use of digital technologies triggers a transformation in firms activities (Bharadwaj et al., 2013; Ross et al., 2016; Autio et al., 2018; Kraus et al., 2019). These transformations are occurring both at the internal and external dimensions of firms. Indeed, innovation through digital technologies not only applies to products and services, but also extends to organizational dimensions related to infrastructure, processes, human capital, as well as customer relationships (Weinman and Euchner, 2015). In that regard, the use of emerging technologies might offer new opportunities to adopt strategic behavior and develop entrepreneurial activities through more innovativeness, proactiveness and risk-taking. However, as outlined by Nambisan (2017), scientific research has neglected to theorize their role in shaping entrepreneurial opportunities, decisions, actions and outcomes. Based on the insights of prior studies, we expected the use of digital technologies in external and internal dimensions of firms to provide new competencies and resources for consolidating strategic orientation and, thus, positively affect the EO of MSMEs. Thus, we developed the first hypothesis:

Hypothesis 1: The degree of digitalization of MSMEs is positively associated with their EO

1.3. At the individual level – entrepreneurial self-concept traits in a digital context

Within the entrepreneurship domain, particularly in a context of rapid technological advances, many researchers have been interested in profiling the specific characteristics that define the entrepreneur and her/his entrepreneurial actions (Schumpeter, 1934; Shane, 2000; Rauch and Frese, 2007; Gruber et al., 2012). In his previous research, Schumpeter (1934) considered the entrepreneur as a central driver to taking advantage of technological changes and defining competitive strategies. It has been acknowledged that the individual perceptions that shape entrepreneurial behaviors about what the firm can achieve with its technological resources are paramount to better explaining and predicting the growth options pursued by an entrepreneur (Gruber et al., 2012). Although technological change presents numerous possibilities to transform production, distribution, as well as organization processes, it does not generate obvious entrepreneurial opportunities that anyone can discover (Shane, 2000). It is individual characteristics that influence the discovery and exploitation of opportunity (Schumpeter, 1934) and, thus, personal traits, prior knowledge, technology and managerial capabilities are required (Shane, 2000; Grégoire and Shepherd, 2012; Gruber et al., 2012).

As outlined by Shane (2000), psychological research has developed theories in which entrepreneurship represents stable characteristics that are not accessible to everyone. Indeed, EO is motivated and driven by diverse personality traits that characterize the entrepreneur (Miller and Friesen, 1982). Following this perspective, numerous personal attributes, such as the need for achievement, the willingness to take risks, self-efficacy and locus of control are closely associated with entrepreneurial behavior and lead some people to pursue entrepreneurship (Shane, 2000). In other words, EO is perceived as resulting from certain drivers related to entrepreneurs' behavioral traits (Miller and Friesen, 1982). Thus, because we were interested in the role of individuals in the relationship among the degree of digitalization of firms and their EO, we investigated two of these human attributes; self-efficacy and locus of control. As many authors have studied the influence of these individual motivation concepts on strategic behavior of firms and have supported significant positive relationships between these dimensions (Miller, 1983; Boyd and Vozikis, 1994; Mueller and Thomas, 2001; Zhao et al., 2005; Poon et al., 2006; Rauch and Frese, 2007; Khedhaouria et al., 2015; McGee and Peterson, 2019), we suggested a new perspective on these links in a context of digitalization.

Self-efficacy. In entrepreneurship research, there are many factors influencing one to become an entrepreneur. These factors are based mostly on combinations of personal attributes, such as traits, background, experience, and disposition, (Gist, 1987; Wood and Bandura, 1989; Boyd and Vozikis, 1994; Chen et al., 1998). Self-efficacy is one of these personal attributes and is an important determinant of human behavior (Bandura, 1986; Boyd and Vozikis, 1994; Ajzen, 2002; Zhao et al., 2005; McGee et al., 2009). According to Bandura (1986), it refers to one's perceived ability to successfully reach a certain level of performance in various roles and tasks of entrepreneurship. More accurately, self-efficacy is defined as "people's judgements of their capabilities to organize and execute courses of action required to attain designated types of performance" (Bandura, 1986). In their research, Wood and Bandura (1989) offered a slightly different definition and described self-efficacy as "beliefs in one's capabilities to mobilize the motivation, cognitive resources, and courses of action needed to meet given situational demands". As it concerned people's beliefs in their capabilities to generate given attainments, this concept is distinguished from the skills one possesses and from outcome expectations. It is more reflective of what individuals believe they can do with those skills (Ajzen, 2002). Thus, because it influences an entrepreneur's choice of activities, aspirations, skill acquisition, goal levels, perseverance, performance and effectiveness, this motivational construct is a useful and dynamic approach that illustrates the process of evaluating and adopting entrepreneurial behavior (Boyd and Vozikis, 1994; Zhao et al., 2005). In the literature, researchers distinguished the concepts of general self-efficacy from that of entrepreneurial self-efficacy. General self-efficacy refers to an individual's confidence in successfully meeting the demands of a variety of tasks in a variety of situations, while entrepreneurial self-efficacy refers to an individual's belief in successfully performing the roles and tasks of an entrepreneur associated with new-venture management (Boyd and Vozikis, 1994; Chen et al., 1998; McGee et al., 2009; McGee and Peterson, 2019). However, as entrepreneurial activity includes many potential tasks and associated skills, it has been acknowledged in scientific research that general self-efficacy is much easier to measure (McGee et al., 2009; Khedhaouria et al., 2015; McGee and Peterson, 2019). Thus, because it more closely reflects a consistent disposition, we used general self-efficacy in our study.

The efficacy belief system is not holistic, but rather consists of a differentiated set of personal beliefs related to distinct areas of functioning. The acquisition of self-efficacy differs according to each person's areas and activities (Bandura, 2006). It is developed gradually through experience and affects skills development as well as effort expenditure and level of persistence (Gist, 1987). Mastery experiences and repeated performance accomplishments are effective ways to acquire a strong sense of self-efficacy (Gist, 1987; Wood and Bandura, 1989). It has been acknowledged in scientific research that the more deeply individuals believe in the effectiveness of their work and ability to successfully accomplish any task or the more positive their perception that they can overcome the difficulties they encounter, the more they aim for ambitious goals and make a stronger commitment to achieving them (Wood and Bandura, 1989). Thus, individuals tend to be attracted to and to perform better in activities for which they have high self-efficacy. Inversely, they tend to avoid activities for which they have low self-efficacy (Wood and Bandura, 1989; Boyd and Vozikis, 1994; Chen et al., 1998; McGee and Peterson, 2019). To this end, because the infusion of digital technologies into a company's operational functions has refined the uncertainty in entrepreneurial processes and outcomes (Nambisan, 2017), entrepreneurs become more confident in their entrepreneurial activities. Hence, because they believe in their abilities and perceive themselves to be efficacious, entrepreneurs may be more likely to manage their business with entrepreneurial behaviors (Chen et al., 1998; Zhao et al., 2005), and would be more willing to encourage new innovative offers and experimentation, to act proactively on their environment and to engage in risky actions (Poon et al., 2006; Khedhaouria et al., 2015; McGee and Peterson, 2019). Given these findings, we developed the second hypothesis:

> *Hypothesis 2: General self-efficacy mediates the relationship between the degree of digitalization and the EO of MSMEs*

Locus of control. As self-motivated individuals, entrepreneurs rely primarily on themselves to start a business and achieve their goals. Thus, many personal attributes are closely associated with entrepreneurial values and behavior, including the self-concept of locus of control (Mueller and Thomas, 2001). Developed in the field of psychology research by Rotter (1966), this construct is significant for measuring perceived control and defining its impacts on human behavior. Because self-efficacy differs greatly from perceived behavioral control, which is related to the capacity to perform a particular behavior (Ajzen, 2002), researchers in the field of entrepreneurship distinguish between the concepts of self-efficacy and locus of control (Boyd and Vozikis, 1994; Chen et al., 1998). First, even if these concepts are both cognitive and about control (Rotter, 1966; Ajzen, 2002), self-efficacy is task- and situation-specific, whereas locus of control is a generalized construct that includes a broader range of situations

(Gist, 1987). For instance, an individual might have a strong locus of control in general, while demonstrating low self-efficacy in performing specific tasks at a specific level of expertise. Second, although both concern behavioral control, locus of control also measures outcome control (Rotter, 1966; Ajzen, 2002). Whether results are determined by one's own actions or by external factors, locus of control is concerned with belief about outcome contingencies and not with perceived capability (Bandura, 2006).

This belief-based personality variable is a relevant indicator of a small firm's performance and more specifically, represents the disposition of a manager to perceive control (Boyd and Vozikis, 1994; Ajzen, 2002). Based on his belief that behavior is learned through social interaction, Rotter (1966) built his insights on the role of reinforcement in determining behavior. According to his research, the outcome of an event can be perceived either as contingent upon an individual's own behavior and under his or her personal control and understanding, or as being dependent upon external factors beyond their control and understanding. Consequently, Rotter (1966) distinguished between the internal locus of control – the perception that rewards depend on an individual's own behavior, and the external locus of control – the perception that rewards depend on outside factors (Boyd and Vozikis, 1994; Boone et al., 1996). In other words, individuals with an internal locus of control perceive that the reward is contingent upon their own behavior and believe they are able to control what happens in their lives, whereas individuals with an external locus of control tend to believe that most of the events in their lives are controlled and result from a chance occurrence. The personality trait of locus of control, especially the internal one, can be considered as a prerequisite for action orientation and can be related to proactiveness and leadership (Boone et al., 1996; Mueller and Thomas, 2001). Accordingly, strategies are highly dependent on the level of perceived control. For instance, internal managers show more transformational leadership and are more task-oriented than external managers, who are more emotion-oriented (Boone et al., 1996). Scientists have thus made an association between entrepreneurial behavior and an internal locus of control orientation. Indeed, it has been widely acknowledged in scientific research that individuals who demonstrate a high level of perceived locus of control (internal) are more associated with entrepreneurial behavior and innovative strategies, while individuals with a low level of perceived locus of control (external) are mainly related to conservative behavior and low-cost strategies (Boone et al., 1996; Mueller and Thomas, 2001; Poon et al., 2006). In this regard, because digital technologies have refined the nature of uncertainties in entrepreneurial activities (Nambisan, 2017), entrepreneurs would be more inclined to believe that rewards depend on their own behavior. Consequently, they would be more willing to adopt entrepreneurial behavior to launch innovative ideas, to exploit new opportunities, to anticipate changes and to take risks (Miller, 1983; Mueller and Thomas, 2001; Poon et al., 2006). Based on these results, we developed the third following hypothesis:

Hypothesis 3: Internal locus of control mediates the relationship between the degree of digitalization and the EO of MSMEs

2. Research framework

As discussed, our proposed model aimed to test how individual behaviors – that is, general self-efficacy and internal locus of control – mediate the relationship between the degree of digitalization of MSMEs and their EO (Fig. 1). We thus address the following model, which can be tested using parallel mediation analysis including more than one mediator (Hayes, 2013):

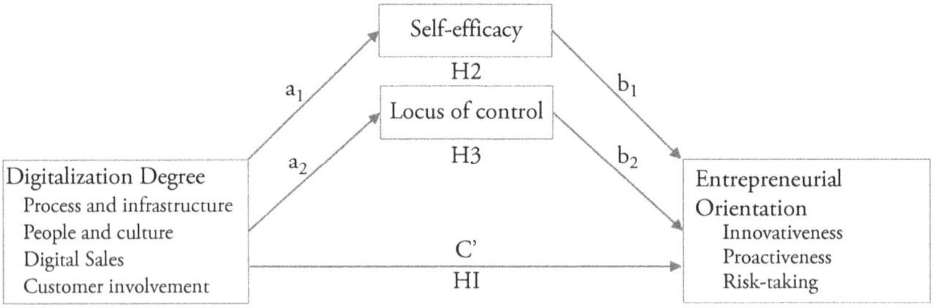

Fig. 1: Research model
Source: from authors

3. Methodology

3.1. Sample and data collection

Our study is based on a quantitative research model that draws on empirical data collected from Swiss MSMEs active in foreign markets.

One half of the sample is represented by manufacturing industries and the other half is adequately representative across other industries, including logistics, professional services, personal and consumer service, IT and communications, heath, as well as wholesale and retail businesses. Highly competitive in terms of innovation and strongly involved on the international stage, Switzerland is exemplary in meeting the objectives of our research. By possessing a competitive and high-level infrastructure of new technologies, the country is a driver of innovation and is a particularly interesting setting regarding digitalization. The use of digital technologies allows Swiss MSMEs and the country to remain both entrepreneurial and internationally competitive (GDS, 2018). Another interesting aspect for our study is that the majority of Swiss companies are MSMEs, representing almost 99 % of the economic fabric. This large proportion constitutes a particularly diversified entrepreneurial universe of firms and highlights the country's strong entrepreneurial spirit.

The data were collected through a secondary data base from 8,000 Swiss internationalizing MSMEs, randomly selected and surveyed. Because our study focused exclusively on high-level insights, we identified executive decision-makers and business founders to fill out the questionnaire. In addition, to ensure homogeneity in our sample, we took into consideration only the responses received from MSMEs reporting 250 or fewer employees, as well as firms that generated at least 5 % of their total sales revenue in foreign markets. After removing responses with missing data or contradictory answers, our final sample includes 143 MSMEs that met our research criteria. The selected MSMEs averaged around 60 employees and generated more than 55 % of their total revenue abroad. Respondents demonstrated a wealth of experience in terms of internationalization and have been trading in foreign markets for an average of 30 years. Furthermore, decision- makers in the respective firms are mainly men (95 %), aged between 18 and 70 years (average 40 years old), who demonstrate a strong entrepreneurial mindset.

3.2. Measures

In our research model, we relied on four constructs – two variables at the firm level and two variables at the individual level. The first one at the firm level is the degree of digitalization. This variable is based on a four-item scale reflecting the company's main strategic dimensions. As part of a digital transformation, firms integrate digital technologies at different levels and spheres of their organization. To differentiate them, we used key variables that include two internal pillars – process and infrastructure and people and culture – and two external ones – digital sales and customer involvement (Greif et al., 2017). Based on descriptive statements, the firms assessed the degree of digitalization of each pillar on a scale of 1–4. In interpreting the results, the higher the selected descriptive statement, the higher the degree of digitalization of the MSMEs surveyed. The second construct used in our study at the firm level is EO. Based on the questionnaire elaborated by Colvin and Slevin (1989), the measurement includes nine items consolidated under three unidimensional entrepreneurial orientations. The first three items are related to firm's innovativeness, the second three assess their proactive behavior and the last three represent their propensity to undertake risky actions. Respondents were asked to evaluate the extent to which the items, formulated by pairs of opposite statements, reflect their firm's strategic posture and answers were recorded on a Likert scale that in our case ranges from 1 to 7. The results were interpreted as follows, the higher the total score, the more firms demonstrate entrepreneurial behavior in their strategic orientation (Covin and Slevin, 1989). The third construct, self-efficacy, refers to the individual and consists of items that articulate a personal position in relation to various skills and competences associated with the topic in question. As outlined by Bandura (2006), scales of self-efficacy have to be tailored according to the specific domain that is the object of interest. In our study, it was measured on the basis of a conceptual framework of task requirements (Chen et al., 1998; Zhao et al., 2005). On a seven-point Likert scale, managers were asked to indicate how confident they were in successfully identifying new business opportunities, creating new products and services, managing innovation within a business, being a leader and communicator, building up a professional network, commercializing a new idea or development and successfully managing a business. The higher the overall score, the higher the respondent's beliefs in her/his capabilities to generate given attainments. Finally, the fourth construct, locus of control, also refers to the individual and was assessed based on the Levenson's (1974) scale, which is an adaptation and refinement of the original construct I-E scale developed by Rotter (1966). Because we were interested in entrepreneurial behaviors of decision-makers, we used the internal control dimension of this belief-based personality variable. Items were written in Likert format, using a seven-point response scale (Sapp and Harrod, 1993). The higher the score, the higher the respondent's belief that outcome contingencies are determined by her or his own actions.

4. Analysis of findings

4.1. Descriptive statistics and construct reliability

In our study, the pattern of bivariate correlations reinforced our hypothesis of a parallel mediation between the variables tested (Hayes, 2013). Tab. 1 reports the means, standard deviations, reliability coefficient, and bivariate correlations between the variables of interest. As expected, the correlation between the level of digitalization and strategic orientation is positive and significant. The results also outlined a positive and significant correlation among the degree of digitalization and the two self-concept traits, as are the correlations between EO and self-efficacy and between EO and locus of control. The correlation between the two self-concept traits is relatively high and also demonstrates a positive and significant result. Moreover, to ensure the adequacy of our model's measurements, we assessed the composite reliability of each construct. Consequently, we conducted a reliability test to define the internal consistency of our measures and used Cronbach's Alpha to evaluate each construct. The major part of the composite reliability scores for measurement scales was above the suggested value of 0.70 (Hair et al., 2006) and ranged from 0.719 for the degree of digitalization, 0.828 for EO to 0.815 for self-efficacy, while the value for locus of control was slightly below, with 0.689. We thus included all of the components in our model.

Tab. 1: Analysis of the means, standard deviation, reliabilities and correlations of the variables

Variables	Mean	Standard deviation	1	2	3	4
1. Degree of digitalization	2.14	0.72	(0.719)			
2. Entrepreneurial orientation	4.35	1.06	.441**	(0.828)		
3. Self-efficacy	5.52	0.90	.219**	.507**	(0.815)	
4. Locus of control	5.62	0.83	.170*	.286**	.647**	(0.689)

Note: values in parentheses are reliability coefficient (Cronbach's Alpha)
**statistical significance at the 0.05 level – **statistical significance at the 0.01 level.*

4.2. Testing our hypotheses

In our study, we relied on parallel mediation analysis to test our hypotheses. As a more complex model than traditional mediation analysis, parallel mediation analysis includes more than one mediator to test the relationship between the independent and dependent variables (Hayes, 2013). There are as many indirect effects as there are mediators. According to Hayes (2013), these mediators are allowed to correlate with one another, but not to influence each other in causality. As we were interested in the mediating effects of individual behaviors in the relationship between the degree of digitalization and EO, we checked if any of the self-concept traits in question drives the mediation more than the others, or if both contribute to it. Indeed, as we have no theoretical reason to assume that one dimension would lead to another, parallel mediation analysis is appropriate (Hayes, 2013). According to Baron and Kenny (1986), an empirical study with a classical mediation must follow a three-step approach and demonstrates that (1) there is a significant relationship between the independent variable and the mediating variable, (2) there is a significant relationship between the independent variable and the dependent variable without including the mediator, and (3) by incorporating the mediator, the relationship between the independent and the dependent variables reduces and the relationship between the mediator and the dependent variable is significant. In our case, to test for a parallel mediated relationship between the dimensions of degree of digitalization and EO, we estimated a series of regression analysis (see Tab. 2). First, the regression of the mediators on the independent variable with the coefficients a1 and a2. Second, the regression of the dependent variable on the independent variable with the coefficient c. Third, the regression of the dependent variable on both the independent variable and mediators with the coefficients b1 and b2.

According to this regression procedure, the mediating effect is proved if the regression coefficient associated with the degree of digitalization and the EO relationship is statistically significant and decreases or goes to zero when the mediators are added to the equation. Results from the parallel mediation analysis demonstrated that the relationship between the degree of digitalization and EO is positive and significant (H1 supported) and transits by self-efficacy (H2 supported) but not by locus of control (H3 not supported). In more detail, there is first a significant relationship between the degree of digitalization and EO ($c = 0.694$;

$p < 0.000$). Second, the degree of digitalization positively affects self-efficacy (a1 = 0.240; $p < 0.01$), which in turn is positively related to EO (b1 = 0.582; $p < 0.000$). Third, we also observed a significant relationship between the degree of digitalization and locus of control (a2 = 0.272; $p < 0.01$), however, no significant relationship between locus of control and EO (b2 = – 0.045; $p > 0.1$) was obtained. Finally, we found that the regression coefficient between digitalization and EO decreases when the mediators are added to the equation (c' = 0.567; $p < 0.000$). Thus, our parallel mediation model (Fig. 2) illustrated a partial mediating effect that transits through self-efficacy (MacKinnon et al., 2007; Hayes, 2013).

Tab. 2: Results of parallel mediation

		Parallel mediation										
		M_1 (SE)				M_2 (LC)				Y (EO)		
Parameters		*Coeff.*	*Standard Error*	*p*		*Coeff.*	*Standard Error*	*p*		*Coeff.*	*Standard Error*	*p*
X (DD)	a_1	0.240	0.097	0.014	a_2	0.272	0.095	0.005	c'	0.567	0.103	0.000
M_1 (SE)		–	–	–		–	–	–	b_1	0.582	0.112	0.000
M_2 (LC)		–	–	–		–	–	–	b_2	-0.045	0.113	0.694
Constant		5.004	0.217	0.000		5.072	0.214	0.000		0.188	0.538	0.727
		$R^2 = 0.042$ $F(1, 141) = 6.182$, $p = 0.014$				$R^2 = 0.055$ $F(1, 141) = 8.136$, $p = 0.005$				$R^2 = 0.391$ $F(3, 139) = 29.760$, $p = 0.000$		

DD = digitalization degree – SE = self-efficacy – LC = locus of control

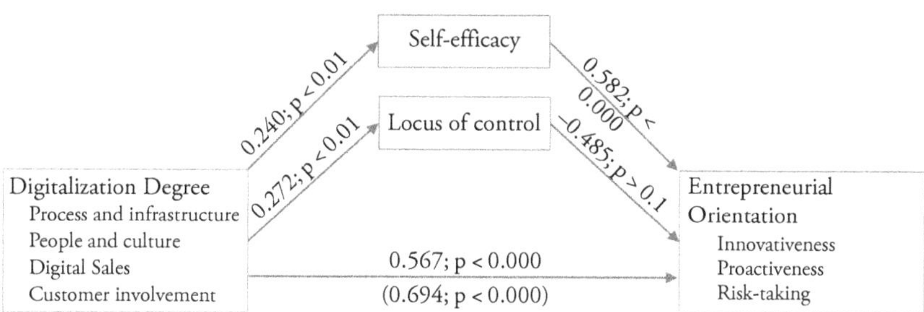

Fig. 2: Final model
Source: from authors

5. Discussion and implications

The main objective of our paper was to empirically test the mediating roles of self-efficacy and locus of control on the relationship among the degree of digitalization and EO of internationalizing MSMEs. Although EO constitutes a broad field of interests, little attention has been paid to empirically investigating associations among the use of digital technologies, self-concept traits and EO in a large sample of entrepreneurs. Based on parallel mediation analysis, we built a model linking key dimensions of a firm's digitalization to EO and self-concept traits. By addressing the call put forward by Nambisan (2017) to progress the function of digital technologies into entrepreneurial activities, our research provided new empirical evidence on the importance of digital technologies in shaping entrepreneurial orientation. Our findings emphasized the mediating role of self-efficacy – the entrepreneurs' beliefs in their capabilities to generate given attainments – in exploiting the opportunities provided by the integration of digital tools at different levels of firms in order to define a strong entrepreneurial strategic posture. Nevertheless, even if we recorded a positive and significant relationship between the degree of digitalization and locus of control – the entrepreneurs' ability to exercise control over the environment – we found no positive and significant results regarding its mediating role on the relationship between the use of digital technologies and the EO of MSMEs. These findings reinforce the important role of personal traits to better perceive the effect of digitalization in entrepreneurial strategic posture. This highlights that the use of digital technologies could be an important source of value creation in the manifestation of entrepreneurial behaviors that in turn, positively increases innovativeness, proactiveness and risk-taking of firms. Importantly, we showed that self-efficacy mediates the relationship between the degree of digitalization of firms and the adoption of EO.

5.1. Theoretical and practical implications

From a theoretical point of view, the major implication to the current literature is the establishment of the parallel mediation model, which tested the interrelationship between the use of digital technologies, self-concept traits and the adoption of EO by internationalizing MSMEs. Indeed, the key contribution of our research includes the analysis of a parallel mediation that paints a different picture on entrepreneurial strategic decision-making and demonstrates that entrepreneurial self-efficacy could be a theoretical explanation for the positive relationship between digitalization and the EO of MSMEs. Furthermore, our research demonstrated relevant empirical evidence that entrepreneurs who digitalized her/his operational functions may lead their firms to a high degree of EO. Furthermore, by considering the degree of digitalization as an antecedent of EO, we provided a new perspective on the EO construct as a dependent variable and highlighted the importance of self-concept traits in building competitive advantage thanks to the digitalization of the operational backbone. This observation concurs with the intrinsic conceptualizations of both self-efficacy and locus of control and contributes to the extension of entrepreneurial theories, especially in DE and EO fields. This integrative perspective is likely to provide new impetus to research on the impacts of emerging technologies in entrepreneurship and on the important role of individuals in shaping these digital opportunities to reinforce an entrepreneurial strategic posture and competitive advantage. From a practical perspective, our study outlined new knowledge for business owners and decision-makers who strive to integrate digital technologies into their operational functions in order to maintain and reinforce their innovativeness, proactiveness and risk-taking in foreign markets. We demonstrated that self-efficacy can be a way forward to strategically use digital technologies in order to reinforce EO and, simultaneously, competitive advantage of internationalizing firms. The parallel mediation analysis foregrounds a new way to help MSMEs enhance their perceived ability to successfully accomplish a certain level of performance in the definition of strategical posture. Indeed, our findings emphasized that the use of digital technologies is imperative in this regard. Consequently, whether it be to improve innovativeness by integrating new actors in the idea-creation process via social networks or by developing new experiments with virtual reality and 3D printers – to enhance proactiveness by collecting and processing data through predictive algorithms or by using the internet of things to optimize the operational process – to securing risky action by using technologies, such as the cloud or the blockchain, many opportunities exist to improve the strategic orientation of internationalizing MSMEs (Hervé et al., 2020a).

As outlined by Schumpeter (1934), it is individual behaviors that influence the discovery and exploitation of opportunities initiated by technological change. Self-efficacy is theoretically significant to explain that entrepreneurs can take advantage of technological means to define competitive strategies. In our results, as this belief-based variable mediates the relationship between the digitalization degree of firms and their EO, we emphasized the significant role of entrepreneurs' perception of their capabilities to successfully achieve a certain level of performance by using digital technologies. In contrast, our results highlighted that locus of control – more precisely, the internal locus of control – has no effect on this relationship. In other words, the disposition of an entrepreneur to perceive control of the environment plays no role in understanding the relationship among the degree of digitalization of MSMEs and their strategic orientation. As acknowledged in the literature, self-efficacy is about individuals' beliefs in their capabilities, whereas locus of control is related to the belief about outcome contingencies (Bandura, 2006). More specifically, self-efficacy is a judgment of the ability to perform given types of performance whereas outcome expectations are judgements about the likely results of that performance (Bandura, 2006). Based on this assumption, we suggest that entrepreneurs are more willing to expend their effort and have more intrinsic interest to make appropriate use of digital technologies in order to drive and run their businesses in an entrepreneurial way. However, it may be currently challenging for them to ensure control of the expected results. In addition, given the pace of digital progress, it may also be difficult for entrepreneurs to perceive an outcome as being contingent upon their own behavior and under their personal control and understanding. By focusing on building and maintaining a meaningful digital operational backbone, we argue that internationalizing MSMEs can build on the personal characteristics of entrepreneurs, and especially on their self-confidence, to improve their existing strategic posture and be driven to seek entrepreneurial opportunities. In this sense, the digitalization of the business is vital to endowing the individual with entrepreneurial behavior.

5.2. Limitations and further research

One limitation of this research is the use of only two measures of self-concept traits. Although self-efficacy and locus of control both represent major human behaviors that influence one to become an entrepreneur, it would be relevant to integrate other personal attributes, like the need for achievement, networking behavior or the willingness to take risks, into the research model. We thus encourage further research to investigate the influence of other personal traits on the relationship between the degree of digitalization of firms and their EO. Furthermore, because we were interested mainly in the entrepreneurial behavior of decision-makers, we took into consideration the variable of the internal locus of control. Since digitalization is an external factor, it might be interesting for future studies to enhance the research model and test the influence of the variable external locus of control. We also pointed out a limitation in our study regarding the independent variable of the degree of digitalization of internationalizing MSMEs. Since we used the average level of digitalization, it was not possible to observe in detail the role of the internal and external dimensions of the firm on the relationship between the variables. Hence, future research might be interested in decomposing this variable and testing each of the dimensions in the model.

Another limitation can be formulated in view of the cross-sectional design of our study. Indeed, we provided an overview of one specific point in time and it would be relevant to take into consideration the impact of change over time. Thus, a longitudinal investigation would contribute to extending views into the dynamic nature of the relationship between the digitalization degree of internationalizing firms and their strategic orientation. In addition, our empirical results were collected from a sample of Swiss MSMEs, which raised questions about the extrapolation of the results to other countries. Future studies could address this issue by collecting empirical evidence in other countries and then providing comparative studies. Finally, as digital technologies are important determinants of competitive advantage, academic researchers need to focus in more detail on patterns of technological change as well as on individuals' competencies required in such a context. Furthermore, given the rapid development of the field of DE and the diversity of knowledge emerging from EO research, we believe it is time to propose a construct in the literature that can measure the digital entrepreneurial orientation of internationalizing firms and thus, offer new insights for advancing knowledge on this domain.

Conclusion

Using a model that links key dimensions of firms and individuals, our research investigated the impact of the degree of digitalization of MSMEs on their EO, and then assessed the mediating role of self-concept traits, i.e., self-efficacy and locus of control, in this relationship. Based on a survey of 143 MSMEs, we empirically tested our model through a parallel mediation analysis. To the best of our knowledge, this research is the first empirical study to consider the mediation role of personal attributes in explaining how the integration of digital technologies into the dimensions of an operational firm affects the EO of MSMEs. Our results emphasized that the degree of digitalization of MSMEs positively affects their entrepreneurial behavior. Moreover, our findings highlighted the mediating role of self-efficacy in exploiting digital technologies to reinforce entrepreneurial strategic posture. However, we found no positive and significant results on the impact of locus of control on the relationship between the degree of digitalization and the EO of MSMEs. By empirically testing the effect of self-concept traits on this relationship, our research demonstrated the importance of considering the behavior of entrepreneurs. Indeed, our research provides a strong basis for future work investigations on the role of an individual's self-confidence in the entrepreneurial process of using digital technologies to reinforce innovative, proactive and risk-taking behaviors of MSMEs. It contributes to the literature on DE and EO by underscoring not only the positive and significant relationship between the degree of digitalization and EO of MSMEs, but also the mediating role of personal attributes. By drawing a new look at traditional theories, these findings provide significant insights for the scholarly community, as well as practitioners and suggest that entrepreneurs should believe in their capabilities of exploiting digital technologies in order to build a strong strategic posture.

References

Ajzen, I. (2002). 'Perceived behavioral control, self-efficacy, locus of control, and the theory of planned behavior 1'. Journal of Applied Social Psychology, 32(4), 665–683.

Anderson, B. S., Covin, J. G., and Slevin, D. P. (2009). 'Understanding the relationship between entrepreneurial orientation and strategic learning capability: An empirical investigation'. Strategic Entrepreneurship Journal, 3(3), 218–240.

Autio, E., Nambisan, S., Thomas, L. D., and Wright, M. (2018). 'Digital affordances, spatial affordances, and the genesis of entrepreneurial ecosystems'. Strategic Entrepreneurship Journal, 12(1), 72–95.

Bandura, A. (1986). Social foundations of thought and action. A Social Cognitive Theory. Prentice Hall, Englewood Cliffs, NJ.

Bandura, A. (2006). 'Guide for constructing self-efficacy scales. Self-efficacy beliefs of adolescents', 5(1), 307–337.

Baron, R. M., and Kenny, D. A. (1986). 'The moderator–mediator variable distinction in social psychological research: Conceptual, strategic, and statistical considerations'. Journal of Personality and Social Psychology, 51(6), 1173.

Bharadwaj, A., El Sawy, O., Pavlou, P., and Venkatraman, N. (2013). 'Digital business strategy: Toward a next generation of insights'. MIS Quarterly, 37(2), 471–482.

Boone, C., De Brabander, B., and Van Witteloostuijn, A. (1996). 'CEO locus of control and small firm performance: An integrative framework and empirical test'. Journal of Management Studies, 33(5), 667–700.

Boyd, N. G., and Vozikis, G. S. (1994). 'The influence of self-efficacy on the development of entrepreneurial intentions and actions'. Entrepreneurship Theory and Practice, 18(4), 63–77.

Business Office Digital Switzerland (GDS). Biel / Bienne. (2018). « Digital Switzerland » strategy. Federal Gazette 2018 5961

Chen, C. C., Greene, P. G., and Crick, A. (1998). 'Does entrepreneurial self-efficacy distinguish entrepreneurs from managers?'. Journal of Business Venturing, 13(4), 295–316.

Covin, J. G., and Miller, D. (2014). 'International entrepreneurial orientation: Conceptual considerations, research themes, measurement issues, and future research directions'. Entrepreneurship Theory and Practice, 38(1), 11–44.

Covin, J. G., and Slevin, D. P. (1989). 'Strategic management of small firms in hostile and benign environments'. Strategic Management Journal, 10(1), 75–87.

Covin, J. G., and Slevin, D. P. (1991). 'A conceptual model of entrepreneurship as firm behavior'. Entrepreneurship Theory and Practice, Fall, 16(1), 7–25.

Davidson, E., and Vaast, E. 'Digital entrepreneurship and its sociomaterial enactment'. In 2010 43rd Hawaii International Conference on System Sciences (pp. 1–10). IEEE. January.

Giones, F., and Brem, A. (2017). 'Digital technology entrepreneurship: A definition and research agenda'. Technology Innovation Management Review, 7(5), 44–51.

Gist, M. E. (1987). 'Self-efficacy: Implications for organizational behavior and human resource management'. Academy of Management Review, 12(3), 472–485.

Greif, H., Kühnis, N., and Warnking, P. (2017). 'Digital transformation: How mature are Swiss SMEs'. PwC CH *http://www.pwc.ch/en/publications/2016/pwc_digital_transform_how_mature_are_swiss_smes_survey_16_en.pdf*

Grégoire, D. A., and Shepherd, D. A. (2012). 'Technology-market combinations and the identification of entrepreneurial opportunities: An investigation of the opportunity-individual nexus'. Academy of Management Journal, 55(4), 753–785.

Gruber, M., MacMillan, I. C., and Thompson, J. D. (2012). 'From minds to markets: How human capital endowments shape market opportunity identification of technology start-ups'. Journal of management, 38(5), 1421–1449.

Hair, J. F., Black, W. C., Babin, B. J., Anderson, R. E., & Tatham, R. L. (2006). Multivariate data analysis, vol. 6. Pearson Prentice Hall, Upper Saddle River, NJ.

Hayes, A. F. (2013). Introduction to mediation, moderation, and conditional process analysis. A regression-based approach. The Guilford Press, New York, NY.

Hervé, A., Schmitt, C., & Baldegger, R. (2020a). 'Digitalization, Entrepreneurial Orientation and Internationalization of Micro-, Small-and Medium-Sized Enterprises'. Technology Innovation Management Review, 10(4), 5–17.

Hervé, A., Schmitt, C., & Baldegger, R. (2020b). 'Internationalization and Digitalization: Applying digital technologies to the internationalization process of small and medium-sized enterprises'. Technology Innovation Management Review, 10(7), 28–40.

Hull, C. E., Caisy Hung, Y. T., Hair, N., Perotti, V., and DeMartino, R. (2007). 'Taking advantage of digital opportunities: A typology of digital entrepreneurship'. International Journal of Networking and Virtual Organisations, 4(3), 290–303.

Khedhaouria, A., Gurău, C., and Torrès, O. (2015). 'Creativity, self-efficacy, and small-firm performance: The mediating role of entrepreneurial orientation'. Small Business Economics, 44(3), 485–504.

Kraus, S., Palmer, C., Kailer, N., Kallinger, F. L., and Spitzer, J. (2019). 'Digital entrepreneurship: A research agenda on new business models for the twenty-first century'. International Journal of Entrepreneurial Behavior and Research, 25(2), 353–375.

Levenson, H. (1974). 'Activism and powerful others: Distinctions within the concept of internal-external control'. Journal of Personality Assessment, 38(4), 377–383.

Lumpkin, G. T., and Dess, G. G. (1996). 'Clarifying the entrepreneurial orientation construct and linking it to performance'. Academy of Management Review, 21(1), 135–172.

MacKinnon, D. P., Fairchild, A. J., and Fritz, M. S. (2007). 'Mediation analysis'. Annual Review of Psychology, 58, 593–614.

McDougall, P. P., and Oviatt, B. M. (2000). 'International entrepreneurship: The intersection of two research paths'. Academy of Management Journal, 43(5), 902–906.

McGee, J. E., Peterson, M., Mueller, S. L., and Sequeira, J. M. (2009). 'Entrepreneurial self-efficacy: Refining the measure'. Entrepreneurship theory and Practice, 33(4), 965–988.

McGee, J. E., and Peterson, M. (2019). 'The long-term impact of entrepreneurial self-efficacy and entrepreneurial orientation on venture performance'. Journal of Small Business Management, 57(3), 720–737.

Miller, D. (1983). 'The correlates of entrepreneurship in three types of firms'. Management Science, 29(7), 770–791.

Miller, D., and Friesen, P. H. (1982). 'Innovation in conservative and entrepreneurial firms: Two models of strategic momentum'. Strategic Management Journal, 3(1), 1–25.

Mueller, S. L., and Thomas, A. S. (2001). 'Culture and entrepreneurial potential: A nine country study of locus of control and innovativeness'. Journal of business venturing, 16(1), 51–75.

Nambisan, S. (2017). 'Digital entrepreneurship: Toward a digital technology perspective of entrepreneurship'. Entrepreneurship Theory and Practice, 41(6), 1029–1055.

Poon, J. M., Ainuddin, R. A., and Junit, S. O. H. (2006). 'Effects of self-concept traits and entrepreneurial orientation on firm performance'. International Small Business Journal, 24(1), 61–82.

Porter, M. E. (1985). 'Technology and competitive advantage'. The Journal of Business Strategy, 5(3), 60.

Rauch, A., and Frese, M. (2007). 'Let's put the person back into entrepreneurship research: A meta-analysis on the relationship between business owners' personality traits, business creation, and success'. European Journal of Work and Organizational Psychology, 16(4), 353–385.

Rauch, A., Wiklund, J., Lumpkin, G. T., and Frese, M. (2009). 'Entrepreneurial orientation and business performance: An assessment of past research and suggestions for the future'. Entrepreneurship Theory and Practice, 33(3), 761–787.

Ross, J. W., Sebastian, I., Beath, C., Mocker, M., Moloney, K., and Fonstad, N. (2016). 'Designing and executing digital strategies'. CISR (Center for Information Systems Research/MIT Sloan School of Management) Working Paper, no. 414 (2016).

Rotter, J. B. (1966). 'Generalized expectancies for internal versus external control of reinforcement'. Psychological Monographs: General and Applied, 80(1), 1.

Sapp, S. G., and Harrod, W. J. (1993). 'Reliability and validity of a brief version of Levenson's locus of control scale'. Psychological Reports, 72(2), 539–550.

Schumpeter, J. (1934). The Theory of Economic Development. Harvard University Press, Cambridge, MA.

Shane, S. (2000). 'Prior knowledge and the discovery of entrepreneurial opportunities'. Organization Science, 11(4), 448–469.

von Briel, F., Davidsson, P., and Recker, J. (2018). 'Digital technologies as external enablers of new venture creation in the IT hardware sector'. Entrepreneurship Theory and Practice, 42(1), 47–69.

Weinman, J., and Euchner, J. (2015). 'Digital technologies and competitive advantage'. Research-Technology Management, 58(6), 12–17.

Wood, R., and Bandura, A. (1989). 'Social cognitive theory of organizational management'. Academy of Management Review, 14(3), 361–384.

Zhao, H., Seibert, S. E., and Hills, G. E. (2005). 'The mediating role of self-efficacy in the development of entrepreneurial intentions'. Journal of Applied Psychology, 90(6), 1265.

Conclusion

Manon Enjolras, Mauricio Camargo,
Christophe Schmitt

In the current context, companies, whatever their size, have to face important upheavals arriving at an increasingly fast pace. If small companies are favored by their agility, flexibility and capacity to adapt, they are, on the other hand, hindered by their difficulty in mobilizing the resources (time, financial means, skills) to make their organizations evolve and structure their mutation in a sustainable way.

The aim of this collective book is to highlight the contribution of innovation and internationalization as drivers of this change, both through the competitive advantage they bring and the dynamics they generate within SMEs. Therefore, the contributors of this collective book are interested in the way innovation and internationalization create synergies, in the manner how the small companies exploit these synergies by adopting specific and varied behaviors, and in the facilitating factors that can catalyze these behaviors to lead to better performance. The conclusive section therefore seeks to synthesize the insights provided by the contributors of this book, by combining them to serve a shared ambition: to support SMEs in their mutation through innovation and international development.

1. Innovation and international: Building opportunities to be exploited

The objective of this book is to study two of the main growth levers for companies in today's economic world: innovation and internationalization. More specifically, the assumption supported in this book is that these two activities are important differentiating factors and that they are intimately linked to each other.

Moving from a dynamic of innovation to the implementation of an international activity is indeed just a step away, mostly because innovation allows companies to improve their performance. This gain can be translated into better financial indicators, more market share or a better image among customers and partners. Thus, innovation represents an opportunity for growth, because it leads to development projects enabled by this increase in performance. In many cases, innovation opens the doors to international markets for companies that are able to identify and transform the opportunities that arise. A good innovation capacity enables companies to pick up on weak market signals, anticipate certain disruptions, and adapt to a dynamic and changing context. Networking, collaborative work, and project management skills are also practices being often associated with innovation, and facilitating the development of international activities. As highlighted in Chapter 3, innovative companies can thus rely on practices that they already master in order to identify and exploit international opportunities and implement a value-creating virtuous circle.

On the other hand, international activities are also a fertile ground for innovation, as they represent a valuable field for experimentation and observation. The conduct of activities in foreign markets allows the company to experience gains in terms of upgrades in know-how, technologies, as well as in processes, products and services (Chapter 2). Depending on the targeted markets, companies may have to comply with more stringent rules or adapt the product's offer to a more sophisticated demand in a specific country. Or perhaps, these upgrades may take another shape, as reverse innovation in the context of emerging countries. In both cases, international activities push companies to adopt a resilient behavior and develop an adaptive capacity to identify opportunities to be transformed. Despite the commitment and effort required, these benefits are not limited to large companies. SMEs are also a favorable terrain because, as Chapter 1 points out, it is not necessary to multiply foreign markets or to have a high international presence to experience these benefits. In fact, more than the degree of internationalization of companies, it is above all the proactive and risk-taking behavior of the management and a strong leadership-based culture that appear to be facilitating factors.

Thus, innovation and internationalization within SMEs act as distinct but interconnected growth strategies based on good practices that create synergies. In the current changing context, both appear as challenges but also as levers for companies to find their place in their ecosystem and to adapt to the upheavals they must face.

If we approach this issue from a methodological point of view, this observation is also raised in the field of strategic management, and may be represented through the Ansoff matrix (Tab. 1). The Ansoff Matrix, created by Igor Ansoff in 1957, is a strategic tool that presents four alternative growth strategies in the form of a 2×2 matrix. One dimension of the matrix considers "product" (existing and new) and the other dimension considers "markets" (existing and new). This traditional tool continues to be perceived as one of the most important tools for business development and penetration into the business activity field. Numerous studies show that the use of Ansoff's matrix in business development is one of the effective variants that entrepreneurs successfully apply (Loredana, 2017).

Tab. 1: Ansoff Matrix (Ansoff, 1965)

Markets / Product	**CURRENT**	**NEW**
CURRENT	Market Penetration	Product Development
NEW	Market Development	Diversification

The first proposed growth strategy is Market Penetration. Companies then focus on selling their existing products or services to their existing markets to achieve growth in market share and improve their competitive advantage. It is therefore an optimization approach, which means doing what we know how to do, but doing it better, or differently, to survive the changes in the context and position ourselves as a key player in the ecosystem.

However, sometimes optimization is not enough. In this case, it is necessary to navigate the matrix and move to another quadrant. This path can be progressive, with different possible entry points.

First, companies can choose to launch or strengthen their international development. In this case, they move to the lower left-hand quadrant: Market Development. In this case, companies focus on developing new markets or market segments for their existing products or services.

Another option consists in focusing on innovation, by reaching the top right-hand quadrant: Product Development. In this way, companies focus on developing new products or services for their existing markets. However, these new products or services are not necessarily new for the customers, they can also be new for the company or for the stakeholders of its supply chain.

Thus, innovation and international represent two distinct growth strategies that allow companies to differentiate themselves in terms of market or in terms of products/services. However, synergies between these activities appear with the objective of moving towards the fourth growth strategy proposed by Ansoff: diversification. In this case, companies focus on the development of new products/services to sell into new markets. It is the riskiest of the four alternatives for the SMEs, especially because it involves a large number of stakeholders within and outside the company and because it is potentially highly resource-consuming. These differentiation strategies are often associated with the notion of disruptive innovation.

However, even in the particular context of small businesses, this strategy can take very specific forms. For example, many small innovative companies position themselves on niche markets, in order to offer a product or a service with very limited competition, targeting a specific clientele. The synergy between market and product-oriented strategies therefore translates into an indispensable internationalization, in order to operate on a market large enough to be sustainable. Thus, the degree of novelty of the innovation that these companies provide implies a global market as a mandatory requirement. In start-up environments and in the literature on entrepreneurship, the terms "born-global firms" or "international new ventures" are also employed. It refers to companies that internationalize immediately and do not follow a gradual path. In this case, internationalization is not a growth strategy, but an intrinsic characteristic of their initial business model, allowing them to build their competitive advantage.

Thus, innovation and internationalization represent accessible growth strategies and powerful levers that SMEs can mobilize. They are also accompanied by their set of challenges and difficulties, which is particularly true for the smallest structures. The implementation of proactive behaviors and the exploitation of synergies to compensate for the lack of resources of these small companies then takes all its sense to consolidate their presence within their ecosystem. The ambition of this book is therefore to follow this path by promoting joint and simultaneous support for both the innovation dynamics and the international activities of smaller companies.

2. Innovative and international companies: Toward resilient and miscellaneous profiles

Despite the difficulties they face, SMEs are able, by relying on their innovation and international activities, to cope with the competition of multinational firms and to establish their presence within their ecosystem. However, rather than imitating the strategies of large companies, successful exporting SMEs develop their own rules, focusing on assets such as flexibility and proximity to the customer.

So, this book also aims to show that there is no single profile leading to maximum performance. On the contrary, depending on structural or market-oriented factors, companies adopt a wide variety of different behaviors to adapt to the environment in which they evolve. These differences may be reflected in the implementation of specific internal practices (Chapter 6), in the strategic orientation of their business model (Chapter 4) or in an adaptation to the geopolitical characteristics of the country in which they are located (Chapter 5).

For example, while the biggest companies seem to adopt more structured and formalized practices in terms of organization, smaller companies may nevertheless achieve strong levels of maturity on internal practices more adapted to their agile and flexible functioning (for example, adaptation of the offer, human resource management, design and openness). Depending on their level of flexibility or structuring, the resources they are able to mobilize and the support they can find within their ecosystem, they build an alignment in the components of their business model giving them a competitive advantage in their domestic and foreign markets.

Moreover, what is valid in one ecosystem will not necessarily be valid in another. Depending on the support or difficulties encountered in their domestic market, companies' practices may vary, and therefore their need for support may not be the same. This observation can thus be directly put into perspective through the theory of contingency (Mintzberg, 1979), particularly when considering the relationship between the structure of a market and the behavior of the companies or organizations that make it up. This school of thought considers that there is no such thing as a good organization "per se". Henri Mintzberg, the main representative of the contingency theory, states that the structure of an organization depends on both its own characteristics and the nature of its environment. There is therefore no universal structure that adapts to all situations. A "good" structure must be adapted to its environment, and an environment shapes the organizations that constitute it. Thus, contingency theory sheds light on the fact that a company's behavior evolves in order to respond to the constraints of its specific market. Its internal regulatory mechanisms must therefore be as varied as the environment with which it must deal. To overcome the constraints of its environment, the firm must adjust its behavior by making strategic decisions that allow it to set up a coherent and specific internal functioning that will enable it to improve its performance and finally, to impact the structuring of its own market.

So, some structural, market-oriented or contextual contingency factors (size, age, business sector, geographical area…) seem to impact the way companies manage their internal practices both in terms of internationalization and innovation, but they are not associated with a specific level of innovation or export capability or performance. There is then a real interest in considering innovation and export activities as a joint challenge that requires specific profiles in terms of internal processes management and that potentially leads to a wide variety of behaviors that can be successful. Thus, support to SMEs should not be limited to targeting companies according to performance criteria such as their degree of commitment to export or their R&D budget, but rather to providing a contextualized support according to criteria that are simultaneously market, structure and context-oriented, and adapted to the companies' behavior regarding simultaneously its innovation and internationalization strategy.

3. Supporting innovation and internationalization: Some key levers to be implemented

To support SMEs in overcoming the difficulties they face and to foster the development of their innovation and internationalization dynamics, several levers of action have been identified by the contributors of this book.

Given the high market openness of the last several decades, most markets already have products that meet the various needs consumers have expressed. Therefore, to create value, companies need to differentiate their products. However, SMEs, unlike large corporations, have access to fewer resources for innovation and are constrained to implement less structured innovation processes. A collaborative innovation approach makes it possible for SMEs to pool resources in order to adopt shared forms of innovation.

Thus, open innovation has become a major strategy for companies aiming at a development dynamic based on novelty and differentiation. It highlights the concept of network. Companies no longer limit themselves to their own resources to innovate, they call on external contributors and rely on partners with varying degrees of proximity. This collaboration is also reflected in the international activities of companies. Strong relationship with its distributors, creation of a joint-venture with a foreign partner, development project with its suppliers or even joint export process with a partner of its domestic market... the forms of international collaborations are also varied and rich for the smallest structures. However, whether it is within innovation or international trade projects, this collaboration requires specific skills and a rigorous preparation to be successful. Indeed, the modes of communication between the contributors, the intellectual property rights, the existence of knowledge management systems are all elements to anticipate (Chesbough and Brunswicker, 2014). Moreover, relational skills, allowing the establishment of a climate of trust between the partners, also appear to be crucial Benham et al. (2018). Thus, as highlighted in Chapter 7, collaboration is a powerful lever for SMEs, allowing them to optimize the value of their innovation and internationalization dynamics, but it must be carefully anticipated and prepared. By relying on a collaborative approach, SMEs can share risks and resources, and access opportunities that they would not have been able to exploit alone.

In the same way, digitalization also appears as an important lever, allowing SMEs to acquire a stronger visibility and international presence, while optimizing the management of their knowledge, processes and resources.

Digital technologies reduce many barriers as regards reaching the global marketplace. This context allows new players to compete and completely transforms the patterns of both domestic and international trade. So, digital tools can be particularly beneficial as they open an opportunity for SMEs to compete with larger companies. First, they can compensate for the weak physical presence on foreign markets. Indeed, SMEs generally have more difficulty to establish their physical presence on a market (or on several simultaneously) and the virtualization of certain processes is an asset to be exploited. Digital marketing, for example, allows them to get closer to their customers and gain visibility (Pergelova et al., 2019). Similarly, the introduction of e-commerce opens up great opportunities to gain market share by facilitating access to products (Cassetta et al., 2019). Secondly, in the era of industry 4.0, digital tools are also a valuable asset to strengthen the performance of the company's internal processes (Mazzarol, 2015). By acting as facilitators, they encourage practices of decentralization, collaboration, information management and specialization of business in the daily routines of SMEs.

Then, digital tools and technologies could indeed be considered as facilitators to be mobilized in order to achieve SMEs' both international and innovation business objectives. However, the digital context also accentuates the competitive landscape all around the world. Therefore, while some digitalization initiatives are indeed differentiating and offensive, others on the contrary appear as "must have" or prerequisite steps through which companies would have to go if they wanted to survive on their market. Additionally, with the current acceleration of digitalization, companies that were ahead of the game in terms of digitalization must renew and reinvent themselves in order to maintain the competitive advantage they had acquired a few years ago. Moreover, the organizational impact of digitalization on SMEs is crucial and needs to be anticipated through a combination of resources, skills, and capabilities to absorb it. Indeed, although we traditionally talk about digital transition, for many companies this is not progressive at all. It is rather a transformation or even a jump into digitalization because the changes induced are generally not incremental. All the elements of this transformation are interconnected and must potentially be implemented simultaneously. Therefore, several companies stressed the importance of relying on a network of partners and institutional support to facilitate their digital transformation. Moreover, the importance of considering the business management and companies' staff behavior regarding digitalization has been pointed out by Chapter 8, highlighting that the individual's self-confidence in the process of using digital technologies could reinforce innovative, proactive and risk-taking behaviors of SMEs. So, digitalization is not only about digital tools implementation, it is also about building new competences, adopting a strategic posture and can be surrounded. It appears as a strong mutation path that companies could take in order to support their innovation and international dynamics.

Through its various contributions, this collective book promotes innovation and internationalization as levers of action for the growth and transformation of SMEs and as an opportunity to consolidate their presence on their domestic and foreign markets. From a cross analysis, mixing both scientific approach and field experience, the insights provided by the contributors have first highlighted the importance of considering innovation and international in a joint way, to emerge synergies creating potential business opportunities. Secondly, the authors have shown that by adopting specific behaviors, practices or business models, SMEs are able to compete with larger companies, through the creation of a strong competitive advantage. Finally, these behaviors can be supported or even transcended by drivers such as digitalization or collaborative approaches to become a key stakeholder of the current dynamic of their ecosystem and to overcome the barriers they may face.

Based on these insights, the ambition of this book is to promote a support to SMEs based on the synergies between innovation and export as levers of growth and differentiation. This support should also consider the multiplicity of innovative and exporting company profiles, by adopting a personalized approach adapted to the strategy and culture of the targeted SMEs. Finally, the support provided by governmental agencies should address digitalization and collaboration as drivers to overcome the difficulties of both innovation and internationalization, while remaining aware of the upheavals that such dynamics can cause within small structures.

Thus, the authors hope that this book will be useful for researchers working in the field of innovation and international trade, but also for practitioners and business consultants seeking to evolve their practices and embrace the opportunities of this evolving context.

References

Ansoff, H. Igor. 1965. Corporate Strategy: An Analytic Approach to Business Policy for Growth and Expansion. McGraw-Hill, New York, USA.

Behnam, S., Cagliano, R., and Grijalvo, M. 2018. "How should firms reconcile their open innovation capabilities for incorporating external actors in innovations aimed at sustainable development?" Journal of Cleaner Production, 170, 950–965.

Cassetta, Ernesto, Umberto Monarca, Ivano Dileo, Claudio Di Berardino, and Marco Pini. 2019. "The Relationship between Digital Technologies and Internationalisation. Evidence from Italian SMEs." Industry and Innovation. https://doi.org/10.1080/13662716.2019.1696182.

Chesbrough, H., and Brunswicker, S. 2014. "A fad or a phenomenon? The adoption of open innovation practices in large firms". Research-Technology Management, 57(2), 16–25.

Loredana, Ecobici Mihaela. 2017. "The use of Ansoff matrix in the field of business." Annals – Economy Series 2; Special: 141–49.

Mazzarol, Tim. 2015. "SMEs Engagement with E-Commerce, e-Business and e-Marketing." Small Enterprise Research 22 (1): 79–90. https://doi.org/10.1080/13215906.2015.1018400.

Mintzberg, Henry. 1979. The Structuring of Organizations. Englewood Cliffs, N.J: Pearson.

Pergelova, Albena, Tatiana Manolova, Ralitsa Simeonova-Ganeva, and Desislava Yordanova. 2019. "Democratizing Entrepreneurship? Digital Technologies and the Internationalization of Female-Led SMEs." Journal of Small Business Management 57 (1): 14–39. https://doi.org/10.1111/jsbm.12494.

List of contributors

Susan ARCE: Instructor Professor at Tecnológico de Costa Rica. Licentiate degree in Business Administration with emphasis in Finance from Tecnológico de Costa Rica and Master in Technology and Educational Innovation from Universidad Nacional, Costa Rica. Her research interests focus on SMEs and export development.

Rico BALDEGGER: Rico Baldegger is Director and Professor of Entrepreneurship, Strategy and Innovation at the School of Management Fribourg (HEG-FR), Switzerland. His specialty area is entrepreneurship and innovation. His academic background includes a Master (Business & Economics), from the University of St. Gallen (1985), and a Ph.D. in SME & Entrepreneurship from the University of Fribourg (1995). Professor Baldegger's broad professional experience in entrepreneurship and management includes the fields of leadership, human resources, IT, and branding. He has created several start-ups and managed SMEs and has also acted as a management consultant. Today, he is on the board of several companies and has experience as a Business Angel. He was Director of the Institute of Entrepreneurship & SMEs and Academic Director of the Master program in Entrepreneurship (Innovation & Growth) at the School of Management Fribourg, Switzerland. Rico Baldegger has more than a hundred publications, including several books. His research is concerned with the innovation process of entrepreneurs, the internationalization process of start-ups and SMEs, new venture creation and technological entrepreneurship.

Germán BENITO-SARRIÁ: Assistant professor at ESCE, France. He holds a PhD in Management from the University of Valencia. His research focuses on business models applied to the internationalization process.

Mauricio CAMARGO: Professor at the "Ecole Nationale en Génie des Systèmes et de l'Innovation" (ENSGSI) in Nancy (France), and Director of the ERPI Laboratory (Research Team on Innovative Processes) at the University of Lorraine. Chemical Engineer from the National University of Colombia and Doctor in Automatic Engineering from the University of Valenciennes (France). His research interests focus on two main areas: the design and management of innovation projects and the management of technology and innovation in general, as well as the design of complex product-process-supply chain systems.

Jean-Paul DAVID: CEO of Mercadex Europe & director of Institut MX. Born in Vancouver (CANADA), Jean-Paul has been active for more than 30 years in international business. In 1994 he founded Mercadex International (Canada) which is dedicated to assisting companies in the development of their activities in the global marketplace. He thereafter founded Mercadex Europe (France) in 2016 and Institut MX in 2018. He holds an MBA in International Management from HEC Montréal and is a graduate of UQTR (Canada). Jean-Paul is also a lecturer in international business at several institutions (notably emlyon business school, TBS, Sorbonne) and is a board member of La Fabrique de l'Exportation, a French Think Tank on exports. He is the author of articles published in international business journals as well as of the book "Comment développer les marchés internationaux".

Manon ENJOLRAS: Associate Professor from the University of Lorraine – ERPI laboratory (France) and coordinator of the LUE Innov4SME project (innovation and export capacities of SMEs), her field of research focuses on the multidimensional metrology of companies' internal processes: innovation, export, industrial property, etc. Her work is based on the application of multi-criteria analysis and data analysis methodologies to design evaluation and decision-making tools. Particular attention is paid to the case of small and medium-sized enterprises (SMEs).

Margie FAITH: Instructor Professor at Tecnológico de Costa Rica. Biotechnology Engineer and Master in Business Administration from Tecnológico de Costa Rica. Her research interests focus on technology transfer management, innovation and digital transformation processes in SMEs.

Daniel GALVEZ: Associate Professor at the University of Santiago de Chile (USACH), Department of Industrial Engineering. Doctor in Industrial Systems Engineering from the University of Lorraine. Coordinator of the LEIND Laboratory (Laboratory of Entrepreneurship and Industrial Engineering) of the USACH. His research areas are Innovation management and decision making. In innovation management, his work focuses on the proposition of assessment models to manage innovation practices and activities in companies. In decision making, his work involves the application of multi-criteria analysis methods to aid in decision making problems.

Jean-Christophe GESSLER: Associate professor at the IAE de Poitiers (University school of management). He started his professional career as an export manager for a French SME which manufactured equipment for wineries. After he switched to an education career, he decided to investigate the topic of collaborative practices between SMEs to go international and devoted his PhD research to it. He is now an expert in this field with a broad scope of collaboration practices ranging from entirely informal to very formal. Jean-Christophe GESSLER is Vice-President of La Fabrique de l'Exportation, the main French think tank dealing with the internationalization of firms and the ability of SMEs to go international.

Annaële HERVÉ: Assistant Professor at the School of Management Fribourg, University of Applied Sciences Western Switzerland (HES-SO), she completed a PhD in Science Management at the University of Lorraine that addresses the research streams of digitalization and internationalization of SMEs. She is currently working on various research projects and is teaching several courses in digital transformation, digital business model, blockchain business model, and business and corporate system. Her main research interests are digital transformation, digital business model, digital entrepreneurship, and international entrepreneurship.

José MARTÍNEZ: Professor at Tecnológico de Costa Rica, Director of CIADEG (Centro de Investigación en Administración, Economía y Gestión Tecnológica). Doctor in Business Management from Universidad de Valencia, Spain. His research interests focus on finances and exporting SMEs.

Camila MUÑOZ: Industrial Engineer of the University of Santiago (Chile) and Master's in engineering sciences. Her research experience has been mainly focused on the relationship between innovation and exports, within the context of Small and Medium Enterprises (SME), looking for common internal capabilities that can be used to exploit this relationship.

José PLA-BARBER: Professor and Chair of International Business at the University of Valencia. He is also associate member at the John Dunning Center for International Business (University of Reading, UK.). He has been the vice-chair of the European International Business Academy (EIBA) (2013–2018) and the Chair of the Western Europe Chapter of the Academy of International Business (2014–2018). His research interests focus on two main areas: the internationalization process and the investment of the European Firms in Latin-America.

Christophe SCHMITT: Professor of entrepreneurship at the University of Lorraine (IAE Metz and CEREFIGE), he holds the "Entreprendre" research chair and is in charge of the PeeL (Lorraine Student Entrepreneurship Cluster). He is also associate professor at the Louvain School of Management (Belgium) and at the "Haute Ecole de Gestion" of Fribourg (Switzerland). His articles and books are mainly based on the notion of value conception and knowledge building for action as well as on the development of entrepreneurial practices.

Cristina VILLAR: Associate Professor in Strategy and International Business at the University of Valencia, and director of the Master in Strategy at the University of Valencia. She holds a PhD in Management and her research focuses on international business management, with a particular interest in innovation and knowledge management processes in both multinationals and SMEs.

Pascal WILD: Associate Professor at the School of Management Freiburg, University of Applied Sciences Western Switzerland (HES-SO). He holds a PhD in Socioeconomics from the University of Geneva (Switzerland). Co-author of the Global Entrepreneurship Monitor (GEM) Report on Switzerland and coordinator of the Swiss International Entrepreneurship Survey (SIES), he is also scientific co-director in a program related to entrepreneurship and appropriate technologies for emerging and developing countries in the global south. His research interests focus on the internationalization of SME and international entrepreneurship, with a particular focus on emerging economies in East and Southeast Asia.

Scientific Committee

Published titles

Vol. 29 – Manon Enjolras, Mauricio Camargo and Christophe Schmitt (Eds.), *Innovation and Internationalization of Small and Medium Enterprises. A Crossroads Perspective*, 2022.

Vol. 28 – Samuel-Jacques Priso Essawe, *Intégration régionale « appropriée » en Afrique. Éléments juridiques d'effectivité*, 2021.

Vol. 27 – Vincent Herbert (dir.), *Tourisme et Territoires. Espaces d'innovations*, 2021.

Vol. 26 – Jean-Alain Héraud et Nathalie Popiolek, *L'organisation et la valorisation de la recherche. Problématique européenne et étude comparée de la France et de l'Allemagne*, 2021.

Vol. 25 – Stéphanie Lachaud-Martin, Corinne Marache, Julie McIntyre, Mikaël Pierre (eds.), *Wine, Networks and Scales. Intermediation in the Production, Distribution and Consumption of Wine*, 2021.

Vol. 24 – Verónica González-Araujo, Roberto-Carlos Álvarez-Delgado, Ángel Sancho-Rodríguez (eds.), *Ethics in Business Communication. New Challenges in the Digital World*, 2020.

Vol. 23 – Didier Caveng, *L'éthique dans la finance. Les banques genevoises à l'épreuve des faits*, 2019.

Vol. 22 – Andre Tiran et Dimitri Uzunidis (dir.), *Libéralisme et protectionnisme*, 2019.

Vol. 21 – Dominique Desjeux, *The anthropological perspective of the world. The inductive method illustrated*, 2018.

Vol. 20 – Benoit Bernard, *Management Public. 65 schémas pour analyser et changer les organisations publiques*, 2018.

Vol. 19 – Dimitri Uzunidis (dir.), *Recherche académique et innovation. La force productive de la science*, 2018.

Vol. 18 – Jean Vercherand, *Le marché du travail. L'esprit libéral et la revanche du politique*, 2018.

Vol. 17 – Dominique Desjeux (dir.), *L'empreinte anthropologique du monde. Méthode inductive illustrée*, 2018.

Vol. 16 – Sophie Boutillier, *Entrepreneuriat et innovation*, 2017.

Vol. 15 – Arvind Ashta, *Microfinance. Battling a Wicked Problem*, 2016.

Vol. 14 – Jean Vercherand, *Microéconomie. Une approche critique : Théorie et exercices*, 2016.

Vol. 13 – Reseau de Recherche sur l'innovation, Blandine Laperche (dir.), *Géront'innovations. Trajectoires d'innovation dans une économie vieillissante,* 2016.

Vol. 12 – Societe Internationale Jean-Baptiste Say, Dimitri Uzunidis (dir.), *Et Jean-Baptiste Say… créa l'Entrepreneur*, 2015.

Vol. 11 – Faiz Gallouj, Francois Stankiewicz (dir.), *Le DRH innovateur. Management des ressources humaines et dynamiques d'innovation*, 2014.

Vol. 10 – Charlotte Fourcroy, *Services et environnement. Les enjeux énergétiques de l'innovation dans les services*, 2014.

Vol. 9 – Remy Herrera, Wim Dierckxsens, Paulo Nakatani (eds.), *Beyond the Systemic Crisis and Capital-Led Chaos. Theoretical and Applied Studies*, 2014.

Vol. 8 – Reseau de Recherche sur l'Innovation, Sophie Boutillier, Joelle Forest, Delphine Gallaud, Blandine Laperche, Corinne Tanguy, Leila Temri (dir.), *Principes d'économie de l'innovation*, 2014.

Vol. 7 – Michel Santi, *Capitalism without Conscience*, 2013.

Vol. 6 – Arnaud Diemer, Jean-Pierre Potier, Léon Walras. *Un siècle après (1910-2010)*, 2013.

Vol. 5 – Sophie Boutillier, Faridah Djellal, Dimitri Uzunidis (Reseau de Recherche sur l'Innovation) (dir.), *L'innovation. Analyser, anticiper, agir,* 2013.

Vol. 4 – Aurelie Trouve, Marielle Berriet-Solliec, Denis Lepicier (dir.), *Le développement rural en Europe. Quel avenir pour le deuxième pilier de la Politique agricole commune* ?, 2013.

Vol. 3 – Sophie Boutillier, Faridah Djellal, Faiz Gallouj, Blandine Laperche, Dimitri Uzunidis (dir.), *L'innovation verte. De la théorie aux bonnes pratiques*, 2012.

Vol. 2 – Faridah Djellal, Faiz Gallouj, *La productivité à l'épreuve des services,* 2012.

Vol. 1 – Abdelillah Hamdouch, Sophie Reboud, Corinne Tanguy (dir.), PME, *dynamiques entrepreneuriales et innovation*, 2011.

www.ingramcontent.com/pod-product-compliance
Ingram Content Group UK Ltd.
Pitfield, Milton Keynes, MK11 3LW, UK
UKHW020710041026
15590UKWH00002B/584

9 782807 618206